D11175394

African Societies

44-10

African Societies

LUCY MAIR

Honorary Professor of Anthropology
University of Kent at Canterbury

CAMBRIDGE UNIVERSITY PRESS

Published by the Syndics of the Cambridge University Press
Bentley House, 200 Euston Road, London NW1 2DB
American Branch: 32 East 57th Street, New York, N.Y. 10022

Library of Congress Catalogue Card Number: 73–93398

ISBN: 0 521 20442 9 hard covers
      0 521 09854 8 paperback

First published 1974

Photoset and printed
in Great Britain by
REDWOOD BURN LIMITED
Trowbridge & Esher

Contents

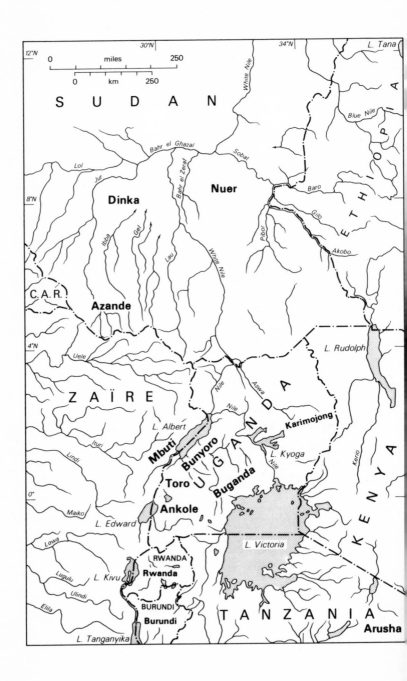

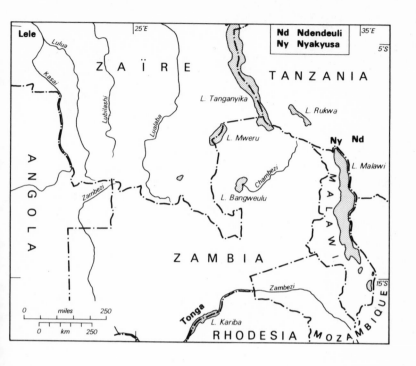
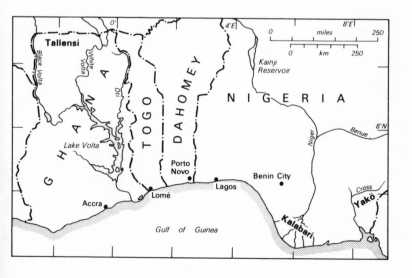

1 African Societies

Social anthropologists study the societies of those parts of the world that have not yet experienced the full consequences of the industrial revolution – societies in which people still get a large part of their living from the food they grow themselves and the animals they herd, in which most of them expect the place where they were born to be their permanent home, and rely for co-operation on their kin and neighbours and not on contracts to do jobs for a money wage. There are a number of reasons for making such studies. Perhaps the most general is the argument that you cannot look critically – or even perhaps understand – your own society until you have seen something very different. This has been the experience not only of anthropologists. It was the novelist Somerset Maugham who said that he only began to understand the English after his travels all over the world. Another, and very different, argument is that the anthropologist is the interpreter to his own countrymen, or, if you like, to other 'Europeans' or 'Westerners', of the cultures of peoples alien to them – of the modes in which such peoples communicate, and above all in which they express their common values and desires. This way of study implies a distinction between 'us' and 'them' – the same distinction, in fact, that we draw when we study the language and institutions of another European country. Yet the latter study is not held to be the business of anthropologists. A good many writers today draw the conclusion that anthropology is, and has always been, a 'colonialist' profession and that it is time to 'decolonise' it; and different ways of doing so are suggested.

The way that is advocated by some French writers (Copans et al. 1971) is to look in what they call 'archaic' societies not for the exotic qualities which differentiate 'them' from 'us', but for what we all have in common. This is not as new as they think; it was the excitement of Malinowski's teaching that he was endlessly reminding us of the common features, disguised under different forms, in 'their' societies and 'ours'. This was the core, and the strength, of his functional theory which has now fallen into such disrepute. He was never tired of repudiating the idea of anthropology as an interest in the exotic.

There is still room to ask where we are to find these common features. The structuralist followers of Lévi-Strauss find it in the unconscious, unrecognised logical laws which lead men everywhere to classify the objects of their experience in terms of opposites that must somehow be reconciled. Marxists, who also argue in terms of contradictions that must somehow be transcended, see what is common to all societies in the exploitation of their fellows by those who control strategic resources. Less committed anthropologists say that a society could not exist as such unless it had some way of maintaining order among its members, some commonly recognised rules governing the holding and transmission of property and the right to exercise authority, some means of passing on to the next generation its moral values and its accumulated knowledge. This is the point of view from which I am writing. It is 'functionalist' in the sense that one looks in the study of alien societies for *their* way of meeting these essential needs; they are not the needs that Malinowski enumerated, but they would be recognised as fundamental by a good many students of society, 'primitive' or 'modern'. We used to call the analysis of these institutions the study of social structure and that of symbols the study of culture; and the sociological theories of Talcott Parsons in America, which are not without a debt to Malinowski, are still called 'structural-functional' and have by no means been snuffed out by the structural anthropology of Lévi-Strauss.

This book, then, is intended to illustrate from different African societies what a British anthropologist sees as the most important aspects of a social system from a structural-functional point of view. We must take as our starting-point the fact that the peoples we are dealing with have not had, until they were brought to them from outside, the techniques of production and communication that the industrial world is used to. They belong to what Peter Laslett has called 'the world we have lost', or indeed to an even remoter world, since the sixteenth-century England to which he was referring knew the skill of writing and the use of money. In such a world people have to adapt themselves to their environment rather than master it. They cannot travel far, and most of them live where they were born, or, if they leave home when they marry, a few miles away at most. Hence their most significant relationships are with kinsmen and neighbours, and an anthropological study must give more attention to the purposes for which people recognise claims and obligations based on kinship than an analysis of an urban industrial society would be likely to do. Indeed our subject has been described as the study of kinship *par excellence* – something of an exaggeration, even though the nineteenth-century anthropologists did give so much thought to the question of different (often imaginary) forms of family and marriage. Another view is that kinship only begins to have meaning when one asks what political or economic or religious behaviour is considered to be appropriate to people in any given kin relationship. But it remains true that the kin relationships provide the rules for all these types of behaviour.

One of the leading students of kinship, Meyer Fortes, distinguishes between the 'domain' of kinship and that of 'politico-jural relations' – the latter being matters of claims to property or to authority, enforceable by sanctions. Within the family, he would argue, obedience to seniors and to the head of the household grows out of the dependence of its members on them. It is accepted as morally right, and the rejection of family or kin-group norms is not a matter to be dealt with by external authority on the human level; many peoples believe that the spirits of the dead are concerned to maintain it. Outside this moral community there must be some coercive means of supporting recognised rights by securing compensation for wrongs suffered. This is the minimal political function. Some would argue further that there is always some body wider than the kin group which has to take decisions for common action, and to act as a unit in relations with outsiders. This would enlarge the field of 'minimal government'. In many African societies there is no difficulty in recognising an embracing authority system with an individual head, though it may be more instructive to study those with a different organisation for law enforcement and the making of decisions.

Finally, African peoples seek to understand the external world on which they are so much more directly dependent than is urban man, whose material needs are all supplied from distant sources. What they cannot themselves control they ascribe to unseen, ultra-human, usually personalised beings whose goodwill they must secure in order to live and prosper, who are concerned with right conduct as their worshippers see it and may punish those who disregard social norms. In addition they may believe that men can obtain, if they know the right formulae and substances, powers beyond the normal to help or harm others. This is the field of religion and magic, the field that symbolism dominates, and that in which the 'translation of culture' has most to say.

First I shall give examples of each of the three main types of subsistence economy: that of the food-gatherers who take their necessities where they find them, that of the herdsmen who rely primarily on their cattle (and other livestock) and that of the cultivators whose main food is a grain crop, though they may herd cattle in addition. Then I shall take different peoples to illustrate different aspects of current theory in its three main fields of kinship, politics and religion, interlinked as they always are in every society.

And what about economics, the Marxist reader is asking. My answer is the same as his. Getting a living is so much the central preoccupation of peoples of simple technology that it is inseparable from any of the aspects of society that I have mentioned.

MODES OF LIVELIHOOD

Only a very small number of people in Africa still live by hunting and gathering wild food, and few if any are now entirely dependent on wild sources. Most of the pygmies of the Congo forests and the Bushmen of the Kalahari desert are attached in serf-like relationships to settled populations on the borders of their hunting grounds, and some Bushmen even have their own settlements under the eyes of their masters, whence they go out on hunting trips for only part of their time. The Hadza of Tanzania have been constantly losing individual members who leave a hunting band to attach themselves to a neighbouring village, and now the government is requiring them to stay in one place and learn to be farmers. An anthropologist,

Colin Turnbull, lived for some time with a band of Congo pygmies, and my example will be taken from his work.

Most of the nomadic cattle peoples are to be found in the
swamps of the upper Nile and the arid country in the north of
Kenya and Uganda. The constraint to which they are subject is
the need for grazing and water. The whole Nuer population
has to move in the dry season to the few sources of permanent
water, and back in the wet season to their homes on the few
ridges that are above flood level. Other peoples – Jie, Turkana,
Karimojong – can leave women and old people in permanent
homes where there is enough water for humans, but must send
their young men away with the herds in search of grazing.
Typical of the cattle peoples is the organisation by age which
allots to all the young men collectively the duty of fighting to
protect their own herds and raid those of others. My example
of a pastoral mode of life will be the Karimojong.

People who practise agriculture – often valuing cattle too –
are the vast majority, and there are many differences among
them. Much of the soil of Africa, particularly in the centre and
east, is so rapidly exhausted that the people who live from it
have to move their villages every few years. Elsewhere there are
permanent settlements in which every household reckons to
have enough land to leave part of it fallow each year. Where
this is the case, rights to land are important among the claims
of kinship, or holders of political authority may have the right
to say who shall cultivate land within their borders. One of the
best descriptions of the effects of different ecologies on the way
of life of culturally similar populations is to be found in the
work of Elizabeth Colson and Thayer Scudder on the Tonga of
Zambia, and I shall take them as an illustration, though not
with any implications that they are typical; there is no 'typical'
African agricultural society.

KINSHIP

Anthropologists conventionally classify kinship systems according to the way in which people reckon descent. Everyone
is descended from two parents, and each of them from two,
and so on . . . But nobody can know all his ancestors, let alone
all his collateral kin, and what is important for a social system

is who is selected for recognition. In many societies, and in most African societies, people trace their descent *unilineally*, that is through father to father's father, or mother to mother's mother, as far back as they can reckon. Persons linked by either mode of descent form *lineages*, which are the source of rights to inheritance and are sometimes held collectively responsible for debts incurred or offences committed by any of their members; in societies which allow private revenge it is lineage mates who have the right and duty of avenging the death of one of their number. If one is counting heads one can say the majority of Africans are *patrilineal* (tracing descent through males), but if one is counting peoples, the balance is different, because there are a very large number of *matrilineal* peoples, most of them with a small population. Most of these are found in a belt stretching across Africa and including a large part of Zaïre, Zambia, Malawi and Tanzania. Many matrilineal peoples live in regions of poor soil, where villages are small and frequently divide when they move. Many inhabit regions where cattle cannot live. But some matrilineal peoples keep cattle, and one, the most populous of all, the Ashanti in Ghana who number over half a million, own valuable land on which they grow cocoa for sale.

The different descent rules lead to a number of other differences between societies of these two types. In particular, patrilineal peoples marry with bridewealth – a substantial payment to a woman's kin which has the effect of making her children the husband's legitimate offspring. In a matrilineal society the children belong to their mother's descent group, and if any marriage payment is made it is usually much smaller. Such societies have to face difficult problems when they enter the market economy; a family may work together to earn a money income, but anything that the father may have saved will go outside the family when he dies. The patrilineal people to be discussed here are the Tallensi, the first African society of which a detailed account of kinship has been given; as examples of matriliny I have chosen the Tonga and Lele.

Some peoples reckon descent through males for some purposes and through females for others. The characteristic distinction is that land is transmitted through males (and therefore patrilineal descent groups tend to live together) and movable property through females (and therefore matrilineal groups make and receive the marriage payments of their members). The first people of this kind to be closely studied were the Yakö on the Cross River in the east of Nigeria, described by Daryll Forde. Others have been found more recently in northern Ghana. The Herero in South-West Africa also have a double descent system, but not much is known about their institutions.

The other possible way of reckoning kinship is to give equal weight to both parents and to one's collateral kin on both sides. This is not common in Africa, but two examples may be quoted. First are the Lozi, the dominant people of the Barotse kingdom in Zambia, and their system illustrates how grouping by descent may lose its importance when a central authority is responsible both for justice and for the allocation of land. Lozi live on little mounds rising above the flood waters of the Zambezi River, each under the authority of a headman who holds his position from the Paramount Chief. A man seeking new land would go to a mound village where he had kin – any kin – and ask the headman to admit him. So the population of such a village would be a body of kin, but not a group based on a fixed principle of descent. A headman's successor would be chosen by the people living on the mound at the time, but not in any fixed line of succession. This type of kinship system is called *cognatic*.

The example to be discussed here is provided by a people very different from the Lozi. They are the Ndendeuli of south-western Tanzania, an amalgam of tribes who were conquered in the nineteenth century by Ngoni invaders from the south, but managed to move out of reach of control by their Ngoni masters as the latters' power became weaker. But Gulliver, who has described their system, does not think their lack of lineal descent rules is the result of mixture or of their subject status; he thinks they never were organised in descent groups. His treatment of their kinship organisation introduces a number of concepts which had not previously been used in analysing African societies.

POLITICAL SYSTEMS

It was in reference to African ethnography that anthropologists first began to ask the question whether every society must have a political system. If there was no chief with a right to command obedience, where should one look for such a system? What, in fact, should it be? The first answer was given in the introduction which Radcliffe-Brown wrote for *African Political Systems*, and was illustrated by the brief account of the Nuer which Evans-Pritchard later amplified in his book *The Nuer*. The definition (abbreviated a little) said the political system of any society was *that part of the total system* which is concerned with the maintenance of order by the use or the possibility of use of physical force, a definition that people have often misquoted when seeking to invalidate it. The Nuer are the classic type of a *segmentary* system, in which descent groups are autonomous, and their 'ordered anarchy' is maintained by the readiness of individuals to fight for their rights and the obligation on kinsmen to support one another. Evans-Pritchard's account of them has indeed sometimes been described as 'classical structural analysis', with the implication that any structural analysis must produce such a model and therefore the method is inadequate for a study of political behaviour. Reinterpretations of it have been offered. But it remains a landmark in the development of social anthropology.

The type of system known as *age organisation* has been mentioned as characteristic of nomad pastoralists. This distributes political functions among the whole population. The entry of boys into manhood is recognised by a formal and often elaborate ritual of initiation, and further rituals mark the stages through which they move as they grow older. Before fighting was forbidden by the overriding authority of colonial powers, the young men were warriors and were expected to spend a large part of their time in raiding neighbouring tribes. Now they exercise coercion to implement the decisions of the elders. The fullest account of such a system, and one which examines it primarily from the point of view of social control and the maintenance of order, is Gulliver's study of the Arusha, a settled agricultural people who may have broken off from a Masai tribe. Gulliver shows how the meeting of the elders is one of a number of alternative venues for the discussion of disputes, and how individuals choose where they will take their quarrels according to their chances of winning support. The Arusha system is much more complex than that of the Karimojong, who were mentioned in connection with the way of life of pastoral peoples.

When we come to discuss kingdoms, we may seem to be on more familiar ground. But in fact there are many differences in the organisation of kingdoms, and some are very unlike those we read of in the history of Europe. There is much argument on the question whether any of them should be called feudal, and words such as 'vassal', which are associated with the feudal period of European history, are sometimes used in describing them. The examples to be discussed are the cluster of Interlacustrine Bantu states, Bunyoro and Buganda, Rwanda and Burundi and the kingdom of Benin in western Nigeria. Every centralised political system contains its own checks and balances, if only those that arise from the competition of rivals for office, or from the need to distribute power by delegating authority. All competitors for power need followers, and although they may get followers by coercion, they must make themselves popular to some degree. This is a crude form of check on abuse, and it becomes less effective with the development of specialised armies and weapons. The Interlacustrine Bantu states had not gone very far along this line of development. They rested on a system of clientage, in which a rich and powerful man would guarantee protection to weaker individuals who offered him their services. As far as we can tell from the records the fortunes of individuals and states fluctuated with their power to keep the loyalty of individual clients and vassal rulers. One effectively centralised state was Rwanda, where the ruler did maintain a standing army, recruited from the pastoral aristocracy and 'serviced' by the commoners who herded the cattle that went with the army to supply its food. Writers have sharply contrasted these kingdoms with the egalitarian segmentary societies that are their neighbours, saying that they take for granted 'the premise of inequality'; they assume that some men are born to rule and others to serve.

The West African example, Benin, is a much more complex one and has a longer recorded history. It belongs to the part of Africa that has been engaged for centuries in a coastal trade with Europeans (not only for slaves) which rival rulers have competed to control. Slave raiding was in fact traditional in West Africa, and his control of a large number of slaves was one source of a ruler's power.

But what is remarkable about West African polities is the complexity of the offices and roles that were recognised. There were councils with a great measure of autonomy whom the ruler was required to consult. There were associations of palace officials, and of others outside the palace, within which individuals strove for promotion. There were bodies of priests on whose performance of ritual the rulers depended for legitimacy and for the prosperity of their domains. These are the kingdoms from which we have hard data on politics as the struggle for power.

RELIGION

African religion has been the subject in recent years of much theoretical discussion. In this field social anthropology has been dominated during its history by a number of different theories. Frazer's were concerned with religion as a means of getting what you want (which it certainly has been to many believers). He saw it as the attitude of people who were disappointed to find that they could not control the forces of nature by applying the 'bastard science' of magic; they must have reasoned, he said, that there were beings stronger than themselves whose will was thwarting their will and must be placated. The individuals who hit on this explanation also claimed to know how to approach these unseen beings; they became priests and dominated their fellows to their own advantage.

Durkheim was writing at the same time as Frazer, but he was concerned not so much with belief systems as with the relation between religious belief and social order. For him the essence of religion was the church, in which believers gathered to assert their faith, and he held, though he did not put it in exactly these words, that the beings towards whom they directed their worship were in fact personifications of the social order conceived as a moral order. This theory led scholars to study the nature of congregations and the occasions on which they meet, and in general it appeared that two main types of ritual were regularly performed: that in which a kin group seeks blessings on some of its members at a time of social transition – a child and its mother at birth, a youth or girl at initiation into adulthood, a couple at marriage, the bereaved and the heir after a death – and that in which a whole community approaches a common divinity to pray for general prosperity. In addition there are 'piacular' rituals performed to appease some being whose anger is held responsible for sickness and other misfortunes.

Malinowski explicitly rejected Durkheim's theory, but his own in fact had much in common with it. Where it contrasts most strongly with some current ideas is in its insistence on the essentially emotional character of religion. Of course it is, as Frazer recognised in the context of a different kind of argument, an expression of man's helplessness, but modern interpreters of African religion would say it was a great deal more. Malinowski insisted that primitive man was a pragmatist, good at observing the objects in his environment that he needed to use, but not interested in speculation about the nature of the world. The French sociologists were already embarked on that study of primitive classification that has culminated in the theories of Lévi-Strauss, and there has now been a revival of interest in the content of religious beliefs. We have not necessarily returned to the 'intellectualist' interpretation of religion as a system of ideas consciously worked out, but we no longer neglect its intellectual aspect.

An earlier interest in religious beliefs for their own sake is connected with Evans-Pritchard's argument that social systems are not, as Radcliffe-Brown saw them, 'natural systems' subject to laws comparable with those of the physical sciences, but symbolic systems in which one can only see patterns. It would seem to follow that the essential aspect of any society is the system of ideas by which people's conduct is governed, and this implies going beyond mere statements that certain actions are pleasing or otherwise to divine beings, and examining all the ideas that are held about the nature of these beings.

Ancestor worship *per se* does not produce very complex

theologies. The ancestors are dead human beings, some of them well remembered as individuals. Peoples with a whole pantheon of other spirits – such as the Nilotes and some west Africans – lend themselves better to the study of religious ideas outside the context of organised ritual. Godfrey Lienhardt, however, in his work on the Dinka has combined the two in a most illuminating study of a Nilotic religion. From West Africa Robin Horton has interpreted Kalabari religion as a theoretical construct comparable to the generalisations that scientists seek to establish.

The serious study of the belief in witchcraft began with Evans-Pritchard's work on the Zande, in which he showed how the ascription of misfortunes to what some people call 'mystical aggression' is a perfectly logical way of thinking. No explanation in terms of general causes accounts for the fact that one person rather than another suffers at a particular time. Evans-Pritchard explored Zande witchcraft and magical beliefs in the same detail as he later examined Nuer religion. Monica Wilson, writing on the Nyakyusa, added to his theory the relation of witchcraft to morality – to the idea that people should not suffer unless they have done something to deserve it.

These then are the examples that I have chosen from the works of British social anthropologists to show how ethnographic work illustrates theoretical positions. Each is taken from the work of an anthropologist who lived for a year or more with the people of whom he writes, speaking their language and joining as far as he could in their activities. It is no good pretending that any of them had seen an African society as it was before the days of European penetration. Every people had been in some way affected by the activities of a European government seeking to prevent the use of physical force, to make their countries productive and to introduce them to 'civilisation' as different European nations interpreted that word. All had been required to pay taxes and therefore had to earn cash incomes in one way or another. European authority replaced that of African chiefs, so that accounts of indigenous political systems could only be reconstructions based on the memories of old men, the casual observations of travellers, and, in exceptional cases, rare documents. Yet we claim to be able to give some kind of account of these systems; perhaps we are weakest when we are trying to judge how far the independent chiefs and kings had the genuine support of their subjects and how far dissent could be expressed and could be effective. Where anthropologists worked, missions had been established, sometimes for longer than secular authority, and some individuals had adopted Christianity. There were also Muslim converts. But traditional rituals had rarely been abandoned altogether.

Particularly in the last thirty years, the population of African cities has enormously increased, partly by permanent emigration from the rural areas, but largely by a to-and-fro movement in which men spend part of their time earning wages in town and part at their home in the village. The life of the town is geared to modern production, and town-dwellers must enter into new types of relationship, with employers, with landlords, with policemen, with work-mates. Modern forms of communication have brought town and country much closer than they used to be. The great expansion of education in the last twenty years has vastly increased the number of people qualified for work that requires literacy.

All these developments have led some people to argue, either that ethnography is no longer worth studying because we should be interested in the problems of change to a 'modern' type of society, or that there is no longer any ethnography to study because no African people still preserves a characteristic culture and social structure. Yet when an anthropologist is able to revisit the scene of fieldwork done thirty or forty years ago, he does not find it unrecognisable; and anthropologists doing their first fieldwork today find themselves observing, with all the money, all the schooling, all the work in town, all the transistor radios, the institutions of non-mechanised societies. This is why most university courses in social anthropology still begin with ethnography.

2   Food-Gatherers: The Mbuti Pygmies *

Some societies are constrained primarily by their environment, others by the limitations of their technology, that is of the tools and methods that they have devised to exploit their environment. In arid country the ultimate limiting factor is the quest for water; herdsmen in such country must organise their whole lives around this. But the largest food-gathering population that is still to be found in Africa, the pygmies of the Ituri forest on the borders of Zaïre and Uganda, are subject to little constraint of this kind. Their way of life is a matter of the techniques that they use to get their food and other necessities, and at the present time they stick to it not because they could not learn, as almost all the rest of humanity has, to destroy the forest and plant food crops in its place, but because they do not want to. 'If we were to cultivate we should die', they say. They like to be in the forest; it is where they feel safe and at ease. They can move in it as they please; there is plenty of water everywhere and there are few insect pests.

What does the forest give them? Animal food of all kinds, from elephants to insects; edible roots, mushrooms, nuts, berries and fruits. Honey has a special place because there is one short honey season in the year, and during the time when they are collecting it they are organised in different groups from those that hunt together for the rest of the year. Their scanty clothing is made from the bark of a tree, which is soaked and then beaten out into strips; and fruits and flowers yield dye to make patterns on it. Their houses are made of leaves on a frame of saplings. Such dwellings can be set up in a few hours and are abandoned when a band moves on, after not more than a month in one camp. People never camp twice in the same place. The forest gives them wood to burn and to make implements and weapons. It seems that they do not know how to make fire, and so must carry embers with them whenever they move camp. There are no metals, but reeds and bamboos can be split to make sharp edges for cutting. Wooden arrows

* *Wayward Servants.* Colin Turnbull, 1965.

and spears have their points hardened by fire, and arrows are smeared with a poison as deadly as any metal tip could be. Vines provide ropes; nets and bowstrings, and baskets for carrying the food they collect, are made of fibres of different kinds.

The forest, then, *can* provide the Mbuti with all the essentials for survival. But there is a catch here. On the edge of the forest live villagers of the different Bantu and Sudanic tribes who have been encroaching on it for centuries. These peoples know how to make pots of clay and metal knives, and they earn money in various ways and buy pots and pans and machets at trade stores. The Mbuti like these durable, labour-saving implements as much as anyone else does, and they get them from villagers in exchange for meat and honey. The villagers claim to exercise authority over the pygmies and try to 'civilise' them – that is to teach them their religious beliefs and rituals and see that they perform them; and individual villagers claim that individual pygmies are their servants, and are obliged to bring them meat and to work for them when they visit the village. But this is another story, and as long as the pygmies are in their forest home the existence of their village neighbours does not affect them.

HUNTING TECHNOLOGY

The essential constraint of technology for the pygmies lies in the kind of co-operation imposed by different methods of hunting. Some use bows and arrows; others drive the game into a net and then kill it with spears. An archer can go out hunting on his own, but Mbuti archers prefer to join in companies of about three men. Hunting with nets needs more man-power, and woman-power as well. Men and boys set up nets in a semi-circle, and women make a line joining the two extremes, and drive the game in front of them, shouting and beating branches on the ground. A net-hunt calls for the co-operation of everyone in a camp except small children and old people, and the fact that people know this is, as will be seen, the strongest force constraining people to keep on good terms with their neighbours. The arc of nets should be neither too narrow nor too wide, and this is what fixes the desirable limits to the size of the band. Every married man has a net of his own. One could reverse this statement and say that every man who has shown that he is a proficient hunter is entitled both to have his own net and to marry; to be allowed to set up house he must kill an antelope and present it to his bride's mother. Either his own mother makes him a net or his father gives him a portion of his, to which his wife will add. A net can be as much as three hundred feet long. It follows then that a net-hunting band needs at least six or seven families and cannot do with more than thirty.

Gathering honey does not need an organised team; it is more important to collect all there is during the short season. At this time, then, a hunting band splits up into two or three sections so as to cover all its territory.

In contrast the band of archers, which for most of the time is divided into sections of three or four families, meets together once a year, actually at the beginning of the honey season, for a communal hunt in which the game is driven towards a line of men without nets. There is no constraint here, either of environment or of technology; this is a custom that archers have chosen to follow. Why? Perhaps, since they regard themselves as belonging to a single band, they feel that they must assert their unity from time to time; our author, who knows less of the archers than he does of the net-hunters, does not tell us.

What then is a band? How does anyone know what band he belongs to? A band is the collection of people who claim the right to exploit a named territory; it is called by the name of the territory, and everyone is a member of the band he was born in and calls that band's territory his home. But there is nothing to stop him spending most of his life with other bands where he has kinsmen, and if he does so he is not treated as an outsider.

So band membership is not a matter of claims based on descent, and this fact supports the view that descent begins to be important only when there is property to be inherited or sectional rights to be defended. It can be important where jural rights are protected only by self-help and vengeance; but the pygmies do not recognise the institution of self-help and vengeance.

It has been argued that patrilineal descent could be expected to develop among hunting peoples because fathers teach their sons to hunt, and the sons stay in the area that they have learned to know. Mbuti sons do tend – 'other things being equal' – to stay in their fathers' bands, which are their home bands, but many things may not be equal. Marriages are generally made between members of different bands, so that everyone has kin in more than one; a hunter may be invited to join a band whose numbers are low, or he may quarrel with somebody in his own band, or he may just feel like paying a visit to kin elsewhere. Sons do not hunt with their fathers, because tasks in the forest are allotted according to age; boys help their fathers to set up nets and learn by watching them, and brothers may stand together in the line of men waiting for the game to charge the net, and get some advantage from knowing how each is likely to react. But the older hunters stand in the middle of the arc, the younger at the ends, so that fathers and sons are separated.

SOCIAL CONTROL

Pygmies are no less aggressive, and no more conscientious about their obligations, than members of other societies, and they need as much as anyone a system of social control that will secure necessary co-operation and respect for accepted norms of conduct, and prevent the 'disturbance of the peace'. Yet they recognise nobody as having authority to command. Wisdom, yes; but even somebody credited with wisdom will be shouted down or 'laughed out of court' if he seems to be trying to impose his will.

So, if nobody 'runs' the band, how is it 'run'? It is held to be the duty of the older men to quiet 'noise' – the noise of quarrelling, which the pygmies believe displeases the forest, and may make it withdraw its protection and inflict on them disasters such as thunderstorms that bring trees crashing down. But their method does not lie in direct rebuke, still less in the infliction of punishment. Indeed they avoid passing judgement on the rights and wrongs of a quarrel.

Quarrels are between individuals, at any rate in the beginning. Failure to meet the obligation to join in the hunt is a failure in obligation to the band as a whole. How is this dealt with?

Laziness, Turnbull tells us, is one of the few failings that the Mbuti explicitly condemn, since it is only the lazy who need go hungry, and a few men's laziness can cause many men's hunger. But sometimes it is damp and chilly at dawn, when the hunt should set out, and since there is no one to give marching orders some people may stay at home. Turnbull witnessed two occasions of this kind. On the first, there was no discussion, but someone who wanted the hunt to go on made an effective protest. This took a form characteristic of the pygmies – a wordless comment, expressed in mime and not directed at any particular person, and intended to provoke laughter as well as to make a serious point. The wife of one of the older hunters came out into the middle of the camp, carrying her husband's spear, and mimed in dance a successful hunt and the general pleasure in the distribution of the food. The silent argument struck home, and the hunt went out.

On the second occasion a number of young men set out only to find that most of the camp had not followed them. This time they came back and abused the lazy ones, particularly the women. The latter retorted that they had their own work and that it was the youths who were at fault. This time there was no hunt, but next day all the women turned out, each carrying her husband's net and spear.

Pygmies can show disapproval of an individual's behaviour in other ways. When a camp is set up the leaf houses are built facing inwards but not aligned on a central point. Friends build close together and with entrances looking towards one another. If someone in your vicinity behaves badly, you add another entrance to your hut facing away from him. A whole complex of alliances and oppositions can be silently proclaimed in this way.

Actual quarrelling is another matter, and here the constraint of technology is all-important. A net-hunting band is utterly dependent on the willing co-operation of all its members. Not only must everyone take part in the hunt, but everyone must do his best; there can be no tripping someone up or letting him down because of a personal grudge. Therefore, it is more important that quarrels should be forgotten, or at best smothered, than that their rights and wrongs should be adjudicated.

This attitude is expressed, in what we should call symbolic terms, in the belief, literally held by the Mbuti, that 'noise displeases the forest'. This statement can be taken in a prosaic sense: noise frightens game and is bad for hunting. But the Mbuti mean more than that. They see the forest as a being, essentially benevolent, a source of protection and of livelihood, but one who can withhold protection if displeased. And the 'noise' of quarrelling – not the actual shouting but the ill-will and disturbance of harmony – is what displeases the forest most. Bad behaviour in general, if it has to be discussed, is called 'noise'. The nearest that people would generally go to a public criticism would be to refer to someone's 'noise'.

Since the Mbuti hold that quarrels should be forgotten rather than settled, they have an institution for dealing with them in this way. This is by allotting to some man in every camp the role of buffoon. The camp buffoon is not formally appointed; he grows into his role. He is usually a rather poor hunter, who is naturally an object of ridicule, and he makes good his technical deficiencies by developing his ridiculous qualities. Turnbull himself occupied this position in the early days when he had not learned the technique of hunting. The camp buffoon is expected, when name-calling seems to be imminent or even before, to distract attention by making people laugh; if necessary he must let them put the blame for anything that is wrong in the camp on his own 'noise'. Above all, he must try to prevent the naming of an individual, even if, and all the more if, that person is clearly in the wrong, because he would be humiliated, and so resentful, and so uncooperative.

People will in fact take sides in quarrels, a process which grows out of, and cements, feelings of personal friendship. They express their feelings, as I mentioned, by the siting and orientation of their huts, and every move to a new camp is an occasion for choosing a new alignment or reaffirming the old one, and by the same token a way of moving out of uncomfortable proximity. The frequent moves thus make some relief of tension possible. Even more so does the division of the band in the honey season, when for a month or two people need only see their friends. At this time a section which is at odds with the rest of the band may leave it altogether, joining another band when net-hunting begins again. And there is yet another possibility: a visit to the village. As the Mbuti see these visits, they periodically raid the village for what they can get; as the villagers see it, the pygmies are their servants, who have a duty to bring their tribute of meat and honey from time to time. There is no fixed time for them, but some respected elder may suggest one if he feels that disharmony in the camp is getting out of hand. While they are in the villages the pygmies do not depend on the co-operation of the hunt. Every individual tries to please, and get what he can out of, the individual villager who claims him as a servant.

RELIGION

The concentration of the pygmies' religion on the forest clearly reflects their way of life, though one could certainly not say that their dependence on the forest *constrains* them to see it as a god. It is more interesting that, in spite of seeing it in this way, they do not appear to perform rituals with the express aim of ensuring the benefits that come from it, as do nearly all peoples who are directly dependent on their environment. They take for granted plentiful game and vegetable foods; if the hunt is not successful the pygmies blame themselves for displeasing the forest. It is not true, as has been recently asserted, that they do not need an explanation for misfortune, though it is true that they do not ascribe it to the malevolent magic or witchcraft of their neighbours, and in this respect they are peculiar, though perhaps not unique, among African peoples.

If things go wrong, in the sense that hunting is bad or there is much sickness, the forest is thought, not to be actively punishing its children, but to have lost interest in them – 'gone to sleep'. Then it must be awakened and caused to rejoice, and the way to do this is by singing. It is the musical sound that pleases the forest rather than any supposed verbal communication with it; Mbuti singing may be almost wordless, but it follows very elaborate patterns.

Malinowski held that the essential function of religion was to give man confidence in the face of death. Others might add further functions, but the Mbuti death ritual, as described by Turnbull, certainly supports the view that this is one. In saying that it is an assertion of the triumph of life over death, Turnbull is saying no more than could be said of any death ritual, but what is peculiar to the Mbuti is their almost complete suppression of the mourning aspect. Their attitude can perhaps be explained by the very small size of the band, which is seriously affected by the loss of a single adult. A dead person is buried by the survivors in his own nuclear family, without any public ritual, and they are expected as far as they can to suppress their manifestations of grief. Immediately afterwards the camp moves on, and as soon as possible after the new one has been built there begins the *molimo* festival, which should last at least a month. While this is going on people must hunt every day and sing for most of the night. The best singer sings through a trumpet which magnifies his voice, and which is also treated as a sexual symbol, and there is other symbolism of sex, therefore fertility, therefore life (as in nearly all primitive death rituals).

The other important ritual occasion for the Mbuti is the *elima*, or girls' puberty ceremony. As the *molimo* is essentially the men's performance, the *elima* is similarly that of the women. The girls are taken to the forest to sing their special songs, and they also visit the camps of other bands, and there make marriage arrangements; there is no ritual for the occasion when a couple actually set up house.

Although this ritual is a prelude to marriage, it includes very marked expressions of sexual antagonism. When the girls go visiting, they invite boys of their choice to come to the hut where they are to sleep at night. But the invitation is a curious one; the girl conveys it by whipping the boy with a young sapling. And when he arrives he is beaten again and sometimes not even allowed to sleep with the girl who invited him. Towards the end of the *elima* period youths may enter the hut without being invited, but to do so they must battle against a company of the girls' mothers armed with sticks and stones.

Sexual antagonism is a feature of other rituals as well. In the *molimo* an old woman has the special role of appearing to oppose its aims; she scatters the ritual fire, which the men then must build up again, and she also tries to 'tie up' the hunt. In a dance known as *ekokomea*, performed both during the *molimo* and in the honey season, each sex adopts the clothes and typical behaviour of the other, even to mimicking copulation with the roles reversed; the dancers make this as comic as possible.

Since the upshot of the *elima* is a series of betrothals, those who wish can say, with Gluckman, that the ritual reaffirms solidarity by allowing the expression of conflict. Turnbull might not say so, but he finds a ritual expression of social order in the allocation of parts in the different types of song, which correspond to the major divisions of the society.

The Mbuti do not believe in the possibility of witchcraft. In this respect they contrast with their village neighbours, who do their best to convince them of it. Why is this? If one accepts the theory that witchcraft is invoked to explain undeserved misfortunes, the answer will be that the Mbuti think *all* misfortune is deserved, since it is an expression of the forest's displeasure. Another theory, that of Mary Douglas, is that people fear witchcraft if they have to live in close contact with their fellows, and she cites the Nuer and Dinka as people with sparse, irregular social contacts, who do not fear it. Can one apply this theory to the Mbuti? The members of a hunting band are in constant close contact; but you can change your band more easily than you can change the village where your food crops have been planted. This is a field where theory is fluid.

THE MBUTI AND THE VILLAGE

The forest is the home of the Mbuti, and they are not obliged to leave it, though they may see their way to getting some advantages from visits to the alien, hot, dusty, crowded world of the village. In this respect they are more fortunate than many of the African peoples who have found themselves forced to leave home and earn money for taxes that they have to pay. Yet it seems that the Mbuti are coming more and more to value objects that they can only get by barter with villagers, just as all the rest of Africa is coming more and more to value the objects that can be bought with a money income.

The villagers have a clear conception of their relationship with the Mbuti, which the Mbuti do not by any means share. As they see it, every individual pygmy is the servant of an individual villager, who is his *kpara* or 'owner'. This is a hereditary status. A villager inherits his father's servants, and a Mbuti inherits his father's master. In reality, individual pygmies choose whom they will recognise as *kpara*. The essence of the relationship is that the pygmy should supply his master with meat and honey. Some have tried, without much success, to make their 'servants' work in harvesting cotton, but all that most of them will do is scare birds from the crops.

The villagers try to control the Mbuti by fitting them into the village social structure. The *kpara* calls his servants his 'children', and seeks to exercise paternal authority over them. This implies having them take part in the same passage rituals – at initiation, marriage and death – as the villagers do, and logically to have gone through the initiation and marriage rituals should give a pygmy the permanent status which these rituals confer. Thus the *kpara* has his servants' sons initiated along with his own sons, and this can be made the occasion for creating a relationship of blood-brotherhood (*kare*) between a village boy and a Mbuti. This relationship should be one in which gifts are exchanged, or goods bartered, as you like to think of it, but it has also ritual aspects; the Mbuti *kare*, for example, has special duties at his village *kare's* funeral. The Mbuti is entitled to seek favours from his *kare*, and a villager, for whom the ritual has a meaning that it does not have for the Mbuti, is more likely to respect his obligation.

The *kpara* and the village *kare* are responsible for the marriage of their Mbuti partners, and they try to insist that it be performed in the village manner. They pay bridewealth to the girl's *kpara* and provide a feast which the Mbuti enjoy, though they do not regard either payment or feast as in any way validating a marriage. At such a marriage the couple are admonished, not on their marital duties as a village couple would be, but on their duties to their respective *kpara*.

Particularly in the ritual of death there is a striking contrast between Mbuti values and practices and those that the villagers impose upon them. The Mbuti death ritual has been described – the quick abandonment of the camp and the turn to the joyful *molimo* festival. The villagers believe that the cause of death, which must be witchcraft or supernatural punishment, must be identified by divination; and if a witch is identified and accused, he or she must go through a cleansing ritual and perhaps pay compensation. This the Mbuti greatly dislike, and they avoid taking part in it as far as they can.

Some village men marry Mbuti girls, and this is part of the process that is everywhere gradually wearing down the numbers of the food-gatherers. But these pygmies seem to have succeeded better in being in the village while not of it than any comparable population has done.

3 Nomad Herdsmen: The Karimojong*

The Karimojong inhabit an unfriendly part of the arid or semi-arid country in the north-east of Uganda; their home is just inside the border with Kenya. They numbered some 55,000 when they were last counted in 1948.

Their country is a plateau about 4,000 feet above sea-level, broken by small rocky hills and some isolated higher mountains rising to 10,000 feet. There is only one permanently flowing river, in the extreme east. The others rise in the mountains, and their rocky upper courses do not hold the rain; water flows there for only a few hours after a storm, except in a few rocky pools that hold it for longer. Lower down the river-beds become sandy and then swampy. In their sandy stretches the water flows for two or three days after every rainstorm, perhaps thirty days in the year; but some of it sinks into the sand and can be reached by digging. A few swampy areas hold water all the year round. Also on the hills and mountains there are scattered rocky pools that hold water for a few weeks.

TERRITORIAL DIVISIONS

The only places where people can live permanently are ridges near the sandy stretches of river-beds, where they can make water-holes, and these are concentrated in a limited area in the eastern part of the country. There there is also alluvial soil where grain can be grown, but not nearly enough to provide a staple food, even when the rainfall is exceptionally good. It is their flocks and herds that enable the Karimojong to live. In the wet season all the stock are gathered at these settlements for a month or two, but as the water shrinks and the grass dries up they must be moved further and further away. Karimojong have names for all the types of water source that I have mentioned, and they know how to recognise the signs of underground water; armed with this knowledge the herdsmen set out, each exercising his own judgement in the light of his fam-

* *Karimojong Politics*. N. Dyson-Hudson, 1966.

25

iliarity with the terrain near his home and the more distant pastures which he will have to seek at the height of the dry season. In the permanent settlements live the women and the small number of men who herd the milch cattle allocated to them and their children. Goats are left with them, since they can browse on thorn bushes; and they can eat porridge made of the millet that the women plant, as long as the rains do not fail altogether.

A settlement is a group of huts neatly thatched with grass in what looks like a pattern of flounces, and surrounded by a stockaded hedge. The herds are brought into it at night. Apart from the outer hedge and cattle gates it is entirely built by women. Ideally it should be the home of an extended family – the head with his wives and unmarried daughters, his sons and their wives and unmarried children. Actually a single settlement often includes a number of separate families who have chosen to build close together. Every settlement must be within reach of water for its herds, but each does not have its own watering-point. Half-a-dozen or so will water their stock at the same place, and this common resource, and the occasion for daily meeting, makes them into what Dyson-Hudson calls 'neighbourhoods'. The neighbourhood he describes in detail comprised seven settlements and 267 people; the number in a settlement ranged from 14 to 61.

Karimojong recognise a wider division of their territory than the neighbourhood: what Dyson-Hudson calls a 'section'. The word literally means 'ridge', but the proper name for each section is the name of the people who belong to it, and in fact some sections (in this sense) have moved considerable distances within the recorded past. Each has a ceremonial ground where important rituals are performed, and this is the most permanent feature of a section's territory. But a time can come when some of them say it is too far to go to this place, and set up a new sacred place of their own; this marks a division of the section.

Whereas Karimojong believe, as a general principle, that in the dry season they are entitled to graze their cattle in any pastures they can find – dispossessing people of other tribes if necessary, as long as the Uganda government does not send police or troops to stop them – the sections have exclusive claims to the pasture adjoining their ridges and dividing them. No one may make a permanent settlement there, and only members of neighbouring sections may graze their cattle there. Such an area is a buffer zone, but between friends, not enemies.

The men on the move build rough camps with thorn hedges to protect the cattle; they sleep themselves in the open. They live entirely from their cattle, except when, if they are near home, a party of girls brings them a little grain. They drink milk, or eat it curdled solid, and they mix it with blood drawn from the neck of an ox. The main practical concern is to keep the numbers of the herd up to the point where there is enough milk for both humans and calves to live on; that is why they cannot be persuaded to cut down the numbers and try to build up smaller herds of 'better' cattle. When cattle die, or when some ritual occasion calls for a slaughter in sacrifice, of course they are eaten; but they are not reared for this purpose and are very seldom killed solely for meat.

CATTLE VALUES

Cattle are a source of other necessities besides food. Their hides make clothing and blankets; their horns and hooves containers of various kinds; their scrota make bags. Their urine is used to cleanse vessels made of wood or of gourds, and to wash human hands, particularly in the cattle camps where there is seldom enough water for this. It is mixed with mud for the floors of huts; it is used to curdle milk, most of which is stored in that form. In the permanent settlements where grain is grown the cattle droppings provide manure. Dyson-Hudson remarks that they have also ritual uses, in that their intestines are the material for divination and their chyme for anointing; but one might comment on this statement that this is possible only when an animal has been sacrificed, and that if it were not for the ritual value that attaches to cattle – of course *because* the Karimojong are so utterly dependent on them – something else could be the object of sacrifice, and something else would be found as the object of divination. In the realm of ritual as opposed to technical activities, there is never any difficulty in finding objects to use.

But the central place of cattle in ritual, and their central place in aesthetic interest, is of course an expression of the close relationship and dependence that links men with their herds; and this is most clearly expressed in the way that human groups are defined in terms of the cattle they herd.

An independent family is essentially one that has complete control over a herd of cattle; but the corollary of this is that if two independently owned herds are normally run together, the two owning groups will call themselves 'one family'. The limits of Karimojong territory, as they themselves see it, are determined not by lines on a map but by grazing needs; they will fight for these, but in the conviction that it is their competitors, not themselves, who are encroaching. When a youth is initiated into manhood the herd from his settlement must be brought to the ceremonial place of his neighbourhood. In rituals involving larger numbers of people, each participant group brings its herds with it.

PROPERTY

It has often been observed that peoples living near the margin of subsistence readily share food in times of scarcity. But it by no means follows that they share the sources of food. If there is little appropriation of property among the pygmies, the reason is that their food supply is given them by the forest; it is there when they find it, not before. In contrast cattle, which have been reared and tended, led to grazing and protected against wild beasts and raiders, are very definitely property. They outlive their owners and must be inherited, and specific persons have rights to the use of them. This seems clearly to be the reason, though not the only one, for the recognition of property claims arising from descent and marriage, and for the unambiguous division of the population into descent groups – lineages – each with rights in a common patrimony. The kinship system of the Karimojong, like those of the other Nilotic and Nilo-Hamitic herdsmen, is significant more in terms of rights to cattle than in any other respect. It illustrates the very important point that a lineage is not a co-operating but a right holding group.

We see then that their environment constrains the Karimojong to a particular mode of life, and a mode of co-operation which contrasts sharply both with that of the pygmies and with that of settled cultivators. Among the latter, subsistence depends on the co-operation of nuclear or extended families with occasional help from neighbours, while with the net-hunting pygmies a whole band hunts together, each member of a family playing a role appropriate to his age and sex. Karimojong men and women have their separate spheres, and for much of the time the members of one family are not even living together.

Nevertheless, there is nothing in the environment that constrains them to adopt the distribution of rights in cattle that they in fact recognise, or to divide their male population into two generations, each with its subdivisions, or to develop the aesthetic interest in cattle which characterises them. These are matters of choice, albeit a choice made many generations ago, or, as some would prefer to put it, of values.

Let us consider first the various people who claim rights to cattle. Inheritance follows the line of patrilineal descent, so that when the owner of a herd dies it is divided among a known number of people, namely all the sons of the owner, wherever they may be. To make a marriage valid – that is to say, to make the woman's children legitimate members of the man's lineage – cattle must be transferred from his side to hers, and the more cattle are handed over the more individuals receive them. Anyone who has received a beast in bridewealth can be called upon to help the giver whenever he is in trouble or difficulty, particularly if he is in need of stock; so that, although the right to inherit is confined to agnates (members of a patrilineage), when the dispersal of a herd is not in question agnates and affines are together considered as 'cattle kin', a body who have a common interest in the cattle gains and losses of their members. Persons who are recognised as kin but do not have claims on a single inheritance, and affines who have not received a share of bridewealth, call one another merely 'water kin'; they recognise an obligation of hospitality but not of giving cattle when called upon.

It is also possible to build up insurance against calamity by giving cattle to unrelated friends, who are then under an obligation to make return gifts, and can be called upon to do so in a crisis. This is an illustration of the principle of reciprocity

which was central to the teaching of Malinowski, though in
these days it is more often associated with the work of Marce
Mauss, *The Gift*. The existence of this 'dyadic contract', a
some writers call it, is regarded by some anthropologists as a
recent discovery ignored by students of social structure. It i
certainly true that where there are no corporate groups based
on descent, individual reciprocities are more important, as wil
be illustrated in Chapter 9; but to suppose that theorists of kin
ship are unaware of their existence is simply nonsense.

Women have certain claims on cattle. When a bride firs
arrives in her husband's settlement he (or his father if he is no
independent) must give her a cow the milk of which will be
used exclusively by her and her children, and more cow
should be allotted in the same way as the number of her chil
dren increases. She does not own these cattle in the sense tha
she could sell them or give them away; but she would have a
legitimate grievance if her husband took them from her to sel
or give away, and if she was one of several wives they would
probably be included in the inheritance claimed by her own
children.

There are also property rights in land and water. Anyone
who has once fenced in and planted an area of land has a claim
against any later comer, even if the land has been left fallow
for many years. Here again the position of women is anomal
ous. It is women who actually plant and grow the crops, but a
woman is only in a settlement in virtue of her marriage. He
daughters leave to be married elsewhere, and new daugh
ters-in-law take their place. If there were to be a disputed
claim it would be the husbands who would fight it out, and i
would be the settlement head, the senior man, who would
decide.

People may also fence the waterholes they have dug at th
permanent settlements. So vital is water to the Karimojong
that nobody should deny another access to it, but there ar
always questions of priority, and in times of severe drough
the herd that is watered first may get all there is. Outsiders ar
expected to ask permission to water stock in the settled area.

AUTHORITY

One possible way of distributing political functions is to allocate responsibility for the defence of herds and grazing grounds – and raiding those of neighbours – to *all* the young men of the tribe, and for the settlement of disputes and the ritual approach to divinity for blessings on people and cattle to *all* the elders. This is the effect of the age organisation – or gerontocracy as it is sometimes called – characteristic of the Karimojong and their neighbours. Where many men are continually travelling far from home and meeting complete strangers, this is a very useful guide to behaviour. Juniors must defer to seniors, and they learn which is which by exchanging age-set names. If there is a quarrel in a camp the senior age-set arbitrate it. If a band of herdsmen come to a place where a ritual or a raid is being organised, they can take part in it because each knows what is his appropriate role.

But although a well-marked ranking by age is convenient in these ways, one could not say that the environment of the Karimojong forces such a system upon them. Still less could this be said of the special features which differentiate the Karimojong age organisation from the many similar systems to be found in this part of Africa. Its fundamental principle is the division of the adult male population into a senior and a junior generation, the senior having authority over the junior, who collectively must obey them as individually they do their own fathers. Such a relationship is more readily accepted in a society that is not rapidly changing, where young men expect to follow in their fathers' footsteps and where there is no source of new knowledge and ideas available only to the young, than it has been in those parts of the world that have been transformed by mechanical inventions.

A youth enters the system through a ritual of initiation, at which he must spear the ox that his father has given to be sacrificed on his behalf, and his mother must make a feast for all the men of the neighbourhood. Once initiated he is entitled to marry and found his own family, and to take part in ritual activities. He will wish to be initiated as soon as he is old enough. But some families cannot spare an ox at this time, and some youths have to wait much longer than their contemporaries. A few men are never able to be initiated at all.

All those who are initiated during a period of five or six years form an *age-set* and are given a common name. Age-sets are distinguished by the ornaments they wear; and when a set wish to adopt a new style of ornament they must beg permission from the next set above, a rule that keeps each junior set constantly aware of the superior status of its seniors. Recruiting to a set, the Karimojong say, goes on until it has 'enough men'. What actually seems to happen is that the oldest section, *Ngibokora*, starts a new set and the rest follow.

Five sets make up a 'generation', and the generation-sets too are distinguished by their ornaments, through the colour of the metals they wear. This is not a matter of seniority, but of position in the endless succession of generations. Alternative generations wear 'yellow' (brass) or 'red' (copper) all through their lives, and this, linking grandparents with grandchildren, is a reminder of the succession of generations and the continuous life of the Karimojong over the centuries.

When five age-sets are complete it is time for the senior generation to retire, and give place to its juniors; by this time many of its older members will have died. The ritual that marks this change is the one great occasion that brings together all the tribe (or all who can travel). It happens only once in anyone's lifetime. If it is long delayed the whole polity may be put out of joint.

The senior generation as individuals are herd owners, controlling the disposal of the stock which is herded by their sons, and arranging the marriage of their daughters. As a body they are held to be alone capable of approaching the deity, Akuj, who is the source of all blessings for the Karimojong and can withhold them if he is displeased. For people who genuinely believe that their lives and fortunes are in the hands of a divine being the performance of the necessary ritual to obtain his good will is no small thing, and the position of the elders as intermediaries with him is what supports their authority in secular matters. Karimojong ascribe disasters that are remembered from the past to curses laid by the elders on juniors who were disrespectful.

Neighbourhoods largely manage their own affairs; sections organise their more important rituals together; it is only the great succession ceremony that concerns all Karimojong at one time. It is the elders who are responsible for such collective decisions as have to be made, and the junior generation who must see that their decisions are carried out if anyone does not voluntarily abide by them.

Essentially the responsibility of the elders is to maintain the welfare of the whole people by their mediation with Akuj, through the performance of ritual for the health of the cattle and for success in raids against the cattle of enemy neighbours. Two major ceremonies for the benefit of the cattle should be held every year. The most important of these is the one called 'Freeing the Cattle', when the rains are coming to an end and it is time for the young men to move away from the settlement with their herds. They beg the elders for permission, and then all the cattle are driven to the ceremonial ground and solemnly blessed before their departure. No doubt most herdsmen feel that they cannot hope to get safely through the long dry season without the blessing, but sometimes one tries to steal a march on his fellows. In that case a band of young men are sent to bring him back, and they beat him and take from him an ox for a sacrifice. At another ceremony, called the 'Beseeching', the young men beseech the elders to approach Akuj for his blessing on the herds. On both occasions the young men must sacrifice cattle which make a feast for the elders.

In these days, when the Uganda government hears of fighting for pastures or the raiding of cattle, it sends detachments of police or even of troops, arrests men who will be charged with murder, and imposes heavy fines. Yet raiding and fighting still go on. Raiding is not a mere pastime. It can arise out of fighting for pasture on disputed ground, and this is a matter of environmental constraint, in that in years of severe drought herds must be driven further afield than their normal pastures. The side which has lost cattle in such a fight will try to get them back in a raid. When such fighting was considered to be as legitimate as wars between nations are held to be today, the young men were given permission by the elders to set out on a raid, and a formal ritual of blessing was performed. Nowadays such a public declaration of intent would not be politic; some individuals among the Karimojong have been appointed as 'chiefs' by the government, and though their authority would not stop a raid, they would have to report such preparations unless they wanted to lose their jobs. Nevertheless, as late as 1958 this ceremony was held to bless an army of 600 warriors.

The elders also have responsibility in every-day matters. It is for the elders of a neighbourhood to decide whether a new-comer may settle there. It is for them also to settle disputes which arise within it; and the type of dispute that arises where people have property rights may be settled by a compromise, but it cannot be simply forgotten as Mbuti disputes can. A typical Karimojong dispute begins when someone seizes stock that he thinks are owed him and the owner does not admit the debt. The question is discussed in a gathering of all the men of the neighbourhood. All may give their opinions, but the elders must decide what is to be done. In most cases the decision is that somebody must hand over stock in compensation for a wrong. If the man adjudged to pay does not do so, the injured party will complain after a time, and the young men will be called on to take the stock from him. It happens sometimes also that a man who is called on to give an ox to be sacrificed at a ritual refuses to do so. Then the young men will be sent to take it, and one of them will spear it himself.

This secular sanction – resting on the command of physical force – may be reinforced by a ritual one. An elder may curse a recalcitrant junior, and the effect of this is greatly feared. The wrongdoer must abase himself before the elder and beg for-giveness, promising not to repeat his offence.

When Dyson-Hudson was among the Karimojong, a suc-cession ceremony had been due for nearly twenty years but had been postponed over and over again. First there was a succes-sion of droughts, during which the herdsmen had all they could do to keep their cattle alive, and could not have driven them all together to the tribal sacred ground. Then there was a series of outbreaks of cattle disease, which the government sought to control by forbidding the movement of stock. By the time Dyson-Hudson arrived there were not more than twenty of the senior generation left in the whole country, and even all the senior set of the junior generation had died. In the section where there were no elders, the 'Freeing the Cattle' ceremony could not be held, so that there was no co-ordination of cattle movements away from the settlements. The young men did no wait to be initiated before they married; indeed they could not, since they could not tell how long it would be before new initiations began to be held. The older of the uninitiated took to raiding, again without the control of the elders' sanction. They would not accept beatings from the initiated men who were still juniors, and sometimes they accused seniors who chastised them of assault, taking them before government-appointed chiefs.

The succession ceremony was held in 1958, soon after Dyson-Hudson arrived in the country. Juniors became elders, younger men were initiated as juniors, and those who had not yet married waited until after their initiation to do so. The long delay had not resulted in the breakdown of the system, though the two years that Dyson-Hudson spent there were not long enough to judge whether it would be restored in exactly its old form. But what is clear is that there was no question of having learned by experience that people could get on without it. To say that this reflects the conservatism of peoples of simple technology is to say very little. In the technical field they may be conservative because they think it wiser not to take risks – and often their methods are the best for their circumstances. But in the field of political institutions we must ask what it is in particular that they value, and the answer, I think, is to be found in the conviction of their dependence on divinity and therefore on persons with the qualifications to approach divinity. Only elders can do this. Nobody attempted to take their place on the ritual field, whereas in secular matters people managed without co-ordination. The belief that man cannot choose who is to approach the gods is found in many African religions: *only* a man whose father is dead can pray to the ancestors, *only* a man who inherits the power can control the weather, *only* a member of the right lineage can, as chief, perform national rituals. But if domination by the elders had been resented as it is in many parts of the world today, we might expect that the younger men would not wish to return to it. One answer here is that it is not so easy to work out new political systems when there are no models to look to; another that the initiated men who were trying to keep their juniors in order had an interest in the return to the traditional order. The facts may suggest too that resentment against authority is not a necessary feature of the relation between the generations, though there may well be, as between individual fathers and their sons, some friction as the younger man begins to wish he was in sole control of his own herd. Certainly none of these questions can be answered by asking what the environment requires.

SEGMENTATION

But there is another field in which it perhaps has more influence. The Karimojong are one of seven peoples in the north of Uganda and south of Sudan whose languages have so much in common that differences between them are merely those of dialect. All have the same division into alternating generations, and all believe in the deity Akuj; though not all of them accord to the senior generation the political responsibilities that the Karimojong do. Yet they have enough in common to suggest a common origin; and the Karimojong preserve a legend which accounts for their different names by incidents when they are supposed to have hived off from a single Karimojong people. The other tribes have their own legends, which do not necessarily corroborate the Karimojong version.

What is more interesting than trying to pin down particular facts is to consider the hiving-off process as such. It could be ascribed to the constraint of the environment, to a climate which sometimes forces people to move so far that they prefer to stay where they are rather than return home. This is more or less what happened to Ngipian, a very large section which has 800 settlements divided into units living near each of five rivers, and two ceremonial grounds. There was an earlier time, around the turn of the century, when all the cattle in eastern Africa were decimated by disease. The Karimojong were beginning to recover when Europeans first met them (and we do not know how this may have affected the succession ceremonies). But meantime Ngipian had taken to elephant hunting to get the cattle which traders offered them in return for ivory, and this led them to scatter widely over the country, a long way from what had been their home when the herds were prospering. As they recovered their cattle they joined together again, but by this time another section had occupied most of their old territory. Migration is frozen now, because the

Uganda government recognises as section territories areas marked on the map. But it would still be possible for the southern sections of Ngipian to assert their ritual independence, and so complete the autonomy that they already have in secular affairs. If they went further and said they were no longer Karimojong at all, they would have accomplished the process through which all the separate tribes of the cluster may have originated.

Can one say it is the environment that produces this near-autonomy of territorial sections? Certainly people have to live in small clusters far apart so as not to strain resources too much; and also the distribution of permanent water fixes the areas of permanent settlement. But on the other hand, it makes it necessary for sections to mingle in the distant pastures, and there only the recognition that all are Karimojong prevents them from fighting. The most that can be said is that environment and the technique of herding favour a loose organisation that may make secession easy.

4 Cultivators: The Gwembe Tonga *

By far the greater number of African peoples live by cultivating the soil, some having cattle and some not. Among them can be found every type of descent system and a wide variety of political and religious systems. A 'typical' cultivating population would be even harder to find than a 'typical' population of food-gatherers or herdsmen. Moreover, the agricultural peoples, almost without exception, have long-established relationships with a world outside their own borders, the world of commercial exchange which today links together almost the whole of mankind. They are incorporated in states to the governments of which they pay taxes, and so they must earn money incomes, which can be done either by growing crops for sale or by finding employment away from home; and they want to have money incomes for the sake of the various imported goods that money will buy. So if one is talking about constraints imposed by the environment one must see the whole world, and not a small geographical region, as the environment, and one must take into account political constraints as well as those of soil and climate. Moreover, we see them when they have themselves modified their environment by generations of cultivation.

The people I have chosen for this chapter have experienced more than the usual political constraints. They are the inhabitants of some villages in the Zambezi Valley who were compelled in 1958 to move to higher ground when the building of the Kariba Dam caused their homes to be submerged. But it was just because they would have to move and adapt themselves to a new environment that a detailed ecological study was made of their old one, which showed how local differences in social structure both could, and could not, be correlated with differences in the nature of their resources.

* *Ecology of the Gwembe Tonga*. T. Scudder, 1962.
  Social Organization of the Gwembe Tonga. E. Colson, 1960.
  Social Consequences of Resettlement. E. Colson, 1971.

GWEMBE ECOLOGY

The people in question are called the Gwembe, or Valley, Tonga. They have much in common with their neighbours further from the river whom we know as the Plateau Tonga, but while they were in their original homes they had access to alluvial soils capable of permanent cultivation without having to be fallowed, the soils which were annually fertilised by the river flood. As a result they recognise property in land and rules for its transmission by inheritance or otherwise, whereas the Plateau Tonga, who expect to abandon an area where the soil is exhausted and never come back to it, have no such rules. Moreover, the distribution of alluvial soils was different in different parts of the river valley, and this affected the distribution of settlements. Colson and Scudder divided the portion of the valley that is now under water into three regions, Upper, Middle and Lower, and also identified an Upland region a few miles back from the river, but their detailed work was done in the Upper and Middle River.

In the Upper River region the Zambezi used to meander through the valley floor so that there was a continuous stretch of land watered by the yearly floods, and here villages were close together all along the river bank just above the flood level. In the Middle River the banks were steeper, and the main areas of annual flooding were the deltas where tributaries joined the Zambezi. Villages were built where there were pockets of alluvial soil, and could be as much as five miles apart.

The Gwembe depend upon three staple foods: sorghum, bulrush millet and maize. Each of these grows best on a different type of soil, so that families who have land of each type are most secure against hunger. Until fairly recently they planted only land near the river – *jelele* and *kuti*, the banks themselves and the flood plains behind them, which would bear two crops a year, and *unda*, a little higher, which was only flooded when the river was exceptionally high, and so had to be cultivated during the rainy season. As population increased, there was not enough *jelele* and *kuti* land for everyone's subsistence. The *unda* needed to be rested after three or four years if it was to keep its fertility, and here, when numbers grew, people ceased to maintain the rotation, so that it began to be worked out.

This presented a problem for people who could not protect distant gardens from the depredations of elephants and baboons; but as the numbers of these creatures were reduced by hunters with guns, men ventured further and began to make gardens in the bush, called *temwa*, from *kutema*, to cut down trees. At the time of the move many of these gardens in the Upper River region, where *temwa* cultivation started first, were already losing their fertility, but they were still the main source of subsistence for the Middle River people.

Some Gwembe own cattle, which they acquire if they want to extend their cultivation by ploughing. Cattle are not important to them for subsistence, and so play no part in their ritual, which is focused on bulrush millet in the Upper River and sorghum in the Middle River and Upland regions. As regards cattle there is a difference between Upper and Middle River which is purely a matter of recent history. In the nineteenth century the whole valley was infested with tsetse fly, and cattle were only introduced after the rinderpest epidemic of 1898, by destroying the wild game, had destroyed the hosts of the fly. After that tsetse returned to part of the Middle but not to the Upper River, and Upper River people were found to be conspicuously better at herding, at ploughing and at protecting their gardens from cattle.

Both *temwa* cultivation and plough owning gave opportunities of building up prestige to men who otherwise had little hope of becoming influential. A man who cleared new land could do what he liked with it, whereas one who looked to a senior kinsman for land was a dependent as long as this man lived, and sometimes even after his death on account of the traditional succession system. A man who had a plough could plant a much larger quantity of grain, and could either sell the surplus, or have his wife brew beer with which he could reward the labour of others in weeding or harvesting. He could let others have the use of his plough in return for cash or labour. Even close kin would be expected to make some return, and they were dependent on his favour in the first place.

All through the valley, but particularly in the Upper River, there was a constant danger of famine from all sorts of hazards. Of course the vagaries of the local rainfall were the most important, but there were also irregularities in the river flood, the consequence of variations in the rain higher up or in the tributary basins. Total rainfall could be up to average and yet its distribution disastrous. Ideally there should have been a shower every four or five days; if instead four-fifths of the total fell on an early day, the grain could be scorched in the ground. Or too much rain might fall late in the growing season and make the plants rot in the ground; or it could fall when harvested millet heads were drying on the ground, so that they grew muddy.

The alluvial gardens depended on the time and height of the flood. An early flood could ruin standing crops. A low flood would not inundate the whole area that should have been planted. If a good flood went down too early the upper level gardens would be parched before the crops could ripen.

Herds of elephant or buffalo could destroy the gardens of a village in a night. Baboons did more damage in a less spectacular way. Birds ate seedlings or ripening grain, and insects and plant diseases could substantially reduce the crop.

Many valley people had moved up to the Plateau where life was not so precarious, and no longer joined with the kin they had left behind in ritual, nor claimed a share in their inheritance. But the latter kept in touch with them by frequent visiting, to ensure that they would not have been forgotten if they had to ask their kinsmen to share food with them.

GWEMBE KINSHIP

Like most of the peoples of Central Africa and the Congo Basin, the Gwembe are matrilineal. There are more differences in the kinship organisation of matrilineal than of patrilineal societies, and the differences depend mainly on the extent to which links through the father are important where people's primary claims are on the property of the maternal lineage. For the Gwembe such links are of great significance, and this is certainly associated with the importance of claims to land and the advantage of being able to obtain land from more than one source.

Rights in land are held jointly by the people who trace descent through women from the man who first cleared it, the matrilineage or *mukowa*. On a man's death his gardens should be divided among the members of his *mukowa*. But of course young men do not have to wait for their inheritance to get land to live on; they must have some from the time when they marry and set up house. They get it from senior kinsmen, often a number of fields from different owners. A man may get land from his father, but in that case he is liable to be dispossessed when his father dies. The only unchallengeable rights are those based on matrilineal descent, as well, of course, as those of pioneer cultivators in their own lifetime.

But the Gwembe accord more recognition to claims based on paternity than would many matrilineal peoples. In the first place, they expect sons to live near their fathers, and this makes it likely that many young men will look to their fathers for land. In the two Upper River villages, at the time of the study, nearly half the men and one-fifth of the women who were culti- vating *jelele* gardens got the land from their fathers, though a larger proportion of men in all the regions had opened new *temwa* land. But the right of children to look to their fathers for land, and of fathers to make allocations to them, even if these are only temporary (and they are not as temporary as all that), is recognised in the existence of a kin group based on paternity that is complementary to the matrilineage.

The latter, known as *mukowa*, is the small group, compris- ing thirty to forty adults, which exercises joint claims on in- heritance as long as its members recognise their common descent. They do not preserve genealogies, and the Upper River people do not distinguish, as those of the other regions do, between the descendants of different sisters. When a member of a *mukowa* dies, the survivors must gather for his funeral and appoint one of their number to inherit his 'shade', as some anthropologists call an ancestor spirit. Those who are living at a distance tend to be forgotten and not summoned to funerals, and thus there comes about that perpetual division, characteristic of all lineage systems, of groups which conceive themselves as perpetually one. The shades are the object of ritual; they receive offerings from their descendants, and can punish their misdemeanours by afflicting them with sickness. So in a sense a group which remembers common shades may be said to recognise a common authority.

There is nothing very peculiar in this, and the undifferentiated Upper River *mukowa* is very like that of the Plateau Tonga. What is peculiar to the Gwembe is the recognition of a group attached to the *mukowa* through its sons. This group, the *lutundu*, comes into existence on the death of a man who leaves adult children. It includes his sons and daughters and all their sons and daughters. These will belong to several different lineages, none of them his own. His own children and their daughters' children will belong to their mother's lineage (that of his wife), and his sons' children to *their* various mothers'. The head of the *lutundu* is not the eldest son, but the man who inherits the father's shade, who, as a member of *his* matrilineage, maintains its authority over its *lutundu* dependents. The *lutundu* has no descent constituent which could make it a continuing group. When all the man's children and grandchildren are dead it ceases to exist, and the land derived from the founder should return to his lineage. But by this time its original source has often been forgotten, and it comes to be considered part of the holding of the last grandchild's lineage.

The inheritor of a shade inherits the dead person's status, and with it whatever claims he may have had to authority (or, as Elizabeth Colson puts it, rights over descendants) and property, both being more important for men than for women. A man's inheritor has all the claims that he himself would have had on the property of his sons (goods or money that they bring home from a wage-earning trip, for example) and the marriage payments of his daughters, and it is for the value of these claims that a man is willing to inherit the shade; since there is no fixed rule of succession no one is either required or morally obliged to do so. In the Upper River, however, there was rivalry for shade inheritance and the advantages that it brought.

An inheritor has the right to use or re-allocate the land held by the man whose shade he inherits, including that of *temva* pioneers, though this is of less value because of its declining fertility. He can thus either increase his own holding or exercise influence over others through his right of allocation. A man who lives to a good old age can inherit several shades and thus acquire considerable power and possessions. Whereas in the Middle River all inherited shades were distributed at each death, in the Upper River it was the rule that one man and one woman in the elders' generation inherited all the shades of their contemporaries, and one man and one woman in the generation of their grandchildren inherited all those of their parents' generation. When one of these died, *all* the shades of remembered dead were passed on to another individual. Clearly this concentrated authority and privilege in a few hands. It seems that, at any rate for men, this was the rule in the Middle River too at a time recent enough for some of Colson's informants to remember it. But later, they told her, as there came to be movable property to inherit, the close kinsmen of a dead man insisted that his shade must go to one of them, and his property claims with it. Thus it came about that shades were redistributed at every death. Colson inclines to doubt this assertion, and considers that the concentration of shade inheritance on the Upper River is directly related to the pressure on valued alluvial land. If she is right, we should have to regard this, and not the Middle River dispersion of shades, as a recent development. On the other hand, if the Middle River people had had to become, like the Upland people, dependent on shifting cultivation, and become accustomed to abandon their fields after a year or two, it is easy to see how they would have come to disregard a system that is primarily concerned with the control of inherited land.

Middle River people regard Upper River people as old-fashioned, and even before the move the latter took seriously a type of ritual leadership (to be described later) that the Middle River folk had abandoned – as Scudder maintains, to the latter's disadvantage. There are differences in the material culture of the two regions as well, unconnected with differences in sources of materials. In general Colson holds that these differences represent divergences from a culture that was once common to both. But what made the culture? No doubt their isolation made the Upper River people conservative, but it did not dictate the details of the culture that they clung to. If the differences that could be observed in the Middle River were innovations, the only one that could be easily interpreted as a response to changed economic circumstances was that in the inheritance of shades. They are the kind of differences that some anthropologists like to ascribe to 'values'; which is just a way of saying that we can't account for them.

In the field of kinship there is just one special feature of the Upper River that seems to have been a response to the more difficult economic conditions there. In many of the African countries where rural populations are largely dependent on the money that young men earn in employment away from home, women are separated from their husbands for long periods; some husbands never come back. Most commonly an abandoned wife eventually takes up with another man; then her husband's kin write to him and he comes home and divorces her. But in the Upper River they used to allot one of the lineage to be a 'pro-husband', and beget children who would be accounted children of the absentee and belong to his *lutundu*; thus, if he did not come back, he would not have lost the kinship status, and any rights going with it, that he could claim through his marriage. This is a variant on the principle that a widow should be inherited by a man of her husband's lineage, which is widely accepted in Africa. It seems clearly to be a solution to the special problems of a region with many absentee labourers; but a solution that is certainly not determined by the existence of the problem, since no other such region has solved it in that way.

As for the advantages that go with the inheritance of shades, the right to allocate land has been mentioned. The property rights that go with the status of parent are also inherited. The most valuable of these are rights in the marriage payments of girls, and here the variation is in the share that women receive. The goods or cash are actually handed over to the girl's father, but there were different rules about distributing them. In the Middle River her mother received a small separate gift, not part of the payment proper. Most of this payment was kept by the father, who passed on perhaps a third of it to his wife's senior lineage 'brother'. In the Upland region the payment is divided between the lineages of the two parents, as it is on the Plateau. In the Upper River the parents themselves divided it, and each made a small gift to the matrilineage 'brother'. It is here that the rights a woman could acquire by shade inheritance were worth most – and here that shade inheritance was concentrated in two women. If the Middle River interpretation is correct, women there must have been slower than men to assert their interests.

SOCIAL CONTROL

Shade inheritors exercised authority partly through their control of property and partly because they could refuse to make the annual offerings on behalf of their dependents if the latter displeased them. Moreover, the shades themselves were believed to punish with sickness persons who offended their inheritors. Thus the latter had the support of ritual sanctions, and this was in fact the only basis for any authority until chiefs with executive powers were appointed under colonial rule. A shade inheritor has authority only within his own lineage, but there is also a ritual authority for each neighbourhood – the cluster of two to seven villages which forms around good alluvial soil. In every neighbourhood there is a shrine where people go to pray for rain to the spirits of the first comers to the area. Its custodian, the *sikatongo*, is supposedly a matrilineal descendant of the first pioneer, and has inherited the shades of his predecessors.

This is where Upper River custom was peculiar. There every important stage in the agricultural cycle was initiated by communal work in a special garden belonging to the *sikatongo*: burning last year's stalks, planting, first weeding, moving to a shelter by the garden to scare off birds and animals from the ripening crops, harvesting. For the staple – the 'ritual cereal' – he should also be the first to eat or brew beer from the new harvest. Each operation was begun on people's own gardens the day after the communal work. If the rains failed, it was apt to be ascribed to the disobedience of people who did not wait for this. Such a person was fined a black fowl, which was given to the *sikatongo* and eaten by all the people assembled to pray for rain.

In deciding the time for all these activities the *sikatongo* sought the advice of a prophet-diviner believed to speak with the voice of the *basangu* spirits who control the rain; such prophets were often women. It was the *basangu* prophet who decided what ritual must be performed if things went wrong; the *sikatongo's* duty was to ensure, through the work in his ritual garden, that they would go right. Agricultural officers have sometimes complained that this kind of dependence on a ritual leader stops intelligent farmers from choosing the time for their operations. Scudder's evaluation, however, is the opposite. As he sees it, *sikatongo* and *basangu*, with perhaps some other old-timers in the neighbourhood, knew the special circumstances and could judge the critical moment, particularly when it was time to prepare for planting. When he was there he observed that in the conservative Upper River, where the *sikatongo* was still taken seriously, people planted in good time for the rains, whereas in the Middle River many left their planting too late and lost the benefit of a record flood.

The *sikatongo* has no right of command in secular affairs unless he happens to have been appointed by the government as a chief or headman, which he may well be, since officials, at any rate colonial officials, tried to choose prominent men for these posts. Chiefs are authorised to hold courts for the settlement of disputes, and Gwembe sometimes take cases to them. But they prefer to deal with such matters by discussion in village gatherings, where they go on talking as long as it needs for agreement to be reached.

Typical matters in dispute would be claims for compensation for actions that are everywhere regarded as wrongs: homicide or serious physical injury, seduction of an unmarried girl, adultery and failure to pay debts. Most debts would have been incurred at some past time by an agreement to pay compensation, but there could be a dispute over failure to make a marriage payment if a young couple had eloped and not sought the consent of their elders. Now that government courts treat assault and homicide as crimes, and deal with them by sending people to prison, the guilty and their kin do not think they need to make amends by payment; the injured do not accept this view. The Gwembe believe that the shades are interested in justice, and will punish with sickness people who reject just claims, or their children. But the shades can be angry with people who are in the right as well, if they refuse to compromise.

In any small self-contained community social control is maintained very largely because people have to depend on one another's co-operation. Gwembe need help outside their own families at busy agricultural seasons, and they need to join in the performance of the rituals that the shades demand. People who think others have failed in their obligations will respond by rejecting their claims. Short of this, public disapproval is an effective sanction; adverse comment hurts when it comes from people whose good-will you need and whom you cannot get away from. The pygmies secure good-will by distracting attention from comments that might anger some member of the band. The Gwembe, on the contrary, have recognised occasions for publicly expressing them. Dances are accompanied by song, and someone who is incensed by another's action can have a song composed to be sung when the young people dance. Wider publicity is given by the neighbourhood drum teams who dance and sing at funerals, outside as well as within their home area.

Visiting drum teams are outsiders, and might in the old days have been called aliens. Although they are all Gwembe, they are out of range of the neighbourhood sanctions that keep the peace when they are at home. Their dances include a war-dance, essentially an expression of defiance against the representatives of other neighbourhoods, particularly if there is some cause of resentment between them, say an elopement. On the whole it is usually a pair of visiting teams who fight; visitors would be too likely to lose if they attacked a home team surrounded by its supporters. If anyone is badly hurt or killed, the two neighbourhoods break off relations. The elders of the side which caused the injury should send a messenger, someone with close kin in the other neighbourhood, to offer to negotiate compensation. Peace is apt to be more quickly achieved between adjacent neighbourhoods where people take constant contact for granted.

There was never any ultimate authority (apart from that of government chiefs, who are still regarded simply as agents of an outside power) over a neighbourhood, let alone a region or the whole Gwembe valley. Shade inheritors have authority over their own kin. The *sikatongo* had authority in the field of cultivation ritual, but he had a rival in the *basangu*, who could ascribe disasters to his inadequacy. There were, as there are everywhere, men who were influential because they were wealthy above the average: men who controlled much land through shade inheritance, or had opened up large *temwa* gardens by using ploughs, or had made it their aim to build up larger than average herds of cattle, and so were called upon for help when their kinsmen had to pay damages. Possibly they found appeals for help irksome, but to be the source of help gave them a hold over others; and this was translated into a general reputation for wisdom in the discussion of neighbourhood affairs.

From one of the few ecological studies that we have, it seems, then, that little in the social arrangements of an agricultural people can be regarded as a direct response to the constraints of the environment. The ritual co-ordination of work in the fields could certainly be interpreted, as Scudder has argued, as a way of making the voice of experienced people effective in timing. But the Middle River people needed this as much as the Upper River, and the Middle River had given it up before the move. If concentrated shade inheritance had been a response to land shortage, it should have developed first in the Upper River, whereas this too seems to have been considered, by some at least, as an 'old custom' that the Middle River had given up. There is no sign that 'progress' or 'modernity' in the Middle River produced institutions better adjusted to the peculiarities of soil and climate than those of their fathers.

RE-SETTLEMENT

It would be gratifying to be able to treat the history of the re-settled populations as a case of adaptation to a new environment, parallel to what we must suppose happened when the Gwembe entered the Zambezi valley. Yes, they did adapt themselves and quickly too; but to a man-made, not a natural environment. None of the new settlement areas was isolated. Roads had been built for lorries to transport the settlers to their new homes. Wells had been sunk, tsetse fly destroyed. A fishing industry was deliberately created.

The nature of the move, too, was unlike anything in the period of the early colonisation of the valley, when we can suppose that people were gradually learning the characteristics of a new country. We know, and shall always know, very little about the details of the migrations that we know have taken place over great distances in the pre-history of Africa. But it is not unreasonable to 'conjecture' that the process was one in which tiny bands of perhaps a dozen pioneers explored new ground and were followed very slowly by others from their homeland; indeed this is a process that can still be observed in sparsely populated regions such as south-western Tanzania. The Gwembe resettlement, in contrast, was an almost instantaneous transfer of many thousands, some moving a hundred miles in a day.

Adaptation was here a matter of seizing new opportunities rather than of coming to terms with new necessities. The move itself was dramatic, but the changes in social relationships that followed it were similar to the changes that have everywhere gone with increasing involvement in the market economy – a loosening of internal ties as individuals became more and more dependent for livelihood and security on sources outside their own community.

The re-settlement had one peculiar feature. It wiped out all existing land rights; in the new homes all men alike were pioneers. Yet this did not level them at a stroke, because they did not start level. Some brought assets with them; these were the elders who had controlled lineage holdings of river land. They brought with them their large families and the grain they had harvested. They started with a larger labour force than their fellows, and were able to recruit more outsiders by offering beer parties, and they could repeat this process each year. Their surplus they sold for cash or bartered for cattle. They bought ploughs which they rented out to neighbours, and thus maintained the local influence they had had before.

People used the same techniques as before, and for some years women lamented the *jelele* gardens where they had been able to get, all through the year, the vegetables that gave a flavour to their rather tasteless porridge. Then someone thought of planting little vegetable gardens near the houses and watering them by hand, and the idea quickly spread. Fruit trees, which had not done well near the river, were planted from seeds given to people when they visited other neighbourhoods. The agricultural service brought the Gwembe new, better varieties of maize and millet, but were less successful in advocating cotton.

Although there were plenty of *basikatongo* in the new

homes, they no longer organised rituals for the stages in the cycle of cultivation. They had had to leave behind the shrines where they had made offerings to the shades of their ancestors, but they might have built new ones; nobody suggested that new shrines must wait until new pioneers had died and left shades. But people who had found the restrictions of a neighbourhood timetable irksome were glad the rituals had been given up, especially as yields were good during the first few years, and there was no need to appeal for spirit help. When new trouble began the Gwembe looked to the *basangu* prophets to find what shade they must placate, and do not seem to have been told to revive the old rituals.

Many of the younger men were exploiting, rather than adapting themselves to, a new environment, both economic and social. In their new homes they grew crops for sale or opened small stores, and a few took to fishing. Many left, temporarily or permanently, for work in the towns, to which they could now go by lorry along the new roads that had been built to open up the settlement areas. A new social environment was created by a historical event unconnected with the resettlement – the independence of Zambia and the replacement of Europeans by Africans in all kinds of government employment. At first most of these posts were held by men from other parts of Zambia where the schools had been better. But those who worked among the Gwembe had a noticeably higher standard of living, which the youth of Gwembe hoped to be able to attain; in doing so they too would become transferable, and members of an all-Zambian society, the 'new elite'.

Whether or not the traditional social institutions had originally been a response to the environment, they now acted in some ways as an obstacle to this new kind of adaptation. It was not thought right for young men to be better off than their elders, and it was supposed that if they became so the elders would resent it and kill them by sorcery. This did not inhibit all ambition, nor divert it into channels outside Gwembe country, but it was used as an argument against investment in conspicuous objects such as a boat or a large herd of cattle.

In their new homes the Gwembe have more movable property for their descendants to inherit, but very little land of long-term fertility. If shade inheritance is primarily significant in relation to the control of land, one might perhaps have expected that it would be forgotten; and perhaps it may still be as more young people go to school and become, if not convinced Christians, at any rate sceptical towards their traditional beliefs. Colson predicted a general loosening of lineage ties when the lineage ceased to be a landholding corporation. At the time of the move, however, the Gwembe were concerned that lineages should not break up. They were also anxious lest, in the dispersion of the move, people should be out of reach of the shade inheritors who alone could make the necessary offerings to secure the shades' good-will. Just before the move people took pains to have funerals performed, and disputes over kinship property settled, while they were still in touch with the shade inheritor. Some inheritors delegated their authority to substitutes.

But travelling became easier with the building of new roads and the appearance of buses and boats, and soon people began to think there were advantages in having a shade inheritor at a distance, where he would keep up the links between separated kinsmen. A visitor to a funeral from a village in the new settlement areas would find himself chosen as shade inheritor just for that reason. People from the Upper River maintained the rule of concentrated inheritance, though now it carried with it no concentration of power. It is possible, however, that at some time in the future shade inheritance may lose all its group significance, and that every individual will have his own guardian shades to whom he makes his own sacrifices; this is the rule among the Plateau Tonga.

To argue, as Edmund Leach does, that the obligations of kinship are of no significance at all except where they coincide with property interests, is going a long way beyond this, and this argument is not supported by the behaviour of the Gwembe at the time of the move. At that time of uprooting, distress and uncertainty, kin who had quarrelled made up their quarrels, and in the new homes brothers shared homesteads, and other kin built close together, to a much greater extent than they had before. As new causes of dissension arose, the new-found amity melted away; but while it lasted it was evidence that in times of crisis the 'axiom of amity', as Fortes calls it, was a live force.

The Gwembe give us the very opposite of an argument for determinism by their environment. What they show is what is in fact a truism: that the greater the technical knowledge, the more the environment is servant and not master.

5   Agnatic Descent: The Tallensi *

What British anthropologists call structural analysis began with the study of lineage organisation in societies where descent is the most important principle of grouping in political matters as well as the source of individual rights and liabilities. The structure of a society, Evans-Pritchard says, consists in those groups which continue through the generations – corporate groups, as Radcliffe-Brown taught us to call them – in which people's membership is fixed at birth. This type of analysis distinguishes lineage structure from kinship, the whole range of relationships derived through common parentage to which recognised rules of behaviour are attached. To give the descent system primacy over the family was a radical departure from Malinowski's method, and *The Nuer* was received with some surprise by the orthodox of that day – 'nothing about the family?'. But their astonishment was premature and their censure missed its mark. The first two analysts of agnatic lineage structure, Evans-Pritchard and Fortes, each wrote two books, the first on lineage and the second on kinship; it was in this second volume that the family, founded by a couple who in most African societies had to be members of different lineages, found its appropriate place.

It has been asserted that 'classical structural analysis' takes no account of relationships formed by individual choice. In fact marriage is such a relationship in every society. The choice may not be that of the contracting parties; it may be that of lineage seniors or other men in authority who have the right to bestow the hands of girls. Even where lineages theoretically exchange their daughters a choice is made among individuals. But when, as is much more common in Africa, there is no expectation that a pair of lineages will constantly renew their marriage links, every new marriage creates a new body of kin for the family that it founds. The persons concerned form a field – some would call it a network – not a group. To be a kinsman of X or Y is not a principle of action, nor a basis of claims,

* *The Web of Kinship among the Tallensi.* M. Fortes, 1945.

except in relation to X or Y; holders of this status, members of this category, have no common interest as such. It is only common lineage membership that gives common property interests. Extra-lineage kinship is dissolved and recreated with every generation. Yet in the life of every day it is within the field of kinship, not lineage, that people move. It is the links of kinship that bind together lineages whose interests may often conflict. Hence Meyer Fortes' choice of the metaphor of a web.

The study of kinship, then, involves more than an examination of lineage structure, which may be more important in matters of jural and political claims than in day-to-day contacts. As anthropologists have come to take lineage structure for granted, interest has turned to the significance of 'complementary filiation', and of the ways in which individuals can look to extra-lineage kin to supplement inadequate shares of lineage property and establish some measure of independence from lineage authority. Male extra-lineage kin, collectively, are 'mother's brothers'. 'The' mother's brother has been a figure in anthropological theory for many years, and many explanations have been offered of his special relationships with his sisters' children when they are not of his lineage. It is because Fortes himself developed the theory of complementary filiation, and because his detailed account of Tallensi kinship gives the mother's brother his full share of importance, that I choose the Tallensi as the example of kinship in a patrilineal descent system.

The Tallensi live in northern Ghana, and numbered about 35,000 at the time of Fortes' fieldwork (1934). At that time they were very remote from the outside world. There were no good roads, and the young men who went to Kumasi or towns further south, or to work on cocoa farms, had to make their way on foot. Perhaps a third of them did make such journeys, but they did not stay away long. The money they earned was spent largely on cotton clothes and on cattle for bridewealth. People could also sell surplus produce at markets at home. Hardly anyone was literate. When Fortes went back in 1963, Taleland had been 'opened up'. Most children went to school, lorries went to and fro over a good road, everyone expected to spend part of his time in employment, and the labourers brought back transistors which gave them news of the rest of Ghana and the world. (Perhaps it is hard for today's readers to realise that radio receivers only began to reach the most populous parts of Africa in the late 1930s.) But kinship expectations, he found, were much what they had always been.

From their fields the Tallensi harvest millet and guinea corn, their staple crops, with sweet potatoes and groundnuts as a supplement. They own cattle and smaller stock, and value cattle particularly because they are used for the payment of bridewealth, and so to continue and increase the lineage by the marriage of its sons; and cattle are sacrificed at important rituals.

HOMESTEAD AND LINEAGE

A Tale homestead is the dwelling of its head with his wives and unmarried children, his married sons and their wives and children. But is it? When a man has just died it is the dwelling of a couple of brothers. If one of these moves out, his homestead will be the dwelling of a nuclear family; but he will hope to live and prosper long enough to marry more than one wife and see his sons grow up and bring their wives home. This is the developmental cycle of the domestic group, a concept which Fortes first introduced to anthropologists.

The homestead consists of a number of cylindrical mud buildings thatched with straw, and linked and surrounded by a mud wall. Within it each member has his place. The head's is immediately inside the gateway, where he can see all the comings and goings and look out on the livestock which represent his wealth. This section, a small part of the whole, is backed by a low wall, and in the middle of this wall is a tall building where the household grain is stored; only the head of the homestead has access to this. Beyond the wall are the quarters of the wives which are also those of the junior men. Each wife has a sleeping-room for herself and her young children, a kitchen and a store. A small hut houses the stones on which they must take it in turns to grind grain for porridge. Close to the entrance gateway of the homestead there is a shrine to the ancestors of the lineage.

The men of the homestead constitute a minimal, or nuclear,

lineage. With their wives and children they make up what some would call an extended, and Fortes calls a joint, family. This whole group is under the secular control of the senior man and the spiritual protection of his lineage ancestors. In the separate housing of the children of different mothers begins that closer association of the children of the same mother in a polygynous family that is characteristic of all patrilineal systems.

As long as the head of the household is the father, all its members work as a team under his direction and all its property – land, livestock and grain – is at his disposal. He is expected to consider the interests of his sons, notably in allocating cattle for their bridewealth, but they must not openly question his decisions. His eldest son, who will eventually succeed him, is subject to a number of strict rules of avoidance which remind him that he must not seek to usurp his father's place. He must never meet his father in the gateway, for this would be a kind of confrontation. He must not eat with his father, as younger sons may. He must not touch his father's bow, nor look into the grainstore; he is formally 'shown' its contents at the conclusion of his father's funeral.

After their father is dead and his fields have been divided between them, brothers may still live in the same homestead, but they farm separately, and separately manage their household affairs. The sons of a junior wife are likely to be the first to separate from their half-brothers and move out altogether. This division gives the pattern for the way in which the segments of any lineage are related; they trace their descent from different wives of the ancestor whose sons are thought to have separated.

Father and adult sons are the elementary unit in the structure of the lineage that they claim to trace back to a remote founding ancestor; all its members call themselves his children – like the 'children of Israel'. They are all cousins, some very distant cousins; closer cousins recall the name of a nearer common ancestor. Every man hopes to be the originator of a segment which will bear his name. The ways in which the members of such groups co-operate depend upon the *depth* of the lineage, as Fortes puts it – their distance in generations from the ancestor recognised as the founder of that segment.

The minimal lineage is, with the men's wives, the producing

and consuming group; all its property is at the disposal of its head. But a wider segment, probably the children of the brothers whose separation has just been described, has a common interest in the property of its members, in the sense that its elders must give formal consent to any dealings with lineage land, and to the transfer of property in bridewealth payments for its male members. The head of such a group – an *inner* lineage – would be at first the brother who had inherited the ancestor shrine of their common father. An inner lineage divides after some generations, often when two cousins, as the older men will be by then, quarrel about the right to inherit the shrine that marks their unity. The new shrine of the now independent segment will be called by the name of its senior man's father, and will also be dedicated to the latter's mother.

Wider groups co-operate only in sacrifices to their ancestors. At any such sacrifice the meat of the offering is divided among representatives of the different lineage segments descended from the ancestor who is being approached; the inner lineage is treated as a single unit.

The widest group of all, the *maximal* lineage, all those who account themselves the 'children of Mosuor' (or whomever) have in common the rule of exogamy, which prohibits marriage among them.

Within the inner lineage a person calls all men of his father's generation father, all women of that generation father's sister, all men and women of his own generation brother or sister, in accordance with the familiar rules of classificatory terminology. Beyond it what is important is the relation of the lineage as a whole to the person speaking. All members of his own lineage are brothers, all those of his mother's are mother's brothers, all those of lineages into which his sisters have married are sister's sons.

MARRIAGE

The formal rule for the conclusion of marriage is that common to patrilineal societies in Africa; the elders of the bridegroom's lineage must agree to pay bridewealth to the guardian of the bride. But only a minority of marriages are arranged by formal negotiation in advance. A father may promise his daughter in marriage while she is a child, especially if he wants to make an alliance with an important man. But for most young people courting is open and is freely allowed, and it is much more usual for a youth to choose his own bride; it is also very usual for the couple to elope with the connivance of the girl's mother, whom the young man will have softened up with presents. Then her father must either fetch her back or accept the situation and demand the bridewealth.

First he must send for the 'placation gift'; this is not a compensation for the act of elopement, but a part of the conclusion of any marriage. It consists of a live cock for the head of a girl's lineage and a slaughtered fowl for the heads of each of the families in it; one of these must have been sacrificed to the bridegroom's lineage ancestors. This announces to them all that the girl's father is willing to have the marriage formalised.

He also initiates the bridewealth negotiations by a demand. Argument then begins on the question how much is to be paid at once. The full payment is three cows and a bull, or their equivalent in small stock or cash. In the way the discussion is carried on we can see how lineage rights in property are recognised. The elders of the bridegroom's inner lineage formally agree to make whatever immediate payment is decided upon. But it is his own father (or guardian if his father is dead) who must provide the stock or cash.

Marriage has its obvious everyday advantages; it lays the foundation for a household and a working team which will eventually be independent under the husband's authority. But the Tallensi value it above all as the source of legitimate descendants who will preserve a man's spirit (his memory) in the ancestor cult. Legitimate descent is determined by the payment of bridewealth or the agreement to pay and receive it. A woman who leaves her husband and remarries when she has small children takes them with her, but at eleven or twelve their own father claims them. He has final authority over his sons' labour and the marriages of both sons and daughters. A widow who can still bear children should be inherited by the dead man's brother so that she adds further to the lineage strength.

If a marriage breaks up it is usually because the woman leaves her husband. In most cases she goes home for a visit and there takes up with another man. Sometimes her father encourages her, if he prefers the new husband. To have paid a part or even the full bridewealth does not, as it does in many African societies, give the husband an absolute claim on his wife's kin to return her to him as long as they think he has treated her properly. A father-in-law who removed his daughter in those circumstances might be held to have behaved badly, but all his son-in-law could do would be to demand the return of the cattle. There are no required 'grounds' for divorce, no formalities, no authority whose permission must be sought.

It is the payment of bridewealth for a woman that makes her children members of their father's lineage, subject to the authority of their living seniors and, beyond them, the ancestors, and entitled to a share of the lineage patrimony. But the mother herself is not incorporated in her husband's lineage; she is still a member of her own, and she keeps up her ties with her parents and siblings and the latter's children. Through their mother the children of the marriage also recognise these ties. This relationship is what Fortes has called *complementary* filiation. Filiation, in his terms, is the relation of a child to both its parents. Descent is a matter of a line of successors, and in a unilineal system one's descent group starts with one's grandfather, as here, or grandmother, as among the Lele, to whom the following chapter is devoted. It is a person's filiation through the parent who is not of his descent group that Fortes calls complementary.

COMPLEMENTARY FILIATION

The closest such relationship is that between a child and its own mother's full siblings – above all her brothers, since it is men who exercise authority and dispose of property. Mother's brother and sister's child are not only related through the mother/sister; they are of common matrilineal descent, a relationship which the Tallensi greatly value and for which they have a word (*soog*, plural *saaret*). A full brother and sister may speak of each other's children as their own, implying an equal affection for them all, and Tallensi say your mother's own brothers are 'like your own father'. Of course the specific obligations between fathers and sons are different from those between uncles and nephews.

This is significant particularly in the field of property. A son has an absolute claim on his father's property – but not until his father is dead. In his lifetime the father has absolute disposal of it, though he is expected to use it in his children's interest as well as his own. A young man can get property of his 'very own' as a gift from a mother's brother – who, of course, if the property is of any importance, must have the approval of his lineage seniors for the transfer.

The most universal 'expectation' is that when a boy is about twelve years old his mother's brother – or more than one – will give him a hen. From these he can raise chickens, and eventually trade them for goats or sheep, and these, if he is fortunate, for a cow. Such gifts are likely to come from his mother's own brother, but where the use of land is in question it is possible to get it from any member of the mother's lineage.

Young men, and also some young women, can borrow unused land for a season at a time from their mother's lineage to plant groundnuts or sweet potatoes, not only if their fathers have none to spare for these individual plots, but so that they can be freer to sell the crops they plant. Men also get more permanent loans of land for bush-farms (at a distance from the homestead), and sometimes a man who is moving out of the family homestead after his father's death gets land for a new homestead from his mother' lineage. This is one way in which half-brothers separate so that their descendants eventually look to them as the founders of different lineages.

Tallensi men do not have such extensive rights to make free with the movable property of their mothers' brothers as we find in many other societies, but they can, without offence, cut a little grain from a mother's brother's field if they are hungry, as people often are during a large part of the year. A Tallensi explains this by saying that if his mother had happened to be a man the grain would have been part of her/his patrimony – an explicit recognition of the principle of the social equivalence of siblings enunciated by Radcliffe-Brown.

Whole lineages and even clans between whom there is some marriage link are thought of as being in the relationship of mother's brothers to sisters' sons. One context in which this is significant is the formal conclusion of a marriage. The request for the placation gift and later for the bridewealth, and the negotiation on the amount of bridewealth to be paid at once or postponed, are entrusted to an intermediary who should be more concerned with securing agreement than with supporting the position of one side or the other. Such a man should be a 'sister's son' of the bride's father – a member of his own clan who has a link through his mother to the bride's. The moral obligations of kinship to both parties should, it is thought, ensure that he does not sacrifice the interests of either.

The one inescapable obligation of a mother's brother is ritual. The ancestor spirits can be approached with sacrifices only by their patrilineal descendants. But a woman's ancestors, if they are angry with her, can send sickness or other disaster to her children, and she, as a woman, cannot make the necessary sacrifice to appease them; only a man of her lineage can do that. To refuse would be tantamount to condemning a sick person to death. So a Tallensi commonly describes his relationship with his mother's lineage in the phrase 'They sacrifice on my behalf.'

The recognition of complementary filiation is common to all unilineal descent systems. It is much less common to find, in a society where all authority and all property is transmitted in the male line, importance attached, not only to kinship through women but also to *descent* through women. This is the *soog* relationship which has been mentioned. *Saaret* cannot marry. *Soog* imposes no jural or ritual obligations, but *saaret* who are also neighbours expect to help one another with advice, comfort and material aid without any calculation of return. People who discover by accident that they are *saaret* are always delighted and sometimes become close friends. It is also believed that the power of witchcraft is transmitted from mother to daughter, but since Tallensi rarely ascribe their misfortunes to witchcraft this belief has little practical significance

It has sometimes been argued that the recognition of the *soog* relationship should place the Tallensi among the societies characterised by *dual unilineal descent* – through males for some purposes and females for others. But if dual descent is taken to mean that lineages of both types are property-holding corporations, such a description would not fit them.

RELIGION AND KINSHIP

Tallensi religion reflects both the total lineage structure and the norms of conduct in the family. At lineage shrines (*boga*, singular *bogar*) sacrifice is offered to the collective ancestors of whatever segment of the lineage is in question. The shrine for the whole lineage is set up at the grave of the founding ancestor, and some of his descendants should always live there. Men who had been living and prospering for years outside Taleland were sometimes 'called home' by an attack of sickness sent by some ancestor, to take responsibility for such a shrine. Shrines of segments are set up in the homestead of the lineage head, and transferred when one succeeds another. A shrine is a cone of mud on which beer and the blood of sacrificed animals are poured. Whenever a sacrifice is made to lineage ancestors all segments of the lineage concerned must be represented, and the participants must come in peace – that is there must be no public unreconciled disputes among them.

But what is more significant in relation to kinship is the number of different individuals among the relatively recent dead for whom shrines are set up, and who are regarded as having an especial concern with individuals among the living. No man whose own father is alive can approach the spirits, since contact with remoter ancestors can be made only through one's own dead father. Thus parental authority is reinforced by dependence on the father in ritual as well as economic matters. The ancestors are in some ways more powerful than a living father. You cannot argue with them, or take a chance on displeasing them; you only know you have done so when a diviner reveals that some misfortune is a punishment. It may have been incurred by some breach of the rules of kinship amity, but more often than not the sin is to have omitted some obligation to make a sacrifice; and it may not be your own sin but that of a dead forebear. The ancestors are always right.

Only the lineage ancestors can cause a person's death. But others, not necessarily of one's own lineage, are thought to have a particular interest in the fortunes of different individuals, and can manifest demands on them by causing sickness.

Every person has a spirit guardian – a lineage ancestor identified by a diviner a few days after his birth. This spirit, if given proper service, will do its best to preserve the child's life. The child's father must dedicate a shrine to it, and make offerings there on important occasions of its life, notably a woman's first pregnancy. A woman's spirit guardian shrine remains always under the control of her father or his heirs. Like a living parent, this spirit, though responsible for the welfare of its child, can punish, and severely, if it is neglected.

Everyone also has a number of ancestors who are believed to be individually interested in his progress through life: the destiny (*yin*) ancestors. A woman's destiny ancestors are considered to be identical with her father's. A young man learns who his *yin* ancestors are when he falls ill shortly after he has done something outside the normal routine – killed a wild animal or even just bought a new hoe. Then a diviner is consulted, and he reveals that some collection of recently dead ancestors is guiding his destiny and want a shrine made for them; as long as his father is alive it is the latter who must make the offerings there. Tallensi explain the rule that a father and his eldest son must not meet in the gateway of the homestead by saying that their *yin* are rivals; as of course they are in the sense that prosperity for the son implies that he should grow up and in due course succeed his father.

A person who consistently fails to achieve what all Tallensi desire – a stable marriage, a large family, a productive farm – is held to have renounced these things before his birth. But the lineage ancestors may be appealed to to drive out this evil prenatal destiny. Most commonly this ritual is performed for a woman who fails to bear children, or whose children have died. Her ancestors are reminded that they have received a share of her bridewealth in sacrifice and that if she has children they too will sacrifice to them (for every man dedicates a shrine to his mother's spirit immediately after her death).

Another explanation of persistent misfortune is more common for a man. This is that members of his mother's lineage, some of them women, will not leave him in peace until he sets up a shrine for them and promises to become a diviner. Fortes found that nine out of ten men over forty had such shrines, though only a few did actually practise as diviners, a profession for which, after all, other qualifications are desirable besides having suffered misfortune.

As Fortes interprets the religion of the Tallensi, it is closely linked to family authority, which it makes absolute in the sense of being supported by powers from whom there is no appeal. Outside the family the unity of the lineage is maintained by the obligation to unite in sacrifice at the shrine of its founder, and to unite in amity. This is an application of Durkheim's theory of religion as a 'collective representation' of those norms of conduct that are most valued in any given society.

People who are farming land that has been inherited down the generations are constantly being reminded of their ancestors by the graves that they see every day. The ideal is that when a new homestead is built the site chosen should have been the home of a patrilineal ancestor, and sometimes, as was mentioned, a man is summoned home after a long absence abroad so that the grave of a lineage ancestor should not be deserted. The people of the Tong hills, who were the last to maintain resistance to British authority, were finally subdued in 1911; their houses were destroyed and they were forced to go down and live in the plains. There some of them were able to produce more food by shifting cultivation than they could on the permanent farms they had left. Yet they went back to the hills as soon as they were allowed.

But perhaps this was not a sacrifice to the principle that the ancestral land must not be deserted. Worsley has argued (1956) that there might be economic advantages in returning to the hills. The hill people went back to land that had had an unusually long fallow period *just because* it had been deserted. Then the plains have the type of soil that is waterlogged in the wet season and parched in the dry; and sleeping-sickness is endemic there. The conclusion of his re-interpretation of the data is that it is economic interdependence which creates the norms and sentiments ascribed to the absolute sanctity of kinship, and that without a community of economic interest kinship obligations are apt to be disregarded and eventually lapse. Obligations of co-operation are expressed in terms of kinship, and supported by the authority of the ancestors, because in the nature of things, as long as people live in small communities and only rarely travel, it is their kin who are around to co-operate. The sacredness of kinship is an ideology built on this economic infrastructure. This alternative explanation is associated largely with the name of Edmund Leach, who has treated the kinship relations of a Ceylonese village in these terms. Most African ethnographers have recorded kinship rules and behaviour without committing themselves as strongly as Fortes to the theory of their absolutely binding character in relations outside those of the immediate family.

6 Matrilineal Descent: The Lele *

Patrilineal descent systems, though they differ in detail, have a good deal in common all over the world. Of matrilineal systems it could be said without much exaggeration that, even within Africa, no two are alike. Given the rule that descent and inheritance claims are transmitted through women, they have to solve a problem that does not arise with patriliny: where is the family home to be? With the husband's kin, to whom his children are outsiders – non-lineage members – or with the wife's, to whom the husband himself is an outsider? Every such society has to make its own compromise, and whatever this is, it usually results in many changes of residence as people are drawn in one direction or another by the pull of different kinship ties. Older men try to attract younger ones to live with them, sometimes for the sake of their manpower, sometimes for their political support. As Mary Douglas neatly puts it, every village tries to keep its own young men at the same time as recruiting those of its neighbours.

People whose livelihood comes from settled farming cannot be so footloose; the Tallensi move gradually as their land is exhausted, but they stay within the framework of the nuclear lineage. No doubt this is the reason why we rarely find matrilineal descent where there is any kind of significant property to inherit.

In Africa the so-called 'matrilineal belt' stretches across the continent all the way through Zaïre, Zambia, Malawi and Tanzania. Much of this area consists of poor soils which cannot be planted for many years in succession; the alluvial land of the Gwembe Tonga was a striking exception. I choose from it two very different examples: the Lele of the Kasai because of the very remarkable total arrangements of their society, and the Plateau Tonga because they illustrate the stresses that are felt when matrilineal people do begin to accumulate property.

The Lele of this study live on the edge of the equatorial rain

* *The Lele of the Kasai.* M. Douglas, 1963.

forest. Their country is on the east of the Loange river, a tributary of the Kasai, which itself flows into the Congo. They are believed to have come from an original home near Lake Leopold II, well within the forest zone. Mary Douglas worked there in 1949 and 1953, and there had been so many changes between her two visits that she has preferred to write her book in the past tense. In 1949 the Lele were still largely self-sufficient. By 1953 many had begun to work for wages or to earn cash by selling palm-fruit to an oil factory, and to buy the articles that are prized everywhere in Africa – bicycles, sewing-machines, guns. A mission station had made many converts who were rejecting some of the most important traditional institutions. The account, then, is of the Lele in 1949 and earlier, so far as earlier times can be known.

At that time they numbered something under 30,000, and lived in small villages with an average population of 170. These villages, in clearings in the forest, were rectangular in shape, and so divided that men of adjacent generations (defined in terms of an age-set system) had their houses on opposite sides; there were reckoned to be four generations living at a time. The houses too were rectangular; they were built of palm ribs and thatched with palm-fronds. Under the palm-tree just outside, men made clearings where they worked, particularly at weaving, and had their meals. Further out were other clearings where women pounded grain, and further away still they worked oil-presses.

Like the Mbuti, the Lele conceived themselves to be utterly dependent on the forest. The staple grain foods, maize and manioc, were planted in clearings made in the forest. Palm wine, the second most important foodstuff, was tapped from raffia palm. Wild game was their only meat. Women got fish and salt from ponds in the forest, and went there for the household wood and water. Like the Mbuti, the Lele preferred the cool of the forest to the heat of the village, even though it was their own village. Their most valuable form of property consisted in cloths woven from raffia palms planted in the forest, and their other valuable was camwood used as a cosmetic, and also got from the forest. The cloths were made into skirts which the men wore; they did not last long in use. The palms themselves – the same that were the source of wine – lasted only five or six years.

The Lele were divided into matrilineal clans, which were distinguished by name and by the rule of exogamy, but had no corporate interests. Common clan membership created a claim to hospitality, and was the way of entry into a village for a newcomer. The significant group in everyday affairs was what Douglas calls the 'local clan section', clan members who were in regular contact, but who, because of the frequent changes of residence, could not necessarily trace relationships among them. They might be a group of no more than four men and three women. Every village was supposed to have been founded by two or three clans who were called the 'owners' of the village, and the headman was the senior by age of the founding clan which counted most members in it. Members of this clan lived in the houses at the four corners of the village, one for each age-set, and members of founding clans were apt to stay in their own villages, and so keep in contact, longer than others. There was no reckoning of near kinship for purposes of inheritance; a dead man's possessions were shared among all members of the local clan section.

MARRIAGE

Lele marriage rules were preferential – that is to say, members of certain clans had a claim on the daughters of certain others as wives. Lévi-Strauss has taught us to see this kind of rule as a form of communication in which brothers exchange their sisters. The Lele do have a notion that women are given and returned, but brothers do not come into the exchange. Their view, which is striking in a matrilineal society, is that it is a *father* to whom a return is due, and this not because he gave a daughter to someone else, but because he gave her to her own clan – by begetting her. This action was conceived as a priceless gift, as is the bearing of children for the lineage in an agnatic society, and as a return for it a man had the right to claim a girl of his wife's line – not, of course, his own daughter but one of *her* daughters – as a wife, or alternatively to allot her to a clansman (a sister's son). This right, far more than anything tangible, was the supreme value for the Lele. Lele fathers also had the final say in their daughters' marriages, and their share of marriage payments was slightly larger than that of the mother's – the girl's own – clan. In practice a grandfather might find himself allotting a girl to a clansman who lived nearer than he did to her mother's home, where her mother in particular would want to keep her. Whoever had the right to dispose of a girl, however, had something valuable to give, and could make young men his dependents; the possibility of finding a wife was one reason for moving to a new village, and the final acceptance of a newcomer was recognised when he was given a wife.

Since old men with claims on girls made second and third marriages for themselves, younger men had to wait a long time before they could be betrothed, let alone marry. Of course one must remember that a girl who married an old man would become available before long as a widow.

Girls were often betrothed as soon as they were born, to youths of anything from 12 to 20, who then had to wait for them to grow up. All through this long period the future son-in-law was expected to do odd jobs for the girl's father whenever he was called on – mending buildings or fences, tapping wine and so on. The marriage was finally ratified by a payment of 90 raffia cloths, 40 to the bride's clan section and 50 (plus another ten reckoned as the equivalent of an axe) to her father. Young men wove some of these cloths themselves, but they needed help from their seniors, and they got it both from their fathers and their own clansmen (mother's brothers).

Before they were married men did no work in the fields, but they tapped wine and wove raffia, and were expected to help their elders, both fathers and mothers' brothers, and they hunted in the forest. They slept together in a bachelors' hut, and their mothers sent food to them there. Their life, as they saw it, was one of discomfort and hardship, and they resented the authority that imposed it. They went about in gangs, helping one another when any of them had work to do for a senior, and planning the seduction of married women, which was celebrated as an exploit.

Their hardships were mitigated by the allocation to the junior age-set of communal wives – an institution peculiar to the Lele and their near neighbours, and one that was bound to meet with severe disapproval from the colonial government and the Christian missionaries. It was still in existence, however, in 1947, when a law was passed making polyandrous marriage a penal offence; by this time a number of young Lele had become Christians and themselves refused to marry, or be married as, village-wives.

A new age-set was formed every fifteen years or so, and youths would join it as they reached the age of about 18. There seems in the past to have been a formal initiation after which the young men were regarded as a fighting force, but if so, this was abandoned when the Belgian authorities forbade fighting. Just before Douglas was there, they simply paid an entrance fee of six to ten raffia cloths to the village treasury or to their age-set seniors, and thereby gained the right to a common wife, for whom they built a house. Some of these girls were 'captured', and no doubt in the days of warfare they may have been seized in raids or ambushed in the forest. But the 'capture' of later days usually consisted in holding a girl who had come to the village on a visit – and it might well have been arranged by collusion. Once such a girl had borne daughters, their daughters could be claimed in turn by the village – their common grandfather – as wives, just as an individual could claim the daughter of his own daughter. At the time of Douglas's work, the great majority of village-wives were village granddaughters.

Some of the girls refused to play their role; some were beaten into it; but though theirs was an enforced marriage it was certainly not enslavement. In the time when polyandry did not have to be concealed, a village-wife was married with elaborate ritual to honour her. This was described by the informants of Georges Brausch, a Belgian official who made an enquiry into the institution at the time when he had the job of suppressing it (in 1947). First, her house was built in the village square, close to those of the age-set who were to be her husbands. She was there to supervise the building, and might even climb on the roof with the young men, something unheard-of for any other women. When it was ready, she was elaborately dressed and decorated by her kinswomen, and formally installed by the young men of the new age-set, singing and beating drums. She was carried round the village in procession and presented to every house in turn; at the four corners she received gifts of raffia cloths from each of the four age-sets. She ate with her husbands a ritual meal of caterpillars, a Central African delicacy.

As Douglas records what *her* informants told her, a girl who had been allotted as a village-wife was made much of, and not at first expected to cook or work in the fields like an ordinary wife. She shared the food that was sent to the young men by their mothers, and sat chatting with them while they wove their raffia cloths in the age-set weaving place. She could 'help' one or other by snapping off loose ends. In return for this help she had to be given the cloth – so that a young man might be heard desperately saying, 'Oh, please go and help my friend!'

During this period each of the young men slept with her for two nights at a time, taking turns in order of age, and each one gave her a raffia cloth when he left. All these gifts were to go to her marriage payment, forty cloths for her mother and fifty for her father. Her husbands also gave the same services to her parents that an individual son-in-law would, such as rebuilding their houses.

When the time came for her to settle down and cook she was told to choose a limited number of men to be her 'house husbands' – say four or five out of a total of ten or twelve. These kept their possessions in her house; she hoed and cooked for them and slept with them in turn as a polygynous husband did with his wives. Gradually their numbers would fall. Two would quarrel, and one move away; one would marry a wife of his own; one would leave the village. Most village-wives ended up with no more than two or three husbands. Since this form of marriage had been forbidden, and also repudiated by Christian converts, when Douglas arrived there, she could not observe the installation of a new village-wife, but she could talk to several women of that status. Although some had been surprised and captured against their will, others had found a capture by collusion a means of escape from a husband to whom they had been allotted, equally against their will. There was in any case no freedom of choice in Lele marriage.

The children of a village-wife were children not of a clan but of the whole village. Village sons could call on every man in the village – not only their mothers' husbands – for help in such payments as they were called upon to make. At the marriage of a village-daughter the village received 100 raffia cloths – twice the amount paid to an individual father – and since he was giving bride-service not to a single father-in-law but to all the men of her village, her suitor had to go and live there for three months and be a servant to them all, weaving, drawing palm-wine, building, carpentering or whatever. But at his marriage he was given the insignia of honour, an eagle feather and a cap of leopard-skin; and it was said that he had the right to intervene and stop a fight between his own and his wife's village.

For the Lele, then, kinship was above all significant in terms of rights over the disposal of marriageable women, rights which carried with them material and non-material advantages: the material in the receipt of marriage fees, the non-material in the dependence of the son-in-law or prospective son-in-law.

Another way of gaining control over the disposal of women was the institution of pawnship. A pawn was a woman given in compensation for a death, by the clan of the person responsible, to the clan or village of the victim. The deaths in question were rarely violent; they were supposed to have been caused by mystical means. If a women died in childbirth it was thought that she must have committed adultery while she was pregnant. During the difficult birth she would be urged to confess, and the adulterer would then be held responsible. The other deaths for which blood compensation was due were those ascribed to sorcery. The debt was paid by the transfer of a woman to the control of the clan which had suffered the loss. She became their pawn (*kolomo*) and they were collectively her lords (*kumu*), and this status passed to all her matrilineal descendants. The lord's clan had the right to dispose of the woman in marriage and could also transfer them in blood payments; for this, however, they needed the approval of the pawn's own clan.

Indeed the pawn was very far from being a slave; his own father and his own clan were still concerned for him, and his village might attack the lord's village on his behalf. Pawns were not expected to work for their lord, and a male pawn had more claims than duties. The lord was responsible for his blood debts and was expected to help him find a wife. If he was dissatisfied he could get back on the lord by having one of his sisters captured as a village-wife. If a lord was held responsible for the death of a pawn, this could be made good by freeing a female pawn. A pawn could himself be the lord of pawns, and two clans could each have members of the other as pawns. Hence there was no question of a superior class of lords with pawns inferior to them. Since it was through their ability to bestow women in marriage that senior men attracted younger ones to their village, every opportunity was taken to establish claims to pawns.

A village too could claim pawns in compensation for injuries to its collective wives and children, and for various other actions regarded as offences against it as a corporate unit. A pawn given to a village became a village-wife.

POLITICAL ORGANISATION

Lele villages were linked by a tangle of marriage and pawnship relations. They obeyed a common 'rule of law' in the sense that they all recognised the same body of norms governing these relations. But they had no institutions for deciding disputed claims. These were dealt with by negotiations between villages, and if negotiations failed, by the armed force of the younger age-sets, as long as this was allowed. Within the village there was some degree of organisation, but no authority with coercive power. We are learning not to expect such authority in a community of two or three hundred people, and it is a moot question whether a Lele village or an Mbuti band can be said to have a political system. Schapera would answer the question for the Lele by saying that they recognised certain offices which deserve to be called political, and that they participated as a body in organised activities. The latter were hunting and ritual, and the ritual was largely directed to the success of the hunt. Failure in hunting was ascribed to the ill-will of peaople who harboured grievances, and since there was normally a hunt. Failure in hunting was ascribed to the ill-will of people under a moral compulsion to make it known and have it talked out. Such a procedure was initiated by the man who considered himself injured; he would proclaim his complaint when everyone was in the village at dusk or dawn, and thus offer it for public discussion.

The office of headman has been mentioned; it fell to the oldest man of the most numerous founding-clan section. He had certain claims on the rest of the village; he should receive a share of all game killed and wine tapped, and from this source he was able, as the representative of the village, to entertain visitors to it. He claimed the respect of his juniors, as did all old men, but he did not give orders. If he was angry, however, it was thought that the village could not prosper, and if failure in the hunt was ascribed to his anger, the person who had caused it had to admit his fault and beg pardon. This in a general way upheld the principle of respect for seniors.

The headman was a sort of chairman, in the sense that it was for him to announce formally decisions reached by all the men of the village in concert. The village as a corporation had business matters to deal with. Meetings for this purpose would be held around dawn, before anyone had set out for the forest, and if the agenda concerned a claim from outside, the claimant came the night before and slept in the village. The revenues of a village came from outside in the marriage-payments of its collective daughters, and from inside in the payments made for initiation into an age-set, and then into the cult associations which most men entered. All these payments were made in raffia cloths, and went in part to the existing members of the associations and in part to the village treasury. As more and more young people became Christians and rejected all these associations and the institution of village-wife, the village revenues steadily declined. Outgoings included marriage payments for village sons and also a type of payment that could not be made by an individual. If someone had a claim for a pawn which was disputed, and thought he was unlikely to get satisfaction, he could sell his claim to a village that might be willing to try to capture a girl by force, as an individual could not do. The payment was made in bars of camwood. It might be simply promised, and paid only by the man's heirs.

The man responsible for keeping village property, paying it out when called upon, and remembering the debts claimed, was the village 'spokesman' (*itembangu*). He was chosen by his predecessor or by the general consensus, and he had other duties besides that of treasurer. It was his business to make announcements of general interest, concerning not only arrangements for hunting or other work, but complaints from individuals who preferred not to speak up for themselves. If the village as a body imposed a fine, as it sometimes did for disturbances of the peace which were held to have angered the forest spirits and spoiled the hunting, the *itembangu* collected it; and it was his task to cut up and distribute the meat brought home from a communal hunt.

The men of the village were divided into age-sets. A new set was formed about every fifteen years, and there would usually be four in a village. The first and third would build their houses together on one side of the village, the second and fourth on the other. These divisions were known as the 'hands' of the village, though they were not called 'right' and 'left' hands as one sometimes finds in age-systems. There was a rough correspondence between the sets in different villages, so that a newcomer knew where he belonged. In practice each division would consist of a senior set of married men and a junior, many of whom were unmarried. The two were expected to be allies. The seniors should allot wives to their paired set and support their demands for village-wives. In a communal hunt each of the two 'hands' would take one side of the area to be surrounded. The age-set, like the village, had its property in fees paid by new entrants, and its *itembangu* who looked after this and disbursed it when required.

Although the villages were autonomous in their internal affairs, and, as long as they were allowed, made alliances and wars with their neighbours, all Lele recognised the superiority of one clan, the Tundu. In contrast to the Tundu all other Lele clans were called Wongo. The Tundu were said to have been the first immigrants into Lele country, and were called the 'owners' of it as founding clans were the 'owners' of their villages. All Tundu were referred to as *Kumu*, the word used of a lord in relation to his pawn. Tundu had claims to certain prized objects – serval and leopard skins and eagle feathers, insignia of honour which were also worn by village sons-in-law and by men who had killed a leopard or a man. Such objects could not be regarded as Tundu property or as tribute which was exacted from Wongo clans; a man who killed such an animal or bird was not punished if he did not hand it over. But if he presented it to a Tundu he was rewarded either by the release of one of his clanswomen from pawnship or by return gifts equal to the value of a man's ransom. Similarly, if a Tundu village headman visited a Wongo village every man in it should give him a raffia cloth. They would escort him back to his own village and there he would present one of his daughters or grand-daughters to them as a village-wife.

In the eastern part of Lele country, where the Tundu were concentrated, the oldest member of the clan had the title of *Nyimi*, which among the Bushong, the Lele's eastern neighbours, was that of a chief with significant political powers. The *Nyimi* was installed with formal ritual, which included an act of incestuous intercourse with a clan sister, supposedly an enactment of the incest of the first Tundu ancestor. After this act he could never look his clansmen in the face again, and had to live in a secluded enclosure for the rest of his life; as he had to be the oldest member of the clan this would probably not be long.

This act of ritual incest was also part of the accession ceremony of the chief of the Bushong. It was supposedly kept secret, and it was not casually referred to, but it was not held to require a life of expiation. The chief of the Bushong was an active political ruler.

How did the Lele come to have a chief who resembled the neighbouring one in name and in a particular aspect of ritual, and yet had no coercive power? Douglas suggests that the Tundu chief may have lost a power that he once had. Luc de Heusch, a Belgian anthropologist who has worked in the same region, applies to the comparison Lévi-Strauss' theory of reciprocity with a Marxist twist. Basic human relationships are a matter of reciprocal exchange; but historical events – that is occasions when someone is able to withhold reciprocity and so gain power – distort this primaeval equality; thus stratified societies appear. The Lele, by insisting on the principle of reciprocal marriage even in the relationship of Tundu and Wongo, have nipped in the bud a structure of superiority and subordination. De Heusch also remarks that clan organisation among the Lele was not strong enough to breach the independence of the highly structured villages.

A British empiricist would ask where the Bushong chiefs got the followers on whom they relied to make and preserve their military conquests, and why the Tundu, who had commoner hangers-on in their villages, did not or could not make such political use of them. But the data that we have do not enable us to answer this question.

Very few monographs have been considered, as this has, in the light of a theory quite different from the author's.

RITUAL

The importance of ritual power as a source of authority was mentioned among the Tallensi in relation to kinship, and it has been referred to in this chapter in relation to the authority of the village headman. The Lele feared the displeasure of the spirits in the forest as much as the Mbuti did that of the forest itself. A number of associations were responsible for rituals to secure from these spirits success in hunting, fertility in women and protection against sorcerers. The first step towards membership was initiation into the association of Begetters, men who had fathered a child in individual wedlock (not a child of the village). Nearly every man entered this group; they did not themselves perform ritual, but they gained the privilege of eating the chest meat of big game. From them a select few could enter the Pangolin cult. This was reserved for men who were themselves members of a founding clan of the village and whose fathers and wives had also belonged to founding clans. Such a man could qualify if he had a son and a daughter by the same wife. In South Homba, the village where Douglas lived, there were four Pangolin men out of a total of 33, excluding Christians. An initiation into the cult could only be held when a pangolin (scaly anteater) had been killed; this was held to be an event of good augury for future hunting. It fell to the Pangolin men to bless the new site when a village moved.

Many men (and a few women) became diviners – that is persons able to communicate with spirits and learn the cause of misfortunes, particularly sickness and bad hunting. Any man could be summoned by a dream or by a fit of 'possession', but it was for those who were already diviners to decide whether his claim was genuine. He would be sponsored by his mother's brother or his father, for divining was a profitable avocation. If he was accepted, he underwent a novitiate of a year or more before he was allowed to practise. The parents of twins, however, were *required* to become diviners, and they were held to gain their power without any initiation or instruction. There were also a few 'diviners of God'. They were believed to be in continuous communication with the spirits, who gave them messages on such matters as the best place to hunt.

In South Homba 16 of the 21 non-Christian men who had reached Begetter status were diviners, so that it was clearly not exceptional to be credited with the power to contact the spirits. But two men were selected as 'official' diviners, the junior one being generally chosen by his senior. It was their business to protect the village from sorcerers by identifying them through the consultation of 'oracles' – objects of various kinds which were supposed to give a yes-or-no answer to questions that were put to them while they were manipulated by the diviner. The Lele, like many other peoples in Africa and elsewhere, believed that most misfortunes were deliberately caused by malicious persons with occult powers, who needed victims to sustain these powers. Diviners rarely identified fellow villagers as sorcerers, and preferred to indicate somebody at a distance, or to attribute the misfortune to ritual pollution or the vengeance of a dead man's spirit. But the sufferers were most likely to suspect the enmity of their neighbours, and they did not regard the diviners as infallible.

Therefore accusations against neighbours were often made. In the past they were settled by the poison ordeal. This consisted in drinking a decoction of the bark of a tree, which was poisonous at any rate to some people. Ordeals were forbidden in 1924; an earlier traveller reported from a neighbouring tribe that they were held almost every day. Both accuser and accused drank the poison, and kinsmen of the accused would drink it too, to testify their confidence in his innocence. Before the proceedings began the men administering the ordeal drank as a demonstration of their own innocence – and informants do not apparently remember that they ever died. Innocent persons were supposed to vomit the poison. One of Douglas' informants had survived the ordeal twice, and had no fear of it; he nevertheless was widely suspected of sorcery. The ordeal finally settled who should give a pawn as blood compensation; the accusers gave one to a man who had been falsely accused.

From time to time Lele country was visited by the kind of cult movement offering total protection against sorcery that was first described in detail by Audrey Richards in 1935. It has often been argued that such movements have arisen to take the place of traditional ways of dealing with sorcerers which colonial authorities forbade. Douglas holds that the Lele would always have liked to get rid of the poison ordeal, and welcomed this alternative. Whether or not this is so, it is clear that a procedure which was supposed to destroy *all* sorcerers and give permanent protection offered something more than traditional methods could, and so would be welcomed in its own right.

THE LELE IN THE MODERN WORLD

The Lele were effectively controlled by European authorities for only a very short time. Only after a road was driven through their country (1931–5) were the Belgians able to suppress the fighting between villages, and although Lever Brothers had an oil-palm plantation with a factory in Lele country from 1923, they had to find all their labour among neighbouring peoples. During the Second World War the Lele were compelled to work either at growing food or cutting palm fruit for sale, or in wage employment, and money began to circulate in the villages. But the compulsion was withdrawn in 1947, and the Lele then proved to be little interested in earning cash. It was only in 1953, when a subsidiary of Lever's set up retail stores in many villages, that they began to be attracted by the possibility of having money to spend.

The first mission school, opened in 1925, was closed for lack of converts. But a second venture in 1939 was more successful, and ten years later had 'vast congregations' for the major Christian festivals. I mentioned that Christian converts had rejected polyandry, and since the main value of age-set membership was by that time the right to a village-wife, they had also ceased to form new age-sets.

But when the Congo (now Zaïre) became independent in 1960, governmental authority almost ceased to function. After only ten years of effective Christian influence and even less of effective experience of a money economy, the Lele were left to their own devices. We have no further news of them. Of course Zaïre is no longer in the state of chaos that followed the transfer of power, but it seems likely that its African rulers are less enthusiastic than the Belgians were in seeking to change traditional institutions.

Douglas observed opposition, sometimes bitter, between pagans and Christians. The Christians had found an ideology which justified their rejection of the old men's control of the women, and while the Belgians were there this had political support. Lele society appeared to Douglas then to be in a process of actual liquidation. The young Christians were making a complete break with the past. The continuity of the generations was actually ruptured by their refusal to enter age-sets; the marriage system and the authority structure were being rejected together. The young men had also crossed the great divide between the non-monetary and monetary economies; they had come to take imported goods for granted as part of their standard of living. What they do today to earn a money income depends on economic circumstances in Zaïre; perhaps they all work for the oil factory, and this above all – the control of an independent income – loosens traditional kinship and authority relations. It was still possible, Douglas thought, that without missionary support the new values might be rejected and the old system revived. The question what happens when external authority is withdrawn after imposing dramatic changes for a very short period is an interesting theoretical problem which no one has investigated.

7 Matrilineal Descent: The Plateau Tonga*

The Plateau Tonga are one section of the Tonga people who extend over much of the Southern Province of Zambia; the Gwembe Tonga, who were moved to new settlements when the Kariba Dam was built, are another. All have in common a system of matrilineal descent, and all, except the few who were lucky enough to live on alluvial land, traditionally practised shifting cultivation with frequent moving of villages. The Gwembe country had been difficult of access from the outside world until the road was built along which the people were transported to their new home, but European contact came early to the Plateau. A railway had crossed it by 1909, and shortly afterwards the land on either side of this for about four miles was alienated to European farmers; Tonga who were living there had to move away into the area beyond this, which was designated as a reserve. Thus some Tonga became neighbours of commercial farmers; many worked for wages on the farms. After the First World War Tonga began growing their own maize for sale, and some became 'progressive' farmers, putting their savings into ploughs and oxen, and sometimes more sophisticated equipment, and building brick houses. Further from the railway area many people were still content with subsistence farming or just selling a little maize. The contrast is one of the themes of Elizabeth Colson's study of Mazabuka District. It shows what difficulties a system of property rights based on matriliny can create for people who derive their incomes from relationships outside the system; but it shows too how the system persists in spite of the difficulties.

Mazabuka District is bounded on the north by the Kafue River and on the east and south by the escarpment of the Zambezi Valley. The railway runs right through it. At the time of Colson's fieldwork (1946–50) its Tonga population was estimated at 90,000 and was believed to be increasing rapidly. The density on cultivable land was 58 per square mile. It was be-

---

* *Marriage and the Family among the Plateau Tonga.* E. Colson, 1958.
  The Plateau Tonga: Social and Religious Studies. E. Colson, 1962.

coming difficult for the new generation to find land, and impossible to rest any land long enough for adequate regeneration. The adoption of maize, which can be sold as well as eaten, in place of the traditional millet, had increased the exhaustion of the soil. Most men owned cattle, though only a minority used them as plough or draught animals.

The Plateau Tonga had been drawn into the market economy first as wage-earners on the railway and then in employment on the farms. But at the time of Colson's work they were not dependent on employment away from home as are so many African populations. They had a market for their own produce, and looked on wage-labour largely as a way of building up capital for farm implements and stock. The government encouraged this development, and paid a bonus to men adopting improved farming methods, proportionate to the area they planted. A few such men had incomes at the time of the field-work of as much as £1,000, but the great majority earned less than £25 a year, and quite a number sold no produce at all. Those who were commercially minded had further resources. They could sell tobacco, beans, groundnuts and livestock; if they had ploughs or carts they could hire them out; some people ran 'tea-shops' by the side of frequented roads, a few went in for retail trade on a small scale; women brewed beer, or made pots or baskets, for sale. At that time, Colson foresaw that opportunities to earn the desired level of income without leaving home might decrease as the population pressed more heavily on local resources. However, if we can judge by other African peoples who had earlier reached this position, the norms of the kinship system are not likely to have greatly changed.

Colonial authorities sought to prevent the dispersal of population by making a rule that no village should have fewer than ten tax-payers, but Tonga villages did not usually fall below this limit. They would comprise perhaps thirty huts and a hundred people. In the east of the country there was a belt of bush between neighbouring villages; elsewhere one could not always see where one ended and the next began. A village had a headman and was called by his name; when he died he was normally succeeded by a member of the same lineage, but the village was not the home of a descent group. Typically people would build (and still do) in clusters of three or four huts; nobody would choose to live where he could not at least see the house of a neighbour.

CLAN AND *mukowa*

Like the Lele, the Tonga recognise common membership of descent groups without seeking to trace the genealogies on which it should logically be based. But whereas the effective group of this kind among the Lele is based on common residence, among the Tonga its members are dispersed. They use the same word – *mukowa* – for the clan and for the co-operating group whose members know one another. Within the *mukowa* in the latter sense, Tonga refuse to make distinctions between closer and more distant kin (brothers and sisters on the one hand and the children of female cousins on the other), not always because they do not know the relationship, but because, when they do, they prefer to regard the *mukowa* as a homogeneous group; and it is possible, as Colson suggests, that this is a way of holding together people who are not necessarily living in close contact, and maintaining moral claims that can be activated in crises, for example in famine. The members in a *mukowa* may range from only a few adult males to over a hundred.

The Plateau Tonga do not recognise any rule of seniority or authority among the members of the same generation. A man has authority over his sister's children but not over herself; *she* is subject to the authority of her (and his) mother's brother, and her marriage payment may be held by any one of these 'brothers'; in the past she was not allowed to know which. All members of a generation are held to be equal, and they are also equated with the generation of their grandparents. This is another form of the principle of the alternation of generations which is expressed in the relation of Lele age-sets and the layout of the Lele village. But the actual equality of the members of one generation, and of alternate generations in the sense that the senior of these exercise no authority over the junior, is in sharp contrast with the Lele assertion of the absolute importance of seniority in years.

Despite their egalitarian ideology, most *mukowa* look to

some individual as their leader, particularly in their dealings with outsiders. This is necessarily an achieved position. To attain it a man must have a reputation for wisdom and diplomacy. In addition he is likely to be the headman of a village; if this is a large one, it is evidence that he knows how to 'keep people together' and not let the community be disrupted by quarrels. Then he may be the priest of one of the neighbourhood shrines to which people go to pray for rain; or a diviner; he may have a larger than average herd of cattle; or, in the colonial period, he might have employment under government, as a member of the Native Authority in which persons who were supposed to have political powers in virtue of tradition were given responsibility for local administration.

Members of a small *mukowa* believe that they have a common body of ancestors after one or other of whom every child born must be named; the spirit of this ancestor becomes the child's guardian and is believed to influence his adult character, not necessarily for good. But this is by no means a way of commemorating known individuals. Some Tonga do not even know the names of their own grandmothers. Members of the same *mukowa* have a common pool of names to draw on, and people who use these names take the fact as evidence that they belong to the same *mukowa*. Every child is given a name from the *mukowa* names of both parents, the father's being actually the first.

In the past the *mukowa* was a vengeance group. The only way in which force could be mobilised to secure redress for an injury was through self-help; the *mukowa* as a body would seek compensation for wrongs done to any one of its members, and in particular would unite to avenge a homicide. Under colonial rule such action was of course forbidden, but an incident which Colson witnessed gives some idea of what might have happened in the past, as well as showing how far traditional attitudes still prevailed when she was there. A man was knocked down in a brawl at a beer-drink and died a few days later. His assailant was tried for manslaughter and sentenced to a prison term, but from the Tonga point of view this had no bearing on the situation. The guilty man, a member of the Eland clan, was a notorious brawler; his kinsmen had seen him off to the war hoping he would not come back, and during the time before his victim (of the Lion clan) died, the leading man of his *mukowa* had sent one messenger after another to express their concern and dissociate the *mukowa* as a body from their member's act. But after the death the messenger had come back saying that the Lions now refused to speak to him; relations between the two *mukowa* had been broken off.

But some Lions were married to Elands, and some Elands lived in villages where many of their neighbours were Lions. The headman of the killer's village had a Lion and an Eland wife, and children, therefore, of both *mukowa*. No doubt in these cases the boycott was not absolute, but Eland people thought it dangerous to go to other villages where there were many Lions.

During this tense period people recalled the old days, and said that then the victim's *mukowa* would have immediately attacked that of the killer, and seized and enslaved their women and children. Eland women living with their husbands among Lion men would have run away to their own *mukowa*, and stayed away until compensation had been paid and peace restored. As it was these Eland women said they were afraid of being attacked by sorcery. It was they in fact who were most concerned that a settlement should be reached, and who urged their kinsmen to offer compensation, while Lion men who were married to Elands were equally strong for acceptance. 'Will it bring that man back to life for us to lose our wives and children?' they said.

The cold war came to an end with the mourning ritual for the victim. Eland husbands of Lion women had a duty to be there, with other husbands of the mourners; it falls to them to cook the food for the funeral feast. They arrived, were not greeted, and sat in a group by themselves. But then the village headman who was an affine of both parties made an offer of compensation, speaking as the envoy of the leading Eland man. It was relayed through an affine of the Lions, and although it was still some time before the two sides agreed on the amount to be paid, relations could now be resumed.

This is one of the rare cases of the development of a state of feud which have been directly observed and recorded in detail. It has significance beyond its intrinsic interest because it was quoted by Gluckman (1955, p. 21) to illustrate

Evans-Pritchard's original discussion of the feuding process among the Nuer (see Chapter 10), and to support his argument that peace is maintained or restored through the influence of people who are bound by kinship to both the feuding lineages. It is possible that the Tonga story does not parallel at all points the development of a Nuer feud, but it certainly allows us to reconstruct in imagination something that Evans-Pritchard was not able to observe. The conflict described did not of course involve the entire Lion and Eland clans, but those members who lived in the neighbourhood of the crime.

The *mukowa* is also a property-holding group. The possessions of a member who has died are shared among the survivors of the senior generation. A successor should be found to take over the homestead and the village, if he had headed one, and to marry his widow, if she does not wish to marry elsewhere. In either case the successor must purify her by an act of ritual intercourse before she can make a new marriage. The man chosen would not be of the same 'womb' – descended from the same maternal grandmother – but it is not always easy to find a successor, since the position carries more responsibilities than advantages. If members of the same 'womb' were obliged to provide a successor they would complain that they were being forced out of the *mukowa*.

Like their Gwembe neighbours and like the Lele, though in a very different way from the latter, the Plateau Tonga attach importance to their patrilateral kin as well as to their own descent groups. The members of the latter are one's *basimukowa*. Those of one's father's *mukowa* are one's own *basyanaushi*. No continuing group comparable to the Gwembe *lutundu* exists, but as long as a person's father is alive his *basyanaushi* are equally important with his *basimukowa*, and are expected to co-operate with them in all matters affecting his interests; and when a man dies they claim a share in his inheritance.

The main significance of clan membership, in addition to the rule of exogamy, lies in the 'joking' relationship which links pairs of clans. This is the typical joking relationship in which the partners may abuse and insult one another in a manner that would not be tolerated in any other context, but it has the special feature that the joking is supposed to reflect antagonisms or contrasts between the animals after which the clans are named. Stories are told of tricks played by one animal on another which are supposed to be the source of the antagonism. Every clan has a number of such partnerships, and they have significance beyond the exchange of insults. The joking partners of a dead man's clan attend his funeral, and play the fool, mocking the grief of the mourners, telling them they don't really care, perhaps they themselves killed their kinsman by sorcery; and this, it is said, helps to relieve the gloom. Another responsibility is that of intervention in certain situations of ritual danger which the Tonga call *malweza*. *Malweza* is sometimes incurred by breaches of social norms, sometimes simply by accident. Then if the appropriate action is not taken, the person involved in *malweza*, or one of his close kin, may die; that is to say, a death is retrospectively ascribed to *malweza* if someone recalls an act or event that might have incurred it. Incest incurs *malweza*; to strike a senior person (or a sister) does so. So does an attempt at suicide. There is *malweza* if someone's grainstore falls down, because this prefigures his death, when his store of grain will be divided among his kinsmen. *Malweza* can be averted by the insults of the clan joking-partners, and where the event which is supposed to have incurred it is a breach of social norms, their public abuse – which would be impermissible for kinsmen or ordinary neighbours, however much they might disapprove of the culprit – is one of the few sanctions that exist in Tonga society; the more so in that the ancestor spirits are believed not to care about the good behaviour of their descendants, so that sickness does not lead to the kind of examination of conscience and canvassing of possible transgressions that we find in many other societies. In such situations, of course, the abuse is not reciprocal but one-sided. The culprits cannot retort because they have lost the sympathy of their own kin. They cannot lose their tempers and fight because that would deny, and so end, the relationship, and it has other advantages, particularly that of safe conduct among strangers. Colson interprets it as another way of creating a network of links among the small populations subject to no central authority of which Tonga society is made up.

RITUAL AUTHORITY

Before an alien authority introduced courts, police and prisons, self-help by the *mukowa* was the only form of coercion on behalf of jural claims that existed. But there were – and there still are, though they have lost their political significance – ritual centres which integrated, and sometimes imposed peace upon, the inhabitants of a wider locality than the village. These are the neighbourhood shrines at which offerings are made every year to pray for rain. A neighbourhood comprises perhaps seven or eight villages. It can be defined only in terms of the rain-shrines which it recognises; there may be several in one neighbourhood. The neighbourhood *is* the collection of villagers who supplicate at the same shrines. Once a year, at the time when the rains are due, all the people of the neighbourhood must go with offerings to their shrine, and during the three days of the ritual, peace is imposed on all the participants, a requirement in nearly all religious rites including the central ritual of Christianity. In the old days self-help was not allowed during that time, and injuries were atoned by the payment of a fine to the elders of the shrine community instead of compensation to the injured. It is still held to be the duty of every person living in the shrine area to take part in this ritual (although missions forbid their converts to do so) and in the past anyone who stayed away would have been fined. It is still the rule that quarrels which have broken out earlier must be patched up, and if feelings run too high for this one party must leave the shrine community and attach itself to another. To leave a quarrel unsettled within the community which supposedly should join in peace and amity is to incur the danger of drought, famine and epidemic disease.

Some of these shrines are dedicated to men who are supposed to have led sections of the Tonga into their present country from somewhere outside. New shrines are constantly being set up at the bidding of prophets who claim to have a message from some spirit of a more recently dead person, demanding that a shrine be made for him. Both the spirits and the prophets are called *basangu*, whereas the ancestor spirits are called *mizimu*. *Basangu* may be either men or women. The fortunes of a shrine depend upon the supposed effectiveness of its spirit in meeting the needs of its worshippers, who approach it in times of drought and other calamities as well as in the regular annual ritual. If it is still frequented when its founder dies, some member of his *mukowa* takes it over. By the time of Colson's visit the new authority structure created by the British had been well established. But the supposedly traditional chiefs to whom they gave executive powers had to emphasise the possession of rain shrines by their *mukowa* in order to make their status legitimate in the eyes of their people. Some tried to deny the authenticity of shrines owned by other *mukowa* in order to gain respect for their new authority.

MARRIAGE AND PROPERTY

Since it is from the marriage of his parents that a person derives his lineage membership and his complementary kinship, one may take the procedure for establishing a marriage as a starting-point for discussion of relationships with the *basimukowa* and *basyanaushi*. Both groups are involved in the making of the contract and in the ritual which marks the union.

Marriages are no longer arranged without the knowledge of the parties, though to have full social approval they must still have the consent of the *basimukowa* and the father of both bridegroom and bride. It is usual today for the couple to come to an agreement first, but the marriage must still be formally negotiated by representatives of the *basimukowa* and *basyanaushi* of both, and any of these can refuse to play their part. Two payments must be offered and accepted. The first, consisting traditionally in six hoes and a spear, authorises the couple to set up house, but not yet independently of their elders. They must be attached to the household of some senior relative, or possibly a man for whom the bridegroom has been working, perhaps in herding cattle. Their elders discuss where they shall go, at the same time as discussing what the amount of the final bridewealth payment shall be; this is paid in cattle, and usually varies between two and four, but is higher in areas where cattle are more plentiful. Both payments are divided equally between the *basimukowa* and *basyanaushi*: no doubt three cattle would be divided by calculating the money equivalent.

Traditionally a girl was not told either who her husband was to be or when she would go to him; she was seized from her home and carried off screaming. Girls are still expected to scream and generally simulate resistance when their husbands' messengers appear. When the bride leaves her home her father casts her off in the name of her *basyanaushi*; although she will always be a member of her own *mukowa*, her husband will now take over her father's authority over her. She is accompanied by two young women representing the descent groups of her two parents, and it is the representative of the *basyanaushi* who asks her next morning whether she is satisfied with her husband.

Until the cattle payment is completed, which may not be before they have one or even two children, the young couple are subject to the authority of the head of the household to which they are attached. The wife works with the senior woman; she may not cook independently for her husband, nor brew beer, which is important not only as a secular activity but also for ritual occasions. When the final payment has been offered and accepted, a member of the wife's *mukowa* and one of her *basyanaushi* together ritually place in her hut the three stones on which the cooking-pot will stand over the fire. Next, they put grain to soak for the first beer. This is offered to the husband's ancestor spirits, who by this rite are installed as guardians of the new independent household. The husband cannot make this offering on his own behalf; only women can brew beer. This ritual dependence is a matter of concern to widowers; they are debarred from making offerings on behalf of their junior kinsmen, whereas a widow, who can make her own offerings, can often get on very well by herself.

Those Plateau Tonga who have taken to commercial farming have found that their traditional system has considerable disadvantages, not only in its rules for the transmission of property but also in the rules, or absence of strict rules, concerning the establishment of new households. The Tallensi homestead is the residence of a productive team that continues in being over the generations as the young replace the old, but matrilineal descent cannot link the generations in this way. The typical producing group consists of a couple with their dependents: their own children, other young people whom they may 'borrow' from kinsmen at busy times, or even sometimes attract from outside by the prospect of plentiful food, and perhaps a newly married couple who will have no obligation towards them when they have attained independent status. Since sons do not inherit their fathers' goods, there is no continuity in the control of capital equipment, which is likely to be dissipated on the death of the man who built it up. Since women do not inherit their husbands' goods, it would make no difference if daughters stayed at home and brought in their husbands (and they don't). An examination of the property rules shows how a man and his wife-and-her-children are necessarily at odds about the disposal of the product of their labour.

The property of husband and wife is kept strictly separate. The husband is responsible for providing clothes for his wife, but his cash income is at his own disposal, and she is not likely to know what it is. The wife has her own share of the grain crop, which her husband must not touch, and she can give away the surplus, a matter of some importance where famine is so frequent and people beg from their *mukowa*. If she *sells* grain, however, her husband may claim half or all the proceeds; however, what he leaves her is entirely at her own disposal. Women have various independent sources of income. They make pots, they may be paid to brew beer from other people's grain, they can be diviners or herbal doctors. They are given livestock in fees and are free to dispose of these by sale or otherwise. A woman may even acquire oxen, and can refuse to let her husband have them for ploughing; she will more likely send them to someone in her own *mukowa*, lest when her husband dies his *mukowa* may think they are part of his estate. It is the responsibility of the wife's *mukowa*, not of her husband, to meet claims for damages against her, and he cannot use her property, except as a loan, to meet claims brought against him.

But the man's property is still the bone of contention. His wife and sons help to build it up, but they know that what he has when he dies will not come to them. His heirs, all of them outside his family, watch jealously to see that he does not divert it from them to his own family. In fact the only way of doing this is by enjoying a higher standard of living; he cannot make them substantial gifts in any other way. Perhaps this is most likely to be noticed when food is short; Colson describes the indignation of his *mukowa* against a man who at such a time bought a bag of sugar for his family and did not share it with them. A son who worked loyally with his father and shared his prosperity was afraid his father's *mukowa* would kill him by sorcery.

Other sons try to get what they can out of their fathers' property before it goes out of the family. They may cheat their father when he entrusts them with the sale of cattle or other business deals. They certainly have no incentive to work for their fathers if they see opportunities elsewhere. Some mothers encourage their sons to get whatever they can by involving themselves in seduction damages which their fathers will have to pay – although their own *mukowa* also pays its share. But despite these difficulties, it must not be supposed that all Tonga households are rent by continuous strife. Most families everywhere have something to quarrel about some of the time.

In 1950 Tonga men were urging that the Native Authority should pass a regulation authorising them to dispose of their property by will, and Colson was of the opinion that matrilineal inheritance was bound to be soon abandoned. At about the same time I heard a meeting of elders in Malawi pass a resolution abolishing matriliny 'from the first of January next'. No such change has yet been made in these two societies, though in Zambia sons sometimes go to law and get a judgement awarding them some valuable property of their father – say a brick house with corrugated iron roof. In Ghana, the home of the five-million-strong matrilineal Akan-speaking peoples, men are allowed to dispose of their property by will, but matrilineal succession is still the rule.

Mary Douglas has argued (1969) that this system is not inherently inimical to economic development. She bases her argument largely on the Ashanti, the most populous of the Akan peoples, whose enterprise has made Ghana one of the most important cocoa producers in the world. Cocoa growing was successfully extended by the migration of the original growers into vacant forest areas, and the kind of friction that has been described among the Tonga is not recorded of them (but nobody has made anything like as detailed a study there as

Colson's of the Tonga). So, Douglas argues, it is only where productive resources (in this case land) are scarce that there is friction; matriliny does very well in an expanding market economy. But what Colson describes is not competition for the resources but for the consumption goods that they produce, and possibly also the capital in ploughs, etc., and this even though land shortage was already a problem when she was among the Tonga. Young men worry about their share of the product that their labour has helped to create. Troubles about the inheritance of *land* do not feature in the story. But if the expansion of the economy depends on agriculture it is bound to lead to scarcity of land in whatever case.

It seems that matriliny is not doomed unless in the very long run; but it is the tenacity of ideas about kinship, and not economic circumstances, that will maintain it.

Double Unilineal Descent: The Yakö*

A number of African societies recognise descent through males for some purposes and through females for others. The importance attached to the *soog* relationship of uterine descent by the Tallensi, who are often thought of as the prototype of a patrilineal society, has been mentioned. The Ashanti, again, transmit property and political office in the female line, but ritual status is inherited from father to son. True dual descent is found where land rights are transmitted in one line and movable property in the other, so that there are corporate lineages of both types. These have been classified into six groups, widely scattered over the continent (Goody 1969, p. 113). The Yakö, to be discussed here, are one of a number of peoples living on both sides of the Cross River in its middle reaches in eastern Nigeria who recognise double descent. They inhabit five villages just east of the river, and just above the bend where its course changes from south-east to due south. The largest of these, Umor, had a population of 11,000 when Daryll Forde was there in 1935 and 1939, and his ethnographic work refers entirely to it.

The staple food of the Yakö is yams, but they also grow bananas, plantains, kola nuts, pawpaws, native pears and coconuts. They gather the nuts of wild oil-palms, and in 1935 they could still hunt in forests near the villages. Oil-palm products, oil and kernels, are their local source of cash, and cash incomes increased considerably in the early years of this century. Already in 1935 some men were making an income as middlemen, and others as retailers of imported goods brought up the river from Calabar.

DESCENT GROUPS

The Yakö are organised in both matrilineal and patrilineal clans, both of these, as everywhere, divided into lineages. The clan as a corporate body has a good deal more significance

* *Yakö Studies.* C. D. Forde, 1964.

than it has for the peoples discussed up to now. The patrilineal clan (*kepun*, plural *yepun*) in addition to being an exogamous and a ritual unit, has joint rights in land. It claims an area in the village for house sites, and a number of blocks of farming land outside. Each of these is reached by a separate path from the village, and most of the land that is actually cultivated is close to the paths. Different *yepun* may have blocks at different points along the same path. Within a *kepun* different lineages usually farm separate blocks. Every *kepun* has a 'farm path elder' for each of the paths on which it has land. He should settle disputes between *kepun* members farming along his path and defend them from encroachment by outsiders; he can also give permission – and his permission is required – to an outsider to make a farm on land surplus to *kepun* needs. Path elders also traditionally organised communal work in clearing the bush for new farms; it was every member's obligation to give a day to this.

Within the village *kepun* members live in a compact block of houses, with a ditch or some other boundary separating them from neighbours of other *yepun*. Houses on the edge of this area are built facing inwards, so that different *yepun* turn their backs on one another. Each *kepun* should have its own meeting house, where ritual objects are kept, rites performed, secular business discussed and messengers from other *yepun* received. Next to it is the shrine of the *kepun* spirit. The shrine is called *epundet*, a word in which *kepun* is combined with *edet*, the name of a kind of spirit which is more concerned with punishing than blessing, and of which there are many in Yakö belief. It is not conceived as an ancestor or as a personified being at all; it is simply the inhabitant of the shrine. Such non-personified spirits are sometimes called fetishes, a word little used in anthropology outside the context of West Africa. The shrine consists of a small heap of rocks on top of which are pots marked with white clay.

By formal definition a *kepun* is an exogamous group the members of which possess a common *epundet*. The number of adult males in a *kepun* varied in 1935 from 50 to 150. A senior man, the *Obot kepun*, is recognised as the head. He is essentially a priest, and his responsibility is primarily to avert misfortune, or to make expiation to the spirit if some wrong action is said to have angered it and so brought down sickness or some other misfortune on a *kepun* member. At the first pregnancy of any *kepun* daughter she is brought to the *epundet* for a rite to protect her in the new home, away from her own *kepun*, where she will live as a wife. Essentially the effect of this rite is to cause the *edet* to punish anyone who may harm her.

The *kepun* head is also the arbitrator in disputes between members of the *kepun*; he hears these in the presence of other elders, and together they sometimes in the past imposed small fines. He has an assistant whom he chooses himself, and this man is thereby designated as his successor. The choice of a *kepun* head is limited by the fact that certain lineages claim that an *epundet* belongs to them; where this is not the rule the chosen successor would be a man who was already head of his own lineage. Therefore, every *kepun* head is a lineage head.

A lineage in 1935 included 15 to 30 households. Although every lineage is a member of some *kepun*, they are not supposed to be descended from a single common ancestor, and sometimes their separate descent is on record. Within the *kepun* area members of the same lineage live close together, often in the same compound (this is the word used in West Africa for a number of buildings forming a hollow square, traditionally the home of an extended family). Each lineage has its head, chosen by his predecessor like the *Obot kepun*. Lineage heads are normally older men, but no one has any claim in virtue of genealogical status. A lineage head must be acceptable to his fellows; he should command personal authority and at the same time be able to calm angry disputants by diplomacy, and he should have the superior wealth that is the mark of success and can be the source of favours. There can be more than one candidate, and in that case the question is decided by the apparent strength of support for each.

The *yepun* are not actually all divided in accordance with the principles that the Yakö state. Two may share a shrine; usually these are neighbours, but not always. People who call themselves members of one *kepun* and share a house area may be divided into exogamous groups each with a shrine of its own. In fact in 1935 only six of the 26 named *yepun* in Umor conformed to the ideal specification. This state of affairs of course reflects a process to be found everywhere; on the one hand new lineages attach themselves to existing ones, and on the other existing lineages divide as their numbers increase. The newcomers are the splinters of older lineages. At first they may move their dwellings but still worship at their original shrine, but complete secession involves the creation of a new shrine. The ritual power of the older shrine is transferred by taking from it some of its pots and boulders to be the basis of the new one. Or these may be taken from the shrine which is supposed to have been set up by the founders of the village. This final act of separation usually follows a quarrel, perhaps over the distribution of land.

More interesting than the universal process of fission is the frequency with which Yakö adopt outsiders into their lineages. This fact is worth noting because it has sometimes been argued, with reference to descent groups outside Africa, that they cannot be described in lineage terms because it is so easy to transfer membership from one to another. In fact the adoption process among the Yakö closely resembles what has been reported from some parts of New Guinea. A boy whose mother dies or leaves her husband is often brought up in the household of one of her kinsmen, and when he is old enough to marry, this man may make the necessary payments for him. This amounts to recognising him as a son of the *kepun*, and he is thenceforward regarded as an adopted member of it; he will be given land to farm, and on his side will have the same ritual obligations as a member by birth.

In addition the Yakö used to acquire foreign children by payment, a practice which was frowned upon by the colonial authorities as a form of enslavement. Such children were sometimes stolen from their parents, sometimes sold by Ibo parents who could not make a living from their poor soil in the areas of densest population; they were brought up the river by middlemen. They were not treated as slaves by the Yakö who purchased them, but just like other children, with full inheritance rights. Girls were much more often purchased than boys, and this helped to make polygyny possible without the intense competition for marriageable girls that has been described elsewhere.

The recognition of double descent makes every person a member of two lineages, his father's and his mother's, and only full siblings belong to the same two. Since the patrilineage is the source of land rights, it is the localised group. Matrilineal kin are dispersed throughout the village, and beyond it; patrilineal ties are not traced outside the village.

The matrilineage (*lejima*, plural *yajima*) is the source of inheritance of movable goods. It is also a unit for rituals which are of greater importance to its members than are their respective *kepun* rituals. Movable property consists in tools and weapons, household goods, livestock (goats and chickens and some cows), the 'brass rods' – actually flexible lengths of coiled wire – that were the medium of exchange in the early days of trade with the coast, accumulated cash and – where inheritance at a death is in question – stores of food. As with the Tonga, these are distributed at the owner's death among his brothers and sisters' sons. The matrilineage is liable to pay compensation for wrongs done by its members, and receives the payments due for wrongs which its members suffer. People look to their matrilineal kin for loans, and a matrilineage can be held responsible for the debts of one of its members. But it has been remarked already that a father is expected to provide the marriage payments for his son, and that this act marks the recognition of an adopted son as a member of the foster-father's *kepun*. The matrilineage contributes only a small share to the marriage payment of its sons, yet it receives the greater portion of that given for its daughters. The father's authority over his children is recognised in the fact that the payment is actually made to him, but he should pass it on to his wife's brother, keeping only a small amount. It is the matrilineal kin who will be called upon to make repayment if their daughter leaves her husband.

It is they also who are entitled to compensation if one of their number is killed, and who claim it from the matrilineage of the killer. There is no obligation to seek vengeance; indeed this is not approved. But the patrilineal kin often do start a fight, and the killer has to take refuge with the village head, who then warns the angry *kepun* to keep the peace. But a payment (in money by 1935) has to be made to the *lejima*, and in addition a woman must be transferred to them so that her children will add to their strength. Until the compensation has been paid, moreover (and this may be a considerable time), a man from the offending *lejima* is also transferred; in the one case that Forde cites this was the killer himself. In the days when the purchase of children was common, the injured *lejima* would sometimes accept a payment with which they could buy a child instead of taking one of the killer's kin; and if the latter had already been transferred, a bought child might later be substituted for him. The implications of the transfer for a man are mainly ritual, but in addition, when he is in his new *lejima* he must lose inheritance rights in his old one, and he presumably gains them in the new. The transfer is formally accepted and made public by a ceremony at the shrine of the new *lejima*.

I have written in the present tense up to now because the stated norms of kinship are very persistent, and people often persuade themselves that they are observed in practice at a time when anthropologists can see that they are being more and more disregarded; also because fieldwork in neighbouring areas done much later gives the impression that this aspect of the social structure of the Cross River peoples has not changed very much. But much of the rest of this chapter will be put in the past tense, because it describes organisations and usages which were already undergoing rapid change at the time when Forde was there. The first subject of which this is true is the procedure for making a legal marriage.

MARRIAGE

The Yakö recognised no rules giving senior kinsmen the right to dispose of girls in marriage, and as far back as we know people chose their own partner. Girls of eleven or twelve used to form gangs for leisure-time amusement. They would spend their evenings together, and then sleep, at the house of the mother of one or another, where each girl could invite a lover. Boys would seek such invitations by making the girls small gifts. Courtships, therefore, began for girls even before first menstruation, though of course neither boy nor girl was committed by the first choice. But the eventual choice was made by the couple themselves, who then sought the approval of their elders, and it was the young man himself, accompanied by some of his age-mates, who presented himself to the girl's father.

The right age for betrothal was said to be two harvests (i.e. between one and two years) after first menstruation, and another two years were supposed to elapse between betrothal and marriage, during which the youth was obliged to give services of various kinds to his future father-in-law. In the more distant past he was expected to come with his age-mates to clear the ground for planting on his father-in-law's farm. In 1935 it was more common to have them weave fresh mats for the roofing of his house. But the bridegroom himself was expected to help at harvest time in gathering and storing yams, and to lend a hand in any major work of his father-in-law. At harvest time he was also expected to give presents to the girl and her parents, and she would give him a bowl of peanuts from a patch that her mother had given her to plant just for that purpose.

Central to the marriage ritual was the girl's *kukpot* or clitoridectomy, which was performed at a special spot belonging to her *kepun* on the edge of the village. Sex relations were permitted between betrothed couples, but they were not supposed to lead to pregnancy, and the ritual for a girl who was already pregnant was performed at a distance from the village, in the bush. This was a mild form of disgrace; for a girl to become pregnant *before* betrothal was considered far more disgraceful. Forde was able to use the division of women into named age-sets as a basis for calculating how far it was true that, as their elders say everywhere and always, girls were disregarding the strict principles that their mothers followed. He found that the proportion who became pregnant before the clitoridectomy rite was increasing, but the memories of the oldest women did not extend to a time when this had been exceptional. Half of the women over 60 in his sample had had the less honourable rite. Of the youngest, aged 17 to 24, however, only one-sixth had not become pregnant before it. He found two reasons for this: that people had become less willing to practise coitus interruptus, and that the age of betrothal was getting later as the price of palm products fell and young men were not sure that they would be able to raise the marriage payment.

Traditionally the payment should have been handed over at the conclusion of this rite. It was formally presented by the groom's age-mates to those of the bride, the actual giver and receiver not being present. But if it was only promised and not paid till later, it would be given directly to the father-in-law by the bridegroom or his father.

After the *kukpot* the bride returned to her mother's house, where she stayed in seclusion until the next harvest, or, if she was pregnant, until the fourth or fifth month of pregnancy. She was not allowed to go out, nor expected to do hard work, though she could cook; she was visited by her friends, and her husband spent most nights with her. She was given plenty to eat, in particular more meat than women usually got at other times. Accordingly the place of seclusion has come to be called in English 'the fatting-house', a phrase that Nigerians today take for granted though it has the look of a derogatory label devised by some early traveller. This was still the practice when Forde was there.

Some time before Forde's visit fathers had begun to insist on keeping their daughters' marriage payments. According to his records, this had happened in about a third of the marriages of women who were then between eighteen and forty. But among the most recently married, of whom there were only eleven in the ward of Umor where he collected his statistics, only two fathers had passed on the payment. A man who did this became liable for repayment if his daughter left her husband, and could not expect any contribution from his *lejima*, since his daughter was not a member of it and her marriage was no affair of theirs. In some cases it appeared to be a demonstration of superior wealth, a proclamation of the father's ability to make the return, if called upon, from his own resources; Forde saw it as a substitute for the older way of publicising one's wealth by buying a foreign child. But he also ascribes it to a general strain imposed on the marriage system by 'increasing individualism and the depression of the external market for palm products' (1941, p. 49).

The motives for this particular change cannot be very closely compared with the sources of that discontent with matrilineal inheritance which has been recorded among the Tonga. But the Yakö resemble them in that as long ago as 1935 sons were claiming to inherit their fathers' property, and Native Courts, with the support of the administration, were deciding in their favour. Even earlier it was said that men buried their possessions on their farms, where matrilineal kin could not trespass, and thus left them to be dug up by their sons. A man who had been adopted into the *kepun* of a *lejima* kinsman – and this was the commonest form of adoption – could inherit as a *lejima* member from his adoptive father, but he could still not claim all his father's goods.

The *lejima*, like the *kepun*, should have its own spirit shrine, and it was the regular rituals at these shrines which publicly proclaimed a unity that was not significant for the conduct of everyday affairs. They also brought together participants from all over the village, and thus demonstrated in visible form what Gluckman would call the 'cross-cutting ties' that linked members of different *yepun* divided by residence and everyday co-operative work. Actually, although there were 23 *yajima* in Umor in 1935, there were only ten shrines. Some sought ritual benefits and protection from spirits which 'belonged' to another *lejima*, that is to say they depended on the offerings made by a priest of another clan. This situation was explained by reference to supposed divisions of clans in the past.

The matrilineal spirits are called *ase* (singular *yose*), and, like the *yepun* spirits, are not believed to be ancestors or personified at all, but thought to be embodied in the objects at their shrines, which are more elaborate than the *yepundet*. They include decorated skulls, brass and copper rings, and pots, and they are kept in a small house in the priest's compound and brought out on ceremonial occasions. The *ase* spirits are the source of fertility and thus of life itself, and it is they who are approached with supplication for blessing, in contrast to the *kepun* spirits from whom people seek protection from, or remedies for, misfortune. A *yose* priest is chosen by the elders of the clan which claims to own the shrine. There is no rule of seniority; when he is appointed he is frequently middle-aged rather than elderly.

RITUAL AUTHORITY

Ase priests are more important persons than the *yepun* heads, and they played a much more significant part in the traditional system of government. An *Obot kepun* has authority within his own clan, but the *ase* priests as a group, along with some others not directly associated with the lineages, exercised authority throughout the village. It was they who were known as the Leaders (*Yabot*, the plural of *Obot*), and the senior among them was the leader of the whole village (*Obot lopon*). The appointment of any new priest had to be approved by the *ase* priests as a body, and they instructed him in his duties.

There is a sense in which Umor could have been called a theocracy. Its leaders were primarily priests, and the sanctions that they could directly invoke were ritual – the anger of the spirits whom they served, or, as Forde sometimes puts it, controlled – at disobedience to their decisions or breaches of generally accepted norms, and particularly at refusal to compromise disputes. Not all spirits, however, were controlled or 'belonged to' *ase* priests. A number of separate cult associations, which people could enter by the payment of fees, had their own spirits, whom they could summon to action against transgressors in particular fields of behaviour with which they were concerned. Some of these cults had been acquired by payment from neighbouring people who claimed to own them, and the result is a somewhat confusing overlapping of agencies of social control. The Yakö illustrate the danger of seeking to explain institutions by their function alone, if that controversial but useful word is taken to mean that whatever custom is observed in a society is indispensable to its maintenance in a satisfactory condition. It might be easier to argue that these new cults would not have been acquired if there had not been some 'need' for them – but in that case the previously existing institutions could not have fulfilled the 'needs' of Umor society. It is self-evident that whoever took the initiative in buying a new cult *wanted* to do so. But do people always need what they want? Perhaps the introducers of new cults competed for members with the older ones. Perhaps this should be called healthy rivalry; perhaps not.

These quasi-independent associations in the main supported the authority of the council of priests, and those – the majority – which had members throughout the village linked its territorial divisions together. They all received the formal blessing of the village priests at the great seasonal rituals. But there was one maverick, a body called *Nkpe*, which was supposed to have acquired a leopard spirit fairly recently. *Nkpe* claimed that the spirit protected its members, and others who paid them a fee, against theft and adultery; for the latter offence it punished women with sterility. The *ase* priests, concerned as they were with fertility, condemned such a claim, and any member of *Nkpe* had to leave it if he became a *yose* priest. Yet 40 per cent of the men were members, and they considered that membership gave them protection against the abuse of (ritual) powers by the *ase* priests and by other leopard-owners.

The council of priests, twenty-four in all, the ten *ase* priests along with some others, and some ritual officers who were not priests in their own right, dealt with secular as well as ritual matters. Its head, the *Obot lopon*, lived next to the open space where village meetings were held, on land not claimed as property by any *kepun*. The council met at his house. Disputes not settled elsewhere were brought to it, and it decided not only when rituals were due but also when clearing and harvesting should begin. It could fine people for offences and for disobedience, though its ultimate sanction was the power to refuse an offender access to the shrines.

Under British administration, Native Courts were set up with limited powers, and with responsibility for settling cases in accordance with native custom in so far as this was not held to be repugnant (i.e. contradictory) to the principles of humanity and natural justice. The members of these courts were appointed not arbitrarily, but after consultation with the villagers, but the Yakö seem to have envisaged this new institution as something unconnected with their own organisation and not to have supposed that the 'natural leaders' (i.e. holders of traditional office) were the right people to be judges; they rather chose forceful personalities who they thought could stand up to the British officials. The only village head to have been a member was the *Obot lopon* at the time of Forde's visit, and he was not the president. This was, then, an alternative body which had been given judicial powers, supported by the administration, to deal with disputes between individuals. But although in 1935 it was taken for granted and many people went there with their cases, others were still brought before the *Yabot*, and they still dealt with ritual matters.

The *ase* priests, then, were the ultimate village authority in the traditional system. But they did not themselves deal directly with all the eleven thousand inhabitants of Umor. The village was subdivided into four sections which Forde calls wards, territorial divisions in each of which there was a number of unrelated *yepun*. In 1935 the number of households in a ward varied from 300 to 600. Each ward had its own head (*Ogbolia*) and leaders called *Yakamben*. The body of leaders included all the *kepun* heads and any *ase* priests who lived in the ward. To enter it a man had to provide a feast and pay a sum of money which was divided among its existing members; the total cost was £5–7 in 1935. When a member died his *kepun* were expected to find a successor; they would tend to look for someone who could pay his own expenses and would not have to look round for contributions. But membership was not acquired solely by succession. Anyone who could pay the entrance fee, and had the approval of the existing members, could join, and at the time when the palm oil trade was booming a good many younger men paid their way in. The office of ward head theoretically rotated among the three or four *yepun* who were believed to have founded the ward, but in practice there was a good deal of hard bargaining, and particular lineages tried to establish hereditary claims to this and other offices. Thus while authority in Umor could certainly not be said to rest on descent alone, claims based on descent played a considerable part in succession to positions of authority. In the ward which Forde studied in detail about 35 per cent of the adult males were *Yakamben*; so that although they were a minority, they could hardly be called a narrow oligarchy.

The *Yakamben* were responsible for the organisation of age-sets in their wards. In each ward an initiation ritual was held every four years, at which small boys were formally recognised as males (though not with any pretence that they were adult) and ceased to observe, as they had before, ritual prohibitions appropriate to women. On the same occasion the *Yakamben* would proclaim the formation of an age-set of youths about to marry. There were about sixteen sets in existence in Umor at any one time; there were very few men left in the older sets, but the practical significance of set membership was in any case a matter for the younger ones. They could be called on for 'public works' of various kinds in their wards – fire-watching in the dry season, keeping paths open, clearing weeds from springs. It may well have been the existence of this kind of system all through eastern Nigeria that enabled the advocates of 'community development' in the period after the Second World War to achieve such spectacular successes; villagers not only agreed to build a road, a clinic or whatever, they had an institution for allotting the work.

Age-set membership was obligatory. In addition most adult men chose to join an association called *Ebiabu*, in which they passed through three grades, juniors (little boys), adults and seniors. Its main purpose was to celebrate the achievements of its members, such as gathering an exceptionally large yam harvest, or giving or receiving a marriage payment; a man who had done this, especially a senior member, was honoured by a feast. But it also had responsibility for quelling disturbances within the ward; when this was necessary the senior members would call up those in the adult grade. They claimed to possess independent authority, but what this meant in practice was probably that communication to them from the *Yakamben* took the form of requests rather than commands.

While the council of priests formed the ultimate authority for the whole village, every inhabitant of which was dependent for prosperity on their ritual approach to the spirits which controlled it, they too received co-operation from village-wide organisations which were formally autonomous. The ward leaders were directly linked in an association called *Okenka* which had its own leopard spirit. Only *Yakamben*, and not all of them, were members of *Okenka*; it had about 50 members in 1935. A new member was admitted whenever one died, but this was not a matter of lineage succession except for the head. He was supposed to come in turn from each of the three older wards (the fourth had come into being fairly recently), and the office was claimed by one *kepun*, believed to be old-established in each. The head's appointment required the approval of the village council, of which he was *ex-officio* a member. In addition, all boys, soon after their ward initiation, were initiated into a village-wide association called *Korta* which also had a leopard spirit. The priesthood of this association, again, was claimed by three *yepun*. The counterpart of *Korta* for women was *Ekao*. This had its own priestesses, but they were not members of the village council.

More recently there had grown up a purely secular association which exercised coercive powers. This body, called *Ikpunkara*, had 40 members in 1935. It was then said to have become more important than *Okenka*. Neither was able openly to exercise punitive powers after British administration had established its own police and judicial system, but *Okenka* still performed its ritual and thus reminded people of the dangerous powers of the leopard spirit. As the activities of *Ikpunkara* were remembered in 1935, the *Yabot* would invite it to punish people who disregarded their decisions, whether by refusing to pay compensation for offences or by disobeying general instructions, such as those imposing a boycott on trade with a neighbouring village. *Ikpunkara* would seize all the livestock of an offender and perhaps of his kinsmen. Its member claimed in 1935 that debt cases and accusations of theft used to be brought directly to them, and that they would seize property from persons who did not accept their judgement. Like *Ebiabu* in the wards, and like *Okenka, Ikpunkara* regarded itself as co-operating with the council rather than carrying out its orders. But the co-operation was close, and here too it was secured in part by overlapping membership. The *Obot lopon* and several other *ase* priests were *ex-officio* members of *Ikpunkara*. Its judgements were reported to the priests' council, though not because they required its approval.

The ritual assertion of the interdependence of all member of the village was made at the seasonal festivals which marked the first planting, the first ripening of yams, and the harvest. On these occasions leaders of all the associations (except *Nkpe*) came in procession to make offerings at the shrine of the major village spirit and receive blessings. At the festival of the new yams, the only one that Forde has described in detail, a prominent part was taken by the head of an association that has not yet been mentioned – the diviners. These were both men and women, and each was supposedly summoned to his calling by the spirit of a deceased diviner, whether in dreams or through some kind of mental disturbance. They were then initiated and taught the process of divination by the colleagues whom they were to join. Thus the qualification for membership of this body was a particular type of personality rather than descent or other status. Their leader was in charge of a shrine of the sky spirit, the creator god, and the blessing of the village by ritual acts, as opposed to spoken words, was in his hands. In this he was assisted by the two women priests responsible for the clitoridectomy of girls; their presence here is associated with the emphasis of the ritual on fertility, and with the fact that the first-ripening yams are always planted by women. The ritual consisted in the 'cooling' of the village by sprinkling sacred water on people assembled at all the shrines.

The political significance of descent in Umor, then, is different from what we find either where there is no political authority superior to autonomous descent groups, as with the Tonga, or where authority rests with a royal descent line and lineages are important only for the regulation of marriage and the transmission of property. In so far as ultimate authority is ritual, descent gives claim to it; in so far as members of different associations with political functions are expected to be succeeded by their agnates, descent plays a part in their constitution too. But this is a system in which there is a good deal of room for achieved status in bodies with political functions: status achieved not by popular acclaim but by ability to pay entrance fees, with the approval of seniors as a limiting factor. Lineages as such provide priests, and all priests have political responsibilities; certain lineages do claim leadership in some associations. The Yakö have been cited as an example to counter the supposed assumption that any political system must rest either on a balance of power between lineages or on central control by a single chief. It is nevertheless of interest, and perhaps of more interest in a discussion of descent systems, to ask how far lineage membership is significant for them outside the field of domestic relations.

9 Cognatic Descent: The Ndendeuli *

The Ndendeuli live in the Songea District of Tanzania, the south-western corner of the country where it borders on Malawi and Mozambique. Their name is supposed to mean 'What shall I do?' It is said to be what the Ngoni invaders in the latter half of the nineteenth century called all the peoples whom they conquered. It was the practice of the Ngoni on their northward march through Africa to take captives from the villages that they raided, and incorporate them as a subject class into the Ngoni polity. So the people who today call themselves Ndendeuli are a mixture of autochthonous inhabitants of the Songea area and descendants of those many captive peoples who managed to migrate out of reach of effective Ngoni control. In 1953, when Gulliver's fieldwork was done, they numbered perhaps 50,000. But his detailed observations were made in a community of thirty-two households.

The staple food of the Ndendeuli is maize. They also plant beans, millet, cassava, groundnuts and sweet potatoes. When Gulliver was there a few grew a little tobacco for sale, but the main source of their small cash incomes was wage labour, for which about a third of the men were away from home at any one time. It is of course possible that since the time of his fieldwork they have become much more dependent on cash incomes and outside employment, and his own account of them is written in the past tense.

The environmental constraints on cultivators were two: the poverty of their soil and a rainfall that, though reasonably reliable in quantity, came almost entirely within the three months from mid-December to mid-April, and not on completely predictable dates within that period. During the dry season the earth was baked so hard that it could not be hoed, so that planting could only start after the rains had begun; and crops that had not ripened before the rains ceased would wither in the ground. Hence the planting season was short and intensely busy.

* *Neighbours and Networks*. P. H. Gulliver, 1971.

110

Four successive crops of maize, cultivated by Ndendeuli methods, exhausted the best land; some was worked out in two years, or even planted only once. Then it had to be left a long time to regenerate. Hence there could be no question of hereditary claims to land, and since the Ndendeuli had no livestock apart from a few goats, there were no herds to be inherited either. As far as the transmission of property was concerned, then, kinship had no significance.

Each year a Ndendeuli cleared some new ground and abandoned some that he had planted earlier. To be able to do this he liked to have plenty of space around his homestead. Hence Ndendeuli did not live in compact villages, but in what Gulliver calls hamlets, about a quarter of a mile apart. Most hamlets included more than one household, but few had more than two. Where there was more than one household the heads were always related by kinship, usually as father and son or brother and brother. A man was expected when he first married to live close to his father, though he worked his own fields quite independently. In the past marriages had been made in the manner associated with some matrilineal peoples, in which the husband lives with his wife's parents and works for them until he is permitted to take her away. Gulliver and some other writers call this suitor-service. It is possible that such a system is associated with the absence of valuable property which can be exchanged, rather than with matriliny as such; it has already been remarked that most matrilineal peoples have traditionally had little property. By 1953 it had become more usual to pay bridewealth from cash earned by work on the sisal plantations; when a marriage was made in this way the husband was free from the start to choose where he would live. Marriages were arranged by the parents of the parties without the intervention of other kin.

Sons did not necessarily stay with their fathers all their lives. Where two brothers were found to be living in one hamlet, they would be men who had stayed with their father and not separated when he died, but as soon as a son of one of these married and came to live beside his father, the other brother would move off. So there was no basis for the development of even a small patrilineage. The Ndendeuli were familiar with lineage organisation among their neighbours, but they thought it an unsatisfactory arrangement, which arbitrarily limited the range of persons from whom an individual could seek help by claiming kinship.

The main reason for moving one's house was the exhaustion of land within easy reach of it. In the busy season people might have to go to and fro from house to fields several times a day, and a walk of a mile in each direction was as much as they could do without taking too much time from necessary work. All kinds of wild animals attacked the crops, and if the fields were too far away the owner could not watch them. He might then simply move his own homestead a short distance, or he could attach himself to another *local community*, or what other writers have called a neighbourhood. The local community which Gulliver studied in detail had gradually moved over a distance of about three miles in twenty years. A quarrel that could not be patched up, or merely the discovery that you had not many people to back you in a dispute, could be another reason for leaving the community.

THE LOCAL COMMUNITY

Local community is Gulliver's name (the term was first used by Evans-Pritchard) for a cluster of hamlets separated from the next cluster by a mile or two of bush. His thirty-two households in Ligomba constituted such a community. This was the continuing unit of Ligomba social structure, and the only recognisable political unit. To join a community a man appealed to some kinship link with an existing member; this had to be one of traceable kinship, but it might be either cognatic or affinal. The Ndendeuli provide a perfect example of what Fortes means by a system in which political divisions are based on territory not descent.

Every community was supposed to have been founded in the past by a number of people each of whom was related in some way to the man who initiated the move to new ground. Probably none was of very old standing. Ligomba had been founded in 1931 by one Nchinda and fourteen others. Six of the fourteen were Nchinda's kin, the rest were kin of his wife (his own affines). Some of these knew of no kin link to any member of the band other than Nchinda.

Such a leader was called the 'owner of the land' where the

band settled, and when he died he was succeeded by a close kinsman, preferably but not necessarily a son. Every community had its 'owner of the land'. His title did not imply that he could allocate land or say how it should be used, still less that he had any claim to tribute or obedience. He was the spokesman of the community in dealings with outsiders, and a newcomer was formally presented to him by the kinsman who wished to introduce him into it.

Men liked to act as the sponsors of newcomers, since this created a debt of obligation which the newcomer would be expected to repay by continuing co-operation, and above all by taking the sponsor's side in matters of disputed claims. A newcomer owed a real debt to his sponsor. The latter helped him to clear and plant his fields, and shared food with him until he had reaped a crop, as well as advising him in his relations with neighbours. The burden on a sponsor's household in time and resources was considerable, and only a very ambitious man would sponsor a series of kinsmen in successive years.

Kinship in this society was not a source of jural claims either to inheritance or to support in seeking redress for offences. Rather it was an idiom in which people sought co-operation from their neighbours; and part of the significance of the Ndendeuli for anthropological theory lies in the light that they throw on the disputed question whether the moral obligations of kinship or economic self-interest are fundamental in the organisation of non-industrial societies.

Before going on to these questions, however, something must be said about the way in which Ndendeuli categorised their kin. Earlier chapters have not given the kinship terminology of the peoples discussed, though it is of course to be found in the books from which the material is taken. But the Ndendeuli set of kin terms is simple enough to be briefly summarised, and is significant for just that reason.

Persons with whom kinship was known or assumed were classified simply by generation – as fathers, brothers, sons and mothers, sisters, daughters. A father might be one's wife's father, a mother, sister or daughter the wife of a recognised kinsman. Gulliver's exposition deals only with male kin because his subject of enquiry is the type of co-operation organised between household heads. One's own father and brothers, one's parents' siblings, one's first cousins, were 'big' kinsmen – the important ones to whom in most circumstances one did really regard oneself as morally bound. But a 'big kinsman' who lived too far away to co-operate, or one who could have done so but refused, would become a 'small kinsman' along with remoter relations. Conversely, a 'small kinsman' in one's own community who frequently joined in work parties and gave his support in dispute cases would be described as 'big'. For the obligation to reciprocate help received was as strong as the claim of kinship in response to which it was supposed to have been given.

Since there were no corporate kin groups, the total system can only be described by tracing out the links joining particular individuals. In a system of this kind every individual has – is not 'a member of' – a *kin-set*, the total field of kin with whom he can and does interact. The majority of people in his set live outside his local community, but a wise man keeps in touch with as many as he can, either so that he can recruit them to his own community or so that, if he wishes, he can join theirs. Those who belong to the same community are *kin-neighbours*. Kin-sets do not only overlap, as they obviously must, they interlock, in the sense that persons who have some obligation towards X also have obligations to one another which may either reinforce, or conflict with, the bonds which link them to him. Or, as it could also be put, everyone in A's kin-set has in his own kin-set somebody who is in the kin-sets of B, C, D . . . So that a series of kin-links runs through the whole population, and they can be conceived as joined in a *network*, a term that has been much used in the study of societies to which the concepts appropriate for lineage systems do not apply. Of course it would be possible to trace out such a network in a small local community where kinship is reckoned unilineally, and this is in fact done whenever an anthropologist shows the population of his village as points on a single genealogy. But the notion of network conveys, in the case of the Ndendeuli, that genealogical positions have little significance for them in the conduct of day-to-day affairs, and that, instead of being anxious to have their genealogies recorded as some peoples are, they regarded the attempt, when Gulliver made it, as a

European's nonsense.

When a Ndendeuli needed support or co-operation in some enterprise, there was no prescribed body of kin to whom he would automatically turn. He would recruit *ad hoc* an *action-set*, consisting of his kin-neighbours with some of *their* kin-neighbours whose genealogical relation to him he would not know or need to know. We learn the everyday significance of kinship for the Ndendeuli as it emerges from a detailed record of the action-sets recruited in Ligomba, and their activities, during a year's fieldwork.

Occasions for recruiting action-sets were of two types, one regular, the other irregular. The former were the work-parties that fall due at various points of the agricultural cycle, the latter the discussion of disputes which could not be settled privately.

WORK PARTIES

In the seasonal work-parties seven or eight men with their wives, and those of their children who were old enough, would join in hoeing and planting the fields of the man who invited them. Every householder would convene one such party, and perhaps another for weeding midway through the growing season. In the dry season similar parties would be held to cut down and burn the bush where new fields were to be planted. In the busy planting season it was not always easy to fit dates so that work-parties with some members in common did not clash. This problem did not arise during the long dry season. There could be other occasions for a work-party, such as building or repairing a house, or fencing fields. The immediate return from the convener to the participants was beer at the end of the day's work; more important was the recognised obligation to turn out for *their* work-parties. There was no rule assigning anyone to a particular set, and their composition was not constant, partly because there was so much coming and going – people went away to work on the sisal plantations, or left the community altogether – and partly because the same man might be committed in two directions and have to choose which commitment he would recognise. A good deal of trouble was taken to fix the days for work parties so as to prevent such clashes. Dates were fixed by friendly discussion, not by any authoritative ruling; there was nobody in a position to give such a ruling. But sometimes two men would choose the same day and refuse to give way, thus forcing any individual whom both had invited to choose between them; this was part of the game of small-scale politics.

Agronomists have argued that the work-parties were not particularly efficient, and very possibly a man who gave to his own fields the time he spent on other people's might have found that he got on as well or better without their help. But the Ndendeuli attached great importance to them, and asserted that it was for the sake of this co-operation that they built their hamlets in clusters instead of spreading them evenly through the bush. Joining in such a party was a declaration of friendly relations with the other members; it was also an assertion that one respected the obligations of kinship.

Every convener of a work-party could count on three or four 'big' kinsmen to respond to his call. Everyone in the community would have such commitments to a number of other individuals, and just because there were no prescribed co-operating groups, the building up of permanent reciprocal commitments was a matter of choosing partners in directions where obligations to one man would not too often conflict with obligations to others. Within the circle of close – 'big' – kin there was least conflict, since each member of such a work-party was equally committed to the others, and regarded these commitments as prior obligations. So if a man needed to extend his range of partners, he would look to those whom his close kin regarded – though he did not – as *their* close kin. Thus every man was linked through his own work-party to those of everyone else in the community, and simply for the sake of convenience most people wanted these links, with the expectation of co-operation when it was needed, to be maintained.

It is here that we are faced with the question whether it really was the moral constraint of kinship that maintained the constant co-operation even of close kin. Might it not have been simply the pressure of the community's desire to maintain the whole system of co-operating groups that forced people to act in the manner held to be dictated by kinship – the fact that if one relationship was broken, many others might be? As Gulliver would argue, the existence of a debt of co-operation, which might have been contracted at some time by an appeal to the moral obligation of kinship, became an independent reason for further co-operation. Ndendeuli might say, 'We do not work together, how can we be kinsmen?' or 'We help one another, so are we not brothers?' So, clearly, genealogical closeness was not the only criterion of claims on others.

DISPUTE SETTLEMENT

In so far as the members of a work-party were friends of the convener, and men who owed him a return for services of some kind, one might expect that a man involved in a dispute would recruit the same people to be his supporters. But this was not always the case. The same difficulties of incompatible commitments could arise as sometimes did when two work-parties clashed, and the way in which they were dealt with throws light on the relation among the Ndendeuli between kinship and politics. Nobody in a local community has any claim to make authoritative decisions, whether in the matter of disputed rights or of the timetable of work in the fields. But certain persons very definitely seek to be looked to as leaders. The Ndendeuli describe them in a phrase that literally means 'big men'; the English phrase has come to be widely used in anthropology since we have become aware of the importance of competition for informal status in New Guinea, where also the successful ones are called 'big men'. In New Guinea the competition follows different lines, and for this reason Gulliver translated the Ndendeuli phrase as 'notables'. There would be two or three such men in any community; the 'owner of the land', it is worth noting, was rarely among them.

One way to become a notable, as has been mentioned, was to sponsor a number of newcomers to the community. The other, and principal, way was to take a prominent part in the discussion of disputes. Such a discussion would be initiated by someone who wanted to bring public opinion to bear on a question that was disrupting community relations. There was no question of a judicial decision, since nobody was regarded as entitled to give such a decision, but simply of talking out the matter and listening to suggestions, which might or might not lead to agreement as to what should be done. A discussion

of this kind, which is characteristic of many small-scale societies, has been called a 'moot' since Bohannan introduced the
work in writing of the Tiv. There were seven moots in Ligomba
in 1953.

Gluckman, writing of the Barotse, a people whose elaborate
political system includes formal judicial institutions, remarks
that African judges do not seek to focus discussion on a single
issue and rule out anything which does not bear on this as irrelevant. Nor do they hold that people who are to try the case
should know nothing of the parties and their relationship outside the question at issue. On the contrary, they think they
should know as much as possible; and they consider how far
the parties have acted reasonably in every aspect of their relationship. Gluckman explains this as a result of the many-
stranded links between any two individuals in such a society;
the same man is one's kinsman, political superior, ritual authority, and so on, and a quarrel over some one aspect of the relationship must affect the whole.

Gulliver is dealing with a society in which the only ascribed
relationship is that between kinsmen, and a community so
small that everyone knows the totality of past relationships
among its members. A Ndendeuli moot does not purport to be
a judicial institution, and in its discussion past events and
grievances are present to the recollection of the participants
even if they are not mentioned; there is no question of submit-
ting a dispute to a remote judge, as the Barotse may. Hence the
discussion is influenced not only by ideas on reasonable behaviour in the abstract, but also by what has happened on earlier
occasions: who supported whom and got support in return?
Who will refuse to join my work-party if I speak against him
now? The seven cases that Gulliver records in detail are a piece
– arbitrarily cut out, as a field study has to be – of the living
tissue of action and interaction that makes up the continuing
life of any small group in constant contact. It is the study of
action in the context of the past decisions that influence those
under the fieldworker's eye that anthropologists call dynamic,
in contrast to static accounts of jural rules in the form of institutions. Modern studies concentrate on the dynamic aspects of
social life, and therefore must examine very small groups in
minute detail. This more recent development of the subject has

been extremely fruitful, but it would hardly have been possible without the earlier institutional studies that provide most of the material for this book.

In an Ndendeuli moot both disputants expected the support of their kin. Each recruited an action-set, half a dozen men who sat with him, spoke up on his behalf, argued against the other side, and advised him what kind of compromise to accept. The only neutrals were outsiders, people with no recognised kin ties to either; neutrals did not often attend a moot, and if they did, they sat on the edge of the gathering and seldom spoke. There would always be one or two men in the invidious position of being equally closely linked to both sides, who would be approached by both. Some men in this situation found it so embarrassing that when the moot was arranged they would find themselves obliged to visit a kinsman in some other community. Those who did attend would sit midway between the two committed sets. They did not in fact always maintain strict impartiality between, say, two first cousins. This might depend on the question whose goodwill a man valued most, but it could also be a matter of his views on the merits of the case; after all, the Ndendeuli, like every other society, recognised standards of right conduct. But these *intermediaries*, as Gulliver calls them, could also be the people best placed to mediate between the disputants and suggest an acceptable compromise. There was no formally recognised mediator, though there might often be some individual who was expected to play this role, and a man sometimes felt that his intermediate position imposed the duty upon him. The mediator would speak up after the accusations and counter-accusations were finished, and the facts seemed to be agreed. A notable was not necessarily a mediator. If one disputant recruited him as a supporter, he would be that side's adviser and advocate. But a notable might take the initiative in calling a moot, and hold it at his house; and he might offer himself as a mediator even without having been invited to the moot. It was largely from their performance at moots that notables gained their standing in the community.

The largest attendance at a moot in 1953 was twenty out of the thirty-two householders in Ligomba; a moot was, then, never a gathering of the whole community. One reason for the large attendance in this case was that the kin-neighbours of the two disputants had few links with one another, so that it was easy for both to call on men who could give them unequivocal support. All but three of the thirty-two took part in at least one moot, and of the three one deliberately stayed away so as not to have to support a kinsman whom he disliked. One man – not a notable – was present at every moot; two, one of them a notable, were at six of the seven; and seven men took part in five moots. The more acknowledged kin-neighbours a man had, the more likely he was to be involved in a dispute affecting any one of them. But the same men did not find themselves always aligned together. This was precluded by the principle that kin links were equally strong in all directions, and by the fact that every man's set of kin-neighbours was different. In one not intrinsically important or difficult case, twelve men turned up to support one side, largely for the very reason that they had been on opposite sides a week before and wished to show that they were not harbouring ill-feeling.

The reason for this was not simply a dislike of uncomfortable personal relations, though this is certainly to be found in small groups. There was the practical consideration that among the supporters of both parties in the earlier dispute were people who belonged to the same work-parties. Since if either side had insisted on what they took to be their full rights there would have been an open breach between them, all possible influence was brought to bear in favour of settlement.

NETWORKS AND CLUSTERS

One might have expected, however, that competing notables would build up factions committed to follow their lead and support their line through thick and thin. This too was prevented by the over-riding need to maintain the friendly relations on which the work-parties depended. Rivals for influence, if they found themselves on opposite sides, would make the most of the opportunity of an encounter; but it was their kinship with the disputants, not the rivalry between the two leaders, that placed them on opposite sides. A notable, however, did have a specially close relationship with those persons who frequently co-operated with him and with one another, and the nucleus of this would be a set of kin-neighbours. These Gulliver calls a *cluster*. If the whole population of Ligomba is thought of as a number of knots in a net, a cluster will be found where these knots bunch together. Such a cluster was not created by the notable, but by the fact that they had become accustomed to interact more frequently with one another than with other neighbours. The cluster created the notable rather than the reverse; though every cluster did not necessarily produce a notable. This was a matter of personality. But once a man was getting the reputation of a notable, he would seek to build it up in various ways, one being by recruiting close kin from other communities.

When a notable scored over a rival, it was by gaining some advantage for a member of his cluster; and to be seen to have that kind of success would attract to his cluster people who did not 'naturally' belong there on grounds of close kinship. But the people who formed a cluster were not turned in on themselves and bound to seek co-operation only from one another, and in fact they recruited neighbours from outside to their individual action-sets. This was what prevented the community from splitting into segments. Whereas in a lineage-based society, a village that gets too large divides by the secession of one lineage (with its hangers-on), there was no fixed line along which an Ndendeuli community should be divided. There are no recorded data on the way in which a pioneer such as the founder of Ligomba gathered the men who went with him. But what happened most of the time was that individuals would move off one by one to join kinsmen in another community.

The notion of a network is of course applicable to all the societies that are discussed in this book, and to any other. Where an individual is born a member of a lineage, a number of kinsmen are ascribed to him in virtue of the fact – sometimes a very large number. But they are not by any means the only people with whom he interacts. He – or his father – may choose his bride from out of a large number of potential spouses; upon his choice will depend who are his affines and who are the kinsmen of his children, and also, as Lévi-Strauss has reminded us, who, in addition to clanswomen, will be prohibited spouses for the latter. He may make pacts of bond friendship, or agreements to exchange gifts of cattle, with unrelated men far from his home. He may offer his services to an important person who will give him favours in return. What is to be learned from Gulliver's study of the Ndendeuli is not so much the importance of thinking about networks as the importance of thinking about choices. This is not in itself a new idea, but what has been done more fully for the Ndendeuli than for most peoples is the examination of the further consequences of each choice. Every time A supports B and not C in a dispute, he ties himself a little closer to B and divides himself by that much from C. If he moves to a new local community some big man there will be bidding for his support, and he will himself be putting out feelers in directions where he can hope to recruit an action-set when he needs one. Even when there is no kind of dramatic confrontation or re-alignment in progress, the whole complex of relationships is in a perpetual state of gentle movement like, say, the surface of a calm sea, or, to distort Gulliver's metaphor, a net floating in such a sea. We have become used to tracing out social changes on a large scale in terms of the choices that individuals make, though these are generally assumed rather than documented choices. The Ndendeuli story does not demonstrate a one-way move towards the adoption of new institutions, but it reminds us that even where this is not in question the choices made today influence the direction of relationships tomorrow.

10 An Acephalous Political System: The Nuer *

The Nuer are a pastoral people whose home is an area of the southern Sudan lying across the White Nile and its tributaries the Bahr-el-Ghazal and Sobat. The extreme east of their country lies within the boundary of Ethiopia. Like the Karimojong, and indeed like most people for whom cattle are more important than crops, they follow a way of life that is dictated by the needs of their herds, but the constraints imposed by the Nuer environment are very different from those experienced by the desert-dwelling Karimojong. They have to take account of floods as well as drought.

Their country is an almost level plain crossed by many water-courses, which flood every year in the rainy season. They build their houses on sandy ridges high enough to be above flood level, and plant their gardens of maize and millet behind the houses. The villages are not isolated by the flood water, and the rainy season is the time for most contact between villages, when young men go courting and rituals are performed. But the cattle must graze on the village land, since to be constantly in water would make them sick. As the floods recede, they can be herded further from home. Soon the clayey ground becomes parched, pools and minor watercourses dry up, and people and herds have to concentrate where there is permanent water, in camps of rough grass huts or shelters. The number of people in a village may be a few hundred or only fifty, and villages are five to twenty miles apart. The numbers at a cattle camp get larger as the dry season wears on; at its height they may be over a thousand.

When Evans-Pritchard visited the Nuer in 1930, they had hardly been brought under effective administration by the British authorities of the Anglo-Egyptian Sudan, but the 'Nuer Settlement', as it was called, had already modified a system of social control which essentially depended on the use of force by individuals to secure their rights, and which regarded fight-

* *The Nuer.* E. E. Evans-Pritchard, 1940.
  A Manual of Nuer Law. P. P. Howell, 1954.

ing between and within tribes as a normal and praiseworthy activity. Such fighting was now forbidden, and killing was treated as murder. Moreover, individuals had to be found who could be held responsible for the maintenance of order among a people who recognised no such roles. There was no man designated as chief and already endowed with the right of command; hence the authorities had to pick for the office of 'headman' or 'chief' individuals who appeared to them to hold positions of leadership; as far as possible they tried to make nominations that would be acceptable to the people, and by 1942 the process of choice was being described as 'election'. One of the principal duties of chiefs was to hold courts for the settlement of disputes without fighting.

Yet Nuer recollections of their independent past – what another warlike people, the Ngoni, call 'the time of peace' – were vivid in their minds as they talked to Evans-Pritchard, and seem to have been no less so ten years later when an administrative officer, P. P. Howell, was making a study of Nuer law. But it may be because they offered an idealised picture to enquirers that their social structure can be represented as one of beautiful symmetry. Indeed a recent French writer, Louis Dumont, has maintained that Evans-Pritchard's achievement in his book lies not in his account of a political system but in his record of the way the Nuer themselves envisage their society. The same writer argues, further, that they and perhaps many other peoples of simple technology cannot be said to have a political system, since the notion of a political system implies the idea of individual struggles for power, which, he considers, are not found everywhere. Yet the detailed stories of fights and feuds which Evans-Pritchard has recorded are just as much the Nuer's view of the operation of their own society.

After the Sudan became independent the Nuer and their pastoral neighbours fought a war of secession which lasted for seventeen years, and was only ended in 1972 by the grant of a degree of regional autonomy. Many of them fled into Uganda or Ethiopia, where they lived in settlements organised by the United Nations. Now a reconstruction programme is afoot for the southern Sudan as a whole, and no doubt it will bring with it paternalistic schemes of development. These may or may not reach the Nuer, and lead to greater or less social changes among them. But films recently made show them living the same pastoral life that Evans-Pritchard saw. In any case, a social system which maintains respect for generally accepted norms without any institutions of government, whether you call it a political system or not, does not lose its significance because it has been modified by external influences.

In 1930 the total number of people whom their neighbours and conquerors call Nuer (they call themselves Nath) was 200,000. All these had in common language, name and customs, but they had no political unity, however that term be defined. They were divided into some forty tribes differing widely in population, which ranged from 9,000 to over 40,000. A tribe was a political unit in Evans-Pritchard's terms, not in the sense that it recognised a common ruler, but in a number of other ways. One can distinguish between its internal and external relations. There was war between tribes, and although this did not – naturally – imply the mobilisation of all fighting men in each, it was the recognised duty of members of the same tribe to give support against outsiders when called upon. Within a tribe men sometimes killed one another, as they do everywhere; among the Nuer homicide called for vengeance, but it was possible for compensation in cattle to be substituted for the payment of a life, and there were recognised procedures for this. This is what Evans-Pritchard means when he says that within a tribe, but not between tribes, the rule of law was recognised.

SEGMENTARY OPPOSITION

Each tribe had its own territory, usually marked off by watercourses. The tribal territory was divided into sections, which might again be subdivided. The larger tribes had primary, secondary and tertiary sections, and these had names and are shown on maps. Each section had its own dry-season camps.

The Nuer conceived a tribe as consisting of the descendants of a single ancestor, and clans and lineages, with their divisions, as segments of one vast genealogy. But since they attached no importance to rights in land, there was no strong reason for people to live in the territory associated with their lineage, and more than half the Nuer lived elsewhere, in places where they were linked to the dominant lineage by some other tie than that of common descent. In Evans-Pritchard's terms a tribe means the population inhabiting a tribal territory, and a tribal section the population of one of its named subdivisions. Thus tribes and tribal segments should be called political units and not units based on descent.

However, every tribe regarded its territory as 'belonging' in some vague sense to one of its clans, which in virtue of this association with the land was of higher status than the rest, and a lineage of this clan held this 'aristocratic' status in every section of the country. Though they might be called the 'owners' of these territories, this did not mean that they could decide who should live there or how the land should be used. There was a word – *dil* – for these aristocrats. A *dil* had no recognised authority; he had prestige on his home ground, but not away from it.

There was often fighting within as well as between tribes, and in relation to such fighting the parties directly concerned looked for allies, if they needed them, in accordance with recognised rules. Members of a tertiary section, or even a group of villages within it, might fight one another, but they were expected to unite against an enemy from outside; so that people who were your opponents one day might be your allies the next. It would be considered wrong to join with outsiders against those who were nearer to you in terms of actual territory and supposed genealogy, or to refuse support to the nearer section if it was called for. This is how Nuer described the rules they were used to observe, though they also recalled occasions when the rules were not followed.

These rules have been held to express the structural principles of a system of balanced opposition such that no section within a tribe, and no tribe within the Nuer nation, could establish political domination over the rest. Whether or not this is the reason, certainly no such sectional domination had been achieved at the time when fighting was suppressed. Tribes drove their enemies away from grazing grounds. They raided the neighbouring Dinka, stole their cattle and took them captive. Sometimes they established themselves in country that Dinka herds had previously grazed, but not as conquerors; Dinka captives were adopted into the families of their captors, and married their daughters. Evans-Pritchard ascribes this absorption of Dinka to the fact that they were closely similar to the Nuer both in way of life and in language. Another reason might be that there was nothing to be gained by making them a subject class. Cattle people have been quick enough to do this when they invaded the country of cattleless grain-growers, as Chapter 14 will show.

The system that is defined by these rules of alliance and hostility is called *segmentary opposition*. Ideally, as the Nuer (still must) see it, lineages descended from brothers (i.e. from a common grandfather) are equal units which may be in conflict; those descended from first cousins (i.e. from a common great-grandfather) are similarly equal units of which brother lineages form part; so that the brother-lineages have a duty to unite if one is in conflict with a cousin-lineage. And this rule should impose similar obligations on the inhabitants of the divisions of Nuerland associated with these descent groups.

The discovery that some acephalous societies can be seen in this way, as made up of segments each inclusive of smaller segments of like structure, marked an important advance in the study of political systems. But the implicit argument that the opposition of segments was peculiar to peoples without chiefs has been criticised by M. G. Smith, who has pointed out that one can find in any political system units which are opposed to one another but unite in opposition to wider units; thus in a bureaucratic hierarchy, officials at the same level are in competition, but they will combine if their interests as a group appear to be threatened by their superiors.

All lineages segment in the course of generations, so that it might be considered tautological to talk of a segmentary lineage system, but Evans-Pritchard's phrase refers to a system in which a hierarchy of segments is recognised which purportedly covers the whole population. Such a way of looking at kinship is not peculiar to the Nuer; it has parallels both in Africa and outside. But nobody has ever asserted that all descent systems are of this kind. No doubt it is the prestige of *The Nuer* that leads anthropologists working outside Africa to explain so painstakingly that the lineages they observe cannot be pictured as segments of an all-inclusive genealogy; but if they think Africanists suppose that this is the only form of lineage system, they are mistaken.

At various times from the latter part of the nineteenth century prophets have appeared among the Nuer, whose influence extended beyond the bounds of a single tribe. These men were supposed to have been possessed by the sky-god and thus endowed with supernatural powers. Only about half a dozen such men are remembered. The earliest, Ngundeng, made his reputation first by his success in curing sickness and barrenness in women. He foretold dangers and sometimes provided supernatural remedies for them, and in dreams and trances he, and his son who succeeded him, learned the most propitious times and directions for raids against the Dinka. They often went with these expeditions, and always received a share of the booty. Prophets organised resistance to Arab slave traders, and later to the British authorities, who effectively destroyed them. Evans-Pritchard sees these men as personifying 'the structural principle of opposition' in its widest form, the unity of all Nuer against non-African invaders. But perhaps this is making too much of the peculiar features of Nuer political structure. Many peoples have united against clearly perceived external enemies without recognising any principle of internal structural opposition.

Evans-Pritchard also suggested that the prophets, since their power was believed to be hereditary, might have developed into hereditary chiefs with political authority. Certainly hereditary rulers are very frequently believed to inherit ritual powers, but their secular authority needs to be reinforced by a personal following of men who will carry out their orders without being inhibited by the obligations of kinship. Perhaps the prophets might in time have gathered such a following if the Nuer had had only other Africans as enemies. But the paradox of their story is that they reached their widest influence when opposing enemies whom they could not effectively resist.

Internal political systems are concerned with decision-making on the one hand and law enforcement and dispute settlement on the other. Nuer recognised no offices which carried with them responsibility for law enforcement. Nor had they any formal institutions for decision-making, though a decision must have been reached somehow before, for example, a large-scale raid was mounted. The only other decision that had to be made for a tribe as a whole concerned the initiation of young men into adult status. Like a great many other East African peoples, the Nuer divided the whole adult male population into sets based on the time of their initiation, and in the past these sets had been clearly distinguished by the alternation of 'open' periods when initiations were performed and 'closed' periods when they could not be. A ritual specialist called the Man of the Cattle was responsible for making known the beginning and end of these periods. He did this, not by making some proclamation, but simply by performing at his own home the rites, alternately, of 'bringing out the knife' and 'hanging up the knife'. As the news that he had done this spread through the tribe, villages made their own arrangements for the initiation of boys of appropriate age, a dozen boys or fewer undergoing the operation together. It consisted in making six cuts across the forehead from ear to ear, and was exceedingly painful; the scars marked a man as a Nuer for all to see.

When Evans-Pritchard was there, initiations were being held every year, but it still fell to the Man of the Cattle to 'cut' the sets – that is to announce that the next year's initiates would start a new set. Age-set membership did not imply any political responsibilities, but it ranked men by age on a principle that extended throughout a tribe and sometimes beyond it. The name of a man's age-set indicated to a stranger whether he was a senior, a junior or an equal. Juniors were expected to defer to seniors, and if they were not asked to obey them, at least they should not quarrel with them.

It was the elders in the age system who collectively took decisions on village affairs and managed relations with other villages. In noisy arguments – for they were no less egalitarian than younger men – they discussed such questions as when the village should begin its move to the dry season camp, and whether some sacrifice should be made. There might be among them one whose influence was pre-eminent, and who would be called the 'bull of the camp'. Such a man would be of a respected lineage, have a large family and many cattle and, as a result of his wealth, be able to attract to his village young kinsmen not of his lineage. He might also have been a famous fighter or be credited with supernatural powers. But even he had no authority outside his own household. They would move away from the village, and others would see what they were doing and follow suit.

SELF-HELP AND FEUD

Law enforcement was a matter of individual self-help, but this definitely does not mean 'the war of each against all'. Evans-Pritchard applied to the Nuer system the term 'ordered anarchy'; anarchy because there was no ruler, order because people knew very well what their rights were. Readiness to get into a fight was the quality most admired among the Nuer, and anyone who clearly lacked it could expect to be put upon. A man who thought he had been wronged or even insulted would challenge his enemy to single combat. Causes for fighting that a Nuer enumerated for Evans-Pritchard may be quoted: 'a dispute about a cow; a cow or goat eats a man's millet and he strikes it [then the animal's owner has a grievance]; a man strikes another's little son; adultery; watering rights in the dry season; pasturage rights; a man borrows an object, particularly a dance ornament, without asking the owner's permission' (1940, p. 151). Some of these quarrels would be likely to arise between members of the same village, some between men in different villages. Within a village men fought with clubs, which may break bones but do not usually cause fatal injuries. Neither duellist could give in before he was down and out, but other villagers would do their best to pull them apart.

Away from the village every Nuer was armed with a spear as sharp as a butcher's knife, and it was in fights between men from different villages that people were apt to get killed. This could happen if a man had gone with his village mates to seize cattle that he considered were owed him – in bridewealth, or in compensation for some past injury; or at the dry season camps, as the informant quoted indicates. Another occasion for fights was the dancing when young men visited neighbouring villages to court the girls. The dance is itself an expression of defiance, even when the participants are not being treated as enemies.

Homicide was not considered by the Nuer to be necessarily wrong; it could be justified, it might even be a duty. But even

then it was an offence against the kin of the victim, and also
had ritual consequences that no other offence had. A man who
had killed another was in ritual danger and must be purified
from the blood he had shed; this applied even to the killer of an
enemy in war. Homicide within the tribe had more extensive
ritual consequences, as well as the jural consequence of liab-
ility for redress. It is in the consequences of homicide that we
can see most clearly the relationship between the commitments
that result from kinship and those that depend on neighbourhood – if you like, between the significance of kith and
kin. The ritual consequences of a killing affected the killer first
of all. He must go for purification to a ritual specialist, the
'man of the earth'; such a man has commonly been referred to
as 'leopard-skin chief', or 'leopard-skin priest', because he
wore a leopard-skin over his right shoulder as a mark of his
status. I use the term 'earth-priest' as Evans-Pritchard himself
does in his later writings, since it conveys his role more directly. This man's ritual powers were hereditary; several lineages
were believed to inherit such power, but not every man of the
qualified lineages actually became a priest. There were large
numbers of them, since most Nuer would have to call on the
services of one at some time or other; say one in every village
where the villages were far apart, perhaps not quite so many
where they were close together. The slayer had to go at once to
him to have blood drawn from his arm – blood that was somehow associated with that of his victim – taking with him an
animal to be sacrificed. Until this had been done he must not
eat or drink; if he did he would die. As long as he was in the
priest's homestead he was safe; it was sanctuary, since the
earth there was sacred and blood must not be shed on it. His
family and cattle would be dispersed among their kin where
avengers could not get at them.

This account presumes that they were all in imminent
danger from the vengeance of the victim's kin. That is how it
should have been, according to Nuer ideals; but the reality was
certainly not always so. It was the duty – ideally an inescapable
duty – of the victim's close kin to kill either the slayer himself
or a close agnate. But more often, it seems, they would hang
about near the priest's home for a day or two, hoping to catch
their enemy if he ventured outside, and then go back to their

ordinary avocations.

However, the homicide had other consequences. [A *state of feud* now existed between the lineages of slayer and victim.] This came into being automatically as a result of the belief that it was ritually dangerous for anyone on the one side to eat or drink from vessels used by anyone on the other; if they did they would die. Now Nuer do not eat and drink only in their own homesteads; they constantly visit neighbours and are given hospitality. So it was dangerous for anybody on the one side even to visit the other side's village. Hence contact between the two villages was cut off.

Although a man's fellow villagers did not all belong to his lineage, they stood alongside him in matters like this. However, those who were not actually involved in the feud would soon come to be irked by the quarantine in which it placed them. Particularly daughters of one village who were wives in the other would miss the usual visiting to and fro. So they would contribute to the development of a general feeling that the injured side had better give up insisting that their honour must be satisfied by a life for a life, and accept compensation in cattle. It was for the priest of the earth first to persuade the slayer and his kin to offer this, and then to get the victim's kin to accept. Honour required them to insist that only vengeance would do, but if the priest could not persuade them he would threaten them with a curse that would destroy them altogether. But much of this was play-acting; the threat was expected, and it enabled the angry kinsmen to yield to spiritual *force majeure*. The number of cattle to be paid was ideally equivalent to that paid in bridewealth, so that the lineage who had lost a man could make a marriage from which more sons would come. The number agreed on was rarely paid at once; so later on somebody would set out with his village mates to collect the cattle still owing; and there would be a fight; and someone would be killed; and so . . .

However, at this point in the story the priest would drive the cattle to the village of the victim's kin, and there make a sacrifice the effect of which was to end the ritual danger of the meeting of the two sides and formally terminate the feud.

Obviously the inconvenience of maintaining a state of feud was greater the more the villages on the two sides were accustomed to regular contacts; that is, the closer together they were. Feuds that arose out of fights between people further from their respective homes – say, at the dry-season camps – might remain unsettled for years, and eventually there might be so many unsettled feuds between sections of a tribe that they came to think of themselves as separate tribes who did not expect to compensate the victims of homicide.

Two comments must be made on these facts. The first is that there was no relation between the state of mind of the injured lineage and the ease or difficulty of ending a feud. This was entirely a matter of the inconvenience that it caused and the pressure that was put on them to settle. The second is that homicide was an injury gravely resented, and not forgotten even when there had been a formal settlement. 'A feud never dies', Nuer would say; and so, just as they sought to reduce the probability of homicide within the village by leaving their spears indoors when they were there, they would seek to avoid occasions when an old feud might be revived. Members of lineages between whom there had been a feud (in their own lifetime or even years ago) would avoid one another, particularly in the dances where an accidental jolt or an angry word shouted in the excitement of the crowd might start fighting all over again.

For injuries short of homicide there was a conventional tariff of compensation, but there was no superior authority to award damages. Every man was expected to get them by force. But since force was likely to be resisted, and resistance might lead to homicide, there were pressures to settle disputes by agreement between members of the same villages or villages with many contacts. In these cases the parties themselves might prefer not to fight it out, and a settlement would be discussed between the elders, or by them and the earth-priest.

Evans-Pritchard's analysis of the Nuer political system anticipates the theories of Lévi-Strauss in a very remarkable way. The 'model' which the Nuer make of their own society represents it as a set of binary oppositions in the manner that Lévi-Strauss holds to be characteristic of *all* human thinking – necessarily so because of the structure of the human brain. Dumont, presenting his work to French readers, offers this as its most valuable aspect, and argues that later English anthropologists have gone astray in pursuing in their ethnographic work the theme of the relations between lineages as it was illustrated in daily life.

POWER STRUGGLES?

Other writers have questioned whether the principle of balanced structural opposition really worked out in such a way that no segment could dominate another, and whether ambitious men never sought to build up influence into power. The latter question Dumont holds to be prompted by an ethnocentric tendency to regard 'primitive' man as a rugged individualist with the same values as those of the anthropologist. However, there is a certain amount of evidence for the theory that the Nuer had their 'big men' as much as many other supposedly egalitarian societies are said to, and even had a word to describe them. If there were such men, they were priests and the prophets who from time to time succeeded in raising all the Nuer in revolt against their Arab or British conquerors. In the tribes among whom Evans-Pritchard worked, the priests of the earth were never members of dominant lineages; thus they could never claim to be 'owners' of the earth as, for example, Tallensi earth-priests might. Evans-Pritchard argues that, in addition to their sacredness, their lack of attachment to the political groups most likely to be engaged in feuds was important for their peacemaking role. But Howell, who worked from 1942 as an administrative officer among the more westerly tribes, found that there the earth-priests commonly belonged to dominant lineages.

The egalitarian ideals of the Nuer are clear from their behaviour as both these writers observed it. They would flatly refuse any request that could be interpreted as an order. The way to get a man to do something for you was to address him as 'brother', and thus appear to be appealing to the norms of kinship. Even the leader of a gang doing a job on government orders would approach his fellows in that way. Nobody treated an earth-priest with deference outside the situation in which his ritual services were needed. Yet the description of the 'bull' of a village does indicate that some men were a little more equal than others. One of the qualities that went to make a 'bull' was ritual power; and an earth-priest, we are told, was more respected if he was a 'bull'.

Since not all men of earth-priest lineages exercised the ritual powers that they all claimed, the question arises what led some of them to do so. Perhaps they were ambitious, and saw profit in their sacred office, as did some Men of the Cattle according to an earlier report by Evans-Pritchard. Beidelman (1971), noting that the ritual experts were apt to be older men, conjectures that they actually built up support through the dependents whom they gathered around them, and so had secular power to back their ritual authority.

In western Nuerland, where Howell worked, the word *ruic* was used of prominent men. Some of these were the prophets who were said to have led whole tribes to war and sometimes to migrate to new country, and who doubtless did encourage them to such action, though it is not easy to picture a whole tribe, let alone all the Nuer, acting in concert; in one recorded confrontation between a prophet's army and government forces, the former numbered three hundred. Nuer came to call the District Commissioner *ruic*, in a way that certainly suggests the idea of supreme authority. Some of the famous prophets of the past are known to have been cattle-priests or earth-priests. But what is significant about *ruic* is that it is closely connected with *rwac*, which means 'speech'. A *ruic* was in Nuer eyes a man who could talk so persuasively that he got large numbers of people to agree with him and act as he suggested. Not all were leaders of whole tribes. *Ruic* in a narrower sphere had the qualities of informal leaders in all societies without hereditary rule: generosity (made possible by wealth in cattle), wisdom and persuasiveness in settling disputes, a reputation as a fighter. In Nuer eyes, as the word shows, it was the persuasive tongue that counted for most; and this is worth noticing because all over East Africa men of influence in acephalous societies are called by some name that can be translated 'spokesman'.

Beidelman also notes that the 'bull' of a village, although not a ritual specialist, is still the one man who makes sacrifices on behalf of his dependents. Thus he too, in his small sphere, combines a ritual status as their mediator with divinity and a secular one as their acknowledged leader. Beidelman suggests, in fine, that 'bulls', priests and prophets are all men who have political ambitions, and that they all combine the personal qualities which Nuer ascribe to the 'good talker' with the means of obtaining a following of men who depend on them both in ritual and secular matters. On this interpretation the Nuer are not unique; they have their power struggles like any other society. These are struggles for informal leadership because there is no formal office to compete for.

Could the Nuer ever have become a kingdom? Their neighbours the Shilluk had (and perhaps still have) a king with little secular authority, supposedly descended from a divine first ancestor. Their neighbours the Anuak had a king who seems to have exercised no authority at all until he was able to trade ivory for guns with the Ethiopians. As long as the Nuer would only unite against an enemy who must inevitably defeat them, they could not recognise a permanent leader. Their dependence on individual force as the prime guarantee of rights led them to value men who could persuade them to keep the peace, but they could never accept anyone who should force them to.

11 Law in an Age-based Political System: The Arusha *

The Arusha live on the western slopes of Mount Meru, one of the two high mountains of Tanzania close to its frontier with Kenya. They are fortunate in their natural environment with its good volcanic soils, plentiful rainfall and streams that can be tapped for irrigation. The first Arusha seem to have arrived in their present home from the south of Mount Kilimanjaro about 1830, and to have spread up the mountain, clearing the forest to plant bananas, maize, beans and millet as their staple crops. They were not then cattle people, though nowadays they own some cattle, enough for cattle bridewealth to be the rule, and other livestock (sheep, goats and donkeys). Today, too, they grow coffee for sale. Later they were joined by refugees from fighting among the neighbouring Meru and Chagga, whose descendants now form more than half the population.

When Britain took over the administration of Tanganyika after the First World War, the upper part of the mountain was declared a forest reserve, and after 1930 people seeking new land had to find it lower down where the country was more typical of Africa, with poor soil and unreliable rainfall. Their expansion was also limited by the alienation of land for European farms. By the time when Phillip Gulliver worked among them (1956–8) the mountain slopes (an area eight miles long by five broad) were densely settled, with an average of over 1,000 to the square mile. The total Arusha population was 63,000 and had been steadily increasing.

The Arusha do not live in villages but in scattered homesteads, each surrounded by its plantation of bananas and by a fence, or in later and more peaceful days a hedge. Groups of such homesteads fall into well-defined areas such as Gulliver calls local communities when writing of the Ndendeuli; for the Arusha he uses the word 'parish', perhaps because it is the one used by British administrators to describe the lowest level of the system of elected local authorities which they set up just before independence. On the mountain slopes parishes are

* *Social Control in an African Society.* P. H. Gulliver, 1963.

compact areas divided by streams; lower down they are simply artificial units whose boundaries have been fixed by the authorities. In the pioneering days young men were expected to strike out and clear new land for themselves; hence one does not find sons living close to their fathers. Nevertheless patrilineal descent is very important in the Arusha conception of their social structure.

The country of the Arusha borders on that of the pastoral Masai, which extends northward into Kenya. The Arusha speak a language of Masai type, and although they have no tradition that they ever were pastoralists, they organise their young men in age-sets on the pattern of the Masai, and indeed they rely on a Masai ritual expert for the timing of their age-set ceremonies. In Gulliver's view the Arusha idea of their lineage structure, which is not characteristic of most peoples organised by age, may have developed after the Masai-type pioneers were joined by the Bantu-speakers from among the Meru and Chagga.

AGE ORGANISATION

The essence of the Arusha political system is that roles in decision-making and dispute settlement are not allotted to a limited number of office-bearers, but diffused among the whole male population according to a general view of the capacities of men at different ages. The entry of young men into this system, and stages in their progress through it, are marked by formal rituals, and different kinds of behaviour are considered appropriate to men in each of the different *grades*, as the different stages are called. As with the Karimojong, particular ornaments, and here also hair-styles, are worn by the younger men and publicly indicate their status. Whereas the Karimojong recognise only a single division into senior and junior generations, and the Nuer only a total body of adult men ranked by their time of initiation, the Arusha divide each of the major grades – that is of young men and 'elders' – into two.

Uninitiated boys herd the stock, and are pushed around by their elders. Initiated youths are called *murran*. This Masai word is often translated 'warriors', and the translation is not inapt for the Masai, who still go on raiding cattle when they can. But the Arusha, though their young men may have gone raiding once, have been far too closely administered for a long time; hence Gulliver has found it better simply to keep the word *murran*.

Junior murran have very little to do, no doubt because they once used to spend their time learning to fight. They have given up herding, but they do not begin farming. They are called on for simple jobs such as collecting firewood for a feast, and may be sent with messages too straightforward to call for diplomacy. They should not attend public discussions or take part in ritual, and they are not expected to marry.

Senior murran attend the meetings of the elders which discuss matters of public concern, but they are not supposed to speak unless they are asked. They are the executive arm of the elders; they summon witnesses, and may be sent to seize an animal which someone has agreed to pay in compensation and then failed to produce, and it is they who take messages of any degree of subtlety. They begin to work in the fields, and may marry and set up their own homesteads.

It is those who have newly become elders – the junior elders – who take the major part in both political and ritual activities, while senior elders are called on for their knowledge of past events which may be in dispute, and for their wise counsel in knotty cases. They have the main ritual responsibilities. They are normally men with adult children. Those whom Gulliver calls 'retired elders' have really been pushed out of the system at the upper end. Such a man is still the ritual link between his descendants and the ancestors, and he must still give his consent to the disposal of lineage property, particularly land; but in lineage affairs this consent is usually merely formal, and he takes no part in public discussion at all.

Murran are subject to certain food restrictions, and above all should not drink beer, which is the prerogative of the elders and their main recreation. Murran are known by their head-dress and the spears they carry; both are different for junior and senior murran. Elders give up fancy head-dresses and do not carry spears.

There is a formal time-table for advancement from one grade to the next, and at fixed points in it everyone moves up a grade; when the senior murran become elders, the senior elders retire. For any one man the procedure begins with his initiation. The time-table is regulated, as it was in the old days for the Nuer, by the alternation of 'open' and 'closed' periods when initiations may and may not be held. For the Arusha these periods are of roughly six years each, and permission to open a new one must be got from the Masai ritual expert. The centre of the initiation rite is the operation of circumcision. Two or three youths are circumcised together at their father's home or that of one of his brothers, and all those of a parish who are circumcised at the same time sleep in a camp away from the homesteads until they have recovered. There should be three spells of initiation during each open period, with lulls between them. The number who are initiated in the first batch is naturally larger than in the two later ones; it can include boys as much as five years apart in age – all those who were just too young for the last period, and possibly even older ones who missed it for one reason or another, perhaps because they were ill, or their fathers could not arrange the feast that is supposed to be held in celebration. Some men are as much as twenty years old before they are formally recognised as adult. Built into the system, then, is the fact that some members of every age-set will be physically and socially too mature for the roles allotted to them. About two years after the end of the initiation period (when the first batch will have been junior murran for eight years) the junior murran are promoted to be seniors, and about eleven years later they become elders. Senior murran are promoted to elderhood a year before the following set of junior murran become seniors. Each of these promotions is celebrated by a public ritual for which the Masai expert gives permission. Gulliver uses the term 'age-set' for all Arusha initiated within the same period, and 'age-group' for the members of the set in any one parish. An age-set never acts as a unit except in the promotion rituals.

Is real life like this? When Gulliver was living among the Arusha, most of the senior murran had given up murran ornaments and were behaving just like elders. Nearly all were married. Nobody stopped them drinking beer; a portion was allotted to them whenever beer was served to the elders. They were encouraged to speak in public assemblies. Some were representatives – 'counsellors' – of their lineages, a point to be explained later. Similarly the junior elders were coming to be more preoccupied with their private affairs and willing to leave responsibility in public matters to the senior murran. Some of them had attained the degree of recognised wisdom and knowledge of affairs that led people to consult them as they would senior elders.

So the formal move to the higher grade is not the entry of a whole cohort into a new phase of life; rather it is the recognition that most of them have already reached the stage that the name of their new grade describes. The ceremonies are not arranged for automatically by some official with his eye on the calendar; they are held in response to pressure from the set seeking promotion. This set can count on the support of the set next but one above it, to whom they stand, metaphorically, in the relation of sons to fathers; and this linkage of alternate sets continues through time, almost as if it really was a matter of descent. The whole series of age-sets is conceived as divided into two streams, the members of each being allies within their own stream and rivals of the other. The everyday significance of this lies in the fact that it provides a man with ready-made allies when he is involved in a dispute.

Although no individual has authority to command, the age-groups are not leaderless. As a new one is being formed, the initiates in each parish choose from among themselves men who will be their representatives in dealing with outsiders, and whom they call by a word that means 'spokesmen'. Each of the three sections of a circumcision-set has two spokesmen, one for the upper and one for the lower part of the parish. Their status is recognised by their right to a special share of the meat killed at a sacrifice, which they are expected to share at once with their age-mates. A spokesman should attend all parish meetings even if the business does not directly concern him, and keep a watch on the interests of his age-mates; and it was the responsibility of spokesmen in the junior elders' grade to convene the meetings, until they were constituted as organs of local government and required to meet at fixed dates.

LINEAGE ORGANISATION

The Arusha differ from most age-organised societies in that to them membership of descent groups is equally important politically – that is, for social control, and for pursuing one's advantage in disputes – with that of age-sets.

All Arusha claim to trace their descent from one or other of the pioneer settlers. This is not difficult, since settlement is so recent; most men's founding ancestors were grandfathers or great-grandfathers of Gulliver's older informants. The descendants of such a man constitute a 'maximal' lineage; they do not necessarily know the genealogical relationships of all members, but they all know one another. The smallest or 'inner' lineage consists of a set of full brothers with their adult sons; it may number between five and ten men.

But the Arusha have a picture of their own society which is much more complex, and which rests, as does that of the Nuer, on the idea of a series of divisions and subdivisions of the whole population, such that in any matter of dispute every man knows whose ally he ought to be. For the Arusha, who condemn self-help and think that resort to force shows that a man's case is weak, this is not a matter of joining in a fight (though that occasionally happens) but of giving support in discussion. The whole Arusha population is divided into two named moieties, associated with divisions of the territory, though this has little practical significance. Each moiety contains two clans. The membership of these is far from equal; one of the four includes more than half of the total. Within these again there are named sub-clans. All these names, and therefore the divisions that they describe, are believed to have been brought by the Arusha from their original home. Each sub-clan contains up to ten maximal lineages grouped in two divisions, and each maximal lineage is divided in the same way into two groups of inner lineages. The families within an inner lineage are similarly supposed to form two groups.

The name used for any such division of a larger whole is *olwashe*. This literally describes a form of grouping of wives with their children in a polygynous household, characteristic of the Masai as well as the Arusha. Where there were more than two wives, they would be grouped so that the whole household, wives with their children, was divided into two and never more than two sections. It is still the Arusha maṇ's ideal to build up such a household, though, as with any other polygynous society, only a minority achieve it in practice.

It is the *olwashe*, and not the whole of which it forms a part, that is significant for an Arusha, for it is within his *olwashe* that he looks for allies. Of course there must always be some *olwashe* to which both he and his opponent belong, even if they have only clanship in common. Then what matters is their membership of different subdivisions. Thus the same men may be allies in one case and opponents in another, as with the Nuer, though not in the context of armed conflict.

Just as every age-set chooses its spokesmen, so every maximal lineage chooses a counsellor, or sometimes two, whose role in the lineage parallels that of the spokesman in his age-group. The choice is made by the lineage elders with the help of leading men from related lineages, and the counsellor is formally installed and presented with a staff which is the sign of his status. A junior elder is usually chosen. Such a man may well be already a spokesman for his age-group; Gulliver found that about 20 per cent of counsellors doubled the parts. Lineage counsellors expect to be informed of transactions, such as marriage and the disposal of land by inheritance or sale, affecting their members; then they can speak with authority when such facts are disputed.

While spokesmen and counsellors are formally chosen, other men gain recognised influence by virtue of their personal qualities, and such men, along with the age-group spokesmen, are referred to collectively as 'the big ones'. There would be two to four such influential men in each elders' group in a parish. They are men whose opinions cannot be ignored, even though they hold no formal position.

DISPUTE SETTLEMENT

Theoretically disputes between neighbours are dealt with by the parish assembly convened by the elders, disputes in matters of kinship by gatherings summoned by lineage counsellors. Whatever the venue, the aim of the discussion is to reach some kind of compromise on the matter at issue; there is no question of an authoritative judgement which must be obeyed, although as was mentioned, a payment which has been agreed to can be enforced by the murran.

Although any discussion of a dispute may be initiated by a complaint or accusation, and although this is likely to be rejected or denied, the primary aim of the gathering is not to ascertain truth but to reach agreement. Supporters are brought there, not to threaten force, but to give visible evidence of the number who believe in the justice of their principal's cause. Everyone knows whom a given individual *ought* to be able to count on, and if such persons are conspicuously absent, the fact is obvious. The one ineluctable obligation of *olwashe* or age-group membership is to deny support to the other side. Supporters are not expected simply to produce evidence or arguments. They may bear false witness or suppress facts. They may try to confuse their opponents by interrupting them, or drag in red herrings. Shouting down a speaker, however, is not approved, and people can be fined for serious disturbance; the payment is made on the spot, in beer which is drunk, or an animal which is slaughtered and eaten, by those present.

Typical disputes to go before a parish assembly might be: an accusation of theft, adultery or the seduction of an unmarried girl; a claim to compensation for injuries received in a brawl; a disagreement about land boundaries, about whether a land transaction was a pledge or an outright sale, about whether a tenant had been permitted to plant coffee trees (which last so long that to plant them makes the land yours for practical purposes). A difference between age-mates should ideally be discussed in a conclave, as Gulliver calls it – a private meeting of age-group members. Hence public disputes are usually between men in different grades. Each party expects to be supported by his own age-mates or those in the linked group; his own if he is an elder, the group linked to his if he is a murran. In the old days anyone who wanted to raise a matter in public had to ask one of the elders' spokesmen to convene a meeting. Now that a parish council has to meet once a week this is not necessary, but he would still be well advised to have the backing of a spokesman in bringing his case. The elders do not expect to deal with matters involving outsiders to the parish, but these are sometimes brought before them.

Disputes concerning the obligations of kinship and marriage are expected to be settled among kinsmen. They may be discussed in private (conclave) or in public, but a public discussion of a kinship matter (what Gulliver calls a moot) is different from a parish assembly; though it is held out of doors, only the disputants and their supporters take part. Such matters might be: failure to pay bridewealth; the amount of bridewealth to be returned on a divorce; division of inheritance; claims that land to which someone has a right has been sold without his knowledge. It is here that the *olwashe* principle becomes important. A man involved in a dispute will invite members of his *olwashe* to support him – not necessarily every one, but those who live near enough to be in frequent contact and are all the time exchanging services of various kinds. He may go further afield for men whose status or personality carries weight. He ought to apply to his lineage counsellor; not to do so is discourtesy, and he could not carry his case very far without the counsellor. A conclave is often held in the house of a lineage counsellor, a moot in the open at the homestead of one of the disputants.

Often a dispute drags on for a long time, and conclaves alternate with moots without any agreement being reached. All this time each man's supporters are giving him advice, telling him what they know of the other's attitude, perhaps trying to influence the opponent through common kin. Every time a new moot is held the parties try to gather more supporters, particularly by calling in important men who live further away, such as counsellors of other lineages in the sub-clan. In lineage matters an important consideration is always to keep the lineage together; an obstinate man may get his own way, or prevent a settlement, by threatening to secede from the lineage with his brothers. Gulliver noted the feeling of relief in a gathering when agreement had been reached.

Since there are two possible ways of dealing with disputes, Arusha in practice choose between them, calculating where they are likely to find most support. Thus a man called Karime quarrelled with his father-in-law about the bridewealth to be returned when his wife left him. Karime had only one brother. By themselves they would have made a very weak inner lineage, and they reckoned to form one inner lineage with five cousins, four of whom lived some distance away. If he asked them to attend a lineage moot and they refused, this would be a public denial of their common lineage membership, and that would be a worse disaster for him than mere withholding of support. So he took the matter instead to a parish assembly, where his age-mates were junior elders and could be expected to back him against his father-in-law, a senior elder.

THE EXTERNALLY IMPOSED SYSTEM

Yet another recourse is available in the externally imposed political and judicial system. All rulers extending authority over a wide area have had to nominate local agents who enforce their laws and administer their policies, who can give them information about local conditions and who can in some sense 'represent' sections of the population, letting the higher authorities know of their problems. This is as true of China or of medieval Europe as it is of colonial Africa. In their own interests they are wise to choose men who authority depends on something more than external support. In most of British Africa this principle was expressed in the theory of 'indirect rule', government through the medium of traditional authorities. It was not easy to put this into practice among peoples such as the Nuer or the Arusha (or indeed the Tonga in Zambia). The Sudan administration sometimes made Nuer earth-priests into political authorities, with the right to hold courts to try minor offences, and enforce their decisions, and the responsibility for charging with murder anyone who killed in vengeance. We know nothing in any detail of the consequences of this change for Nuer political relationships. For Arusha, however, Gulliver tells us of the creation of chiefs, headmen, and, later, magistrates.

The Germans first, and then the British, appointed two age-set spokesmen as the agents of their authority. Between the wars these 'chiefs' were authorised to hold courts. When local administration was reorganised and to some extent democratised after the second world war, a single chief was recognised for all Arusha. He was chosen at first by a newly created tribal council, and later by election. The first elected chief was a Lutheran schoolmaster. It now became British policy to separate the courts from the executive, and three magistrates were substituted for the chief as judicial authorities.

Subordinate to the chief are headmen, one for each parish, also elected; they are usually senior murran. They should be the chief's agents in such matters as tax collection, a role which in some ways reflects the traditional responsibility of murran. But a headman has been chosen for his post by his own neighbours, and what his neighbours expect of him is to end immediate crises by his intervention, when, for example, a man beats his wife, or an enraged farmer finds someone's cattle in his crops. He has no more authority in settling disputes than the next man, but he is a witness to events that have been put on record by an appeal to him.

The magistrates are appointed by the chief, with the approval of the District Commissioner, who in these days is a member of Tanzania's single political party. They have to be literate in Swahili, though each has the assistance of a court clerk who issues summonses and keeps records. They regard the clerks as advisers and colleagues rather than subordinates. Since they must have been to school, they come from a small minority of Arusha, and at the time of Gulliver's fieldwork they were all Lutheran Christians. When magistrates were first appointed they were necessarily younger men, since education had not been long established in Arusha; so that their values in some matters, particularly marriage, were not those of the majority of their fellows, and they had no great standing in the eyes of the pagan, illiterate elders. Nevertheless, they had not lost their respect for the principle of settlement by compromise, and they would sometimes try to bring the disputants together for informal discussion, as chiefs, who are still appealed to, also do.

Nevertheless, the essential of a formally constituted court is that it must give a decision which settles the matter at issue, or at least can only be upset by an appeal to a higher court. Moreover, a party summoned before the court cannot refuse, and so cannot create a deadlock as he could by refusing to attend a moot. These are the considerations that lead some Arusha to take their cases to court, although they know what they are risking in an adverse decision. The court is a convenient forum if your adversary lives a long way away, so that it is hard to persuade your supporters to go with you to his home. To take a case to it is a way of forcing the issue when the traditional methods have dragged on and on without reaching a compromise. It can be the recourse of men who are more concerned with a particular claim than with lineage unity; though of course such a man might lose his case as well as dividing the lineage. Moreover, this is sometimes a way to prevent division by putting the decision in the hands of an outsider; it avoids compelling the whole maximal lineage to stand up and be counted on one side or the other, and as a result, even if the disputants break off relations, other members of the lineage can still remain friendly.

12   Kingdoms

In discussing kingdoms we are on much more familiar ground. There are not many kingdoms left in the industrialised world, and where there are, kings are less powerful than many presidents of republics. But it is safe to say that everyone can envisage a kingdom without any difficulty.

The focus in ethnographic studies of kingdoms in Africa is more distant than that of Gulliver's close study of an Arusha parish, or of any study of kinship with its eye on domestic relations. Their sights are trained on the capital and the court, the centres from which authority extends over a wide domain. They record constitutions. They ask what is the basis of legitimacy for the kingship and the offices subordinate to it, what claims those in authority make on those subject to it, what subjects expect of rulers, how far, and in what way, superior power can be kept in check, what are the resources that keep administration going, what are the rituals that establish the sacredness of kingship and dramatically present the reciprocal relationship of king and people; and some of them ask whether this relationship is one of consensus or one imposed by superior force. If students of kingship trace out personal interactions in detail, it will be in the context of palace intrigues, succession disputes and struggles for power, not of simple folks making claims against their neighbours. Anthropologists have only been able to observe African kingdoms at a time when the rulers had lost much of their power. But this is a field in which much can be learned from historical records, oral and written.

The logical necessities of the maintenance of centralised rule are common to all governments, and fundamental common features can be seen in all African kingdoms. No ruler can directly control all his subjects. He must entrust responsibility for parts of his realm to subordinate officials of some kind, and thus delegate and so share his power. This power is exercised not only in what might be called public policy such as the organisation of public works or warfare, but in the authoritative settlement of disputes between individual subjects. For their services in all these fields the officials must be rewarded from the general resources of the kingdom in manpower and produce; it is their duty to collect tribute and organise labour gangs or army companies, and it is they who deal with most of the dispute cases, and their pay takes the form of a share of the tribute and the right to call on labour for specified purposes on their own account.

These are the basic necessities in logical terms. One cannot similarly demonstrate the necessity of the various other features that are common to African kingdoms. Almost everywhere there is a conception of 'divine right' – that the king holds his position not only because he claims the kingdom as his hereditary possession, nor because he has been chosen from among his brothers by persons authorised to make the choice, but in virtue of a special relationship with the divinities on whom the whole population ultimately depends; these may or may not be his own ancestors. To say this is not to say that all African monarchs have been 'divine kings' in the sense that the Pharaohs were, still less that they were what Frazer meant by the term, incarnations of some spirit of fertility, who must be put to death when their powers began to decline lest the prosperity of the nation decline with them. What is meant is rather what Shakespeare meant by the 'divinity' that 'doth hedge a king'. Christian kings are not born with divine right, nor are they thought to incarnate their ancestors, but they are ritually given a special relationship with God at their coronation; and the same could be said of African kings.

Every African king had his palace, where a great concentration of wives and servants ministered to his needs and to the upkeep of the royal state, organising the supply of food and firewood, looking after the regalia, traversing the country with messages. Here the king entertained foreign envoys or traders, and, later in history, explorers, received the homage of successors to office, issued decrees and heard petitions. His senior chiefs had houses in the capital and were expected to demonstrate their loyalty by spending much of their time there. Particularly in West Africa, where the level of wealth was much higher than in the east, the elaboration of organisation and of material pomp was marked.

In one way or another nearly every African kingdom has recognised some office which represents 'the people' in the sense that it cannot be held by any member of the royal lineage. Such were the 'prime ministers' of East Africa, and the very complex systems of councils characteristic of western Nigeria. In East Africa kingdoms have been destroyed in revolutions made either by their subjects or by national leaders belonging to other tribes; in West Africa their institutions have by no means been completely dismantled. Nevertheless, this is one of the subjects better treated in the past tense.

13 Checks and Balances: Benin *

The history of West Africa as far back as it can be traced is a story of the building up of empires and the rivalry between them. In the rain-forest area of Nigeria the two great rivals were Yoruba-speaking Ife (and later Oyo) and Edo-speaking Benin, the former to the north and west, in the present Western State of Nigeria, the latter in the south-east, extending to the right bank of the Niger and the western part of its delta. Benin was at the height of its power in the sixteenth and seventeenth centuries, after which it lost its predominance to Ife, and by the time it was defeated by the British in 1897, and its capital sacked, it was already in decline. Under British rule an area roughly corresponding to the traditional kingdom from which the expansion started was recognised as a separate unit; this became the Benin Division in what is now the Mid-West state.

The people of Benin believe that when an earlier dynasty had died out, their elders went to the Oni of Ife, the ruler who was regarded as the supreme source of ritual power, and asked them to give them a prince. This was Oranmiyan, who was also said by tradition to have founded the dynasty of Oyo. The legend implies no subordination to Ife, for it goes on to tell how Oranmiyan found that no outsider could rule the Edo, and so returned home after begetting a son Ewera from whom the present Oba is directly descended. Thus the tradition asserts at one and the same time that the Oba is descended from a source of kings and so has 'divine right' in the ritual sense, and that although he is 'over' the Edo, he is not 'of' them. It may reflect a historical event; possibly in the fourteenth century a ruler of Benin did come from Ife. However, the political systems of Benin and the Yoruba kingdoms developed along very different lines. The most striking difference consists in the import

* R. E. Bradbury (1967), *The Benin Kingdom and the Edo-speaking People of Western Nigeria;* 'The Kingdom of Benin' in *West African Kingdoms in the Nineteenth Century*. Forde and Kaberry (eds), 1967; 'Patrimonialism and Gerontocracy in Benin Political Culture' in *Man in Africa*. Douglas and Kaberry (eds), 1969.

152

nce in Benin of age-based authority systems of the type found
ast of the Niger. Such systems are described in the chapter on
he Yakö; those of Benin were much more elaborate.

At the census of 1952 Benin had a population of 292,000, of
whom 54,000 lived in the capital and the rest in villages of vary-
ng size, averaging perhaps four or five hundred people. Here
he mass of the population grow their staple food of yams with
a wider variety of other crops than would be found outside the
ain-forest area – plantains ('green bananas'), maize, coco-
yams, okra, rice, melons, peppers, gourds, beans – and plant
kola trees and coconut palms, and nowadays cocoa as a cash
crop. The village as a whole, and not separate lineages, is the
and-holding body, and it collectively owns oil-palms which
anyone in the village may tap for wine. Well-to-do individuals
cultivate plantations of rubber, cocoa, coconuts and oil-palm,
employing wage labour.

The traditional authority system, the interest of which lies in
ts intricacy, was destroyed at the time of the British conquest.
The Oba who was then reigning was sent into exile. When he
died, in 1914, his son was reinstated as Oba, but the territorial
organisation that the British then 'recognised' was a stream-
ined hierarchy suited to the requirements of bureaucracy, and
quite unlike anything in independent Benin, and they forbade
he performance of the many rituals of kingship which included human sacrifice. The Oba who came to the throne in
933, and at the time of writing is still ruling, is an educated
Christian. It is possible that there has been less change in the
village authorities, although they must have been affected to
ome extent by the local government law of 1952, which set up
elected councils with powers and functions modelled on those
n Britain. Hence the authority system is best described in the
past tense.

VILLAGE AUTHORITIES

n every village the men were graded as youths, warriors and
lders, the members of each grade having their appropriate re-
ponsibilities. The youths, from about 15–30, were responsible
or communal works – clearing weeds from paths and streams
and repairing shrines and council houses; and it was they who

carried the twice-yearly tribute of yams and palm-oil to the capital. The warriors were available for fighting when the Oba called for troops, and they could also be allotted communal tasks requiring special skill. There were no collective ceremonies for the formation of age-sets or promotion from one grade to the next. The elders decided when a boy was to be regarded as having become a youth, and when a batch of youths should move into the warrior grade. They appointed leaders for the men in each grade, through whom they gave their instructions. The elders formed the village council. It was they who controlled access to village lands, collecting dues from outsiders who worked it with their permission, and discussed such matters as the apportionment among the village members of the tribute due to the Oba and contributions to be made for village purposes, the organisation of communal work or rituals and the consultation of diviners in case of misfortune. When Bradbury was there the councils of elders were still active, and would concern themselves with such matters as the building of schools; but in some villages the grades of youths and warriors were tending to be merged. The elders were called *edion*, the same word that was used to describe the ancestors collectively and also for the senior grade of the many associations, some of which will be described. The oldest in actual years was called the *odionwere*; he was the priest of both the earth and the ancestors. When the elders let it be known that it was time for the older men in the warrior grade to join them, each man who wished to do so had to visit all the existing members, making them payments and seeking their blessing. This was the pattern for advance to the highest rank in every association, and in these bodies too the *edion* took decisions for the whole membership and settled disputes among their juniors. Every association also had its shrine for the dead members as a collectivity and believed that they would punish disrespectful behaviour in juniors.

For some villages there was no intermediate authority between the *odionwere* and the capital. But in others, particularly in the north and east of the kingdom, there were hereditary chiefs, most of whom claimed to be descended from the younger sons of former Obas. It was said that in the past every new Oba planted out his younger brothers in this way. Some of these chiefs (*onogie*, plural *enigie*) claimed authority over several villages, and a few had their own titled officials and collected tribute; but many lived in a style indistinguishable from ordinary villagers.

For the purposes of tribute collection and raising manpower for war or for building work in the capital, every village was allotted to a titled chief promoted from among the Oba's retainers. These men did not administer divisions of the country; rather they were intermediaries, in both directions, between the Oba and the general population. One chief would be responsible in this way for a number of widely scattered villages. Their reward consisted in a half share of the tribute collected, and with this they could buy slaves whom they settled in their villages – by agreement with the village head – to work the land for them. They themselves had to live in the capital, under the Oba's eye, and they communicated with their villages through messengers. A man from the country who had business at court would approach the chief under whom he came, offering a present for his advocacy; this was another source of wealth.

THE CAPITAL

Politics in Benin consisted largely in competition among the Oba's retainers for the titles which carried with them privileges of this kind. R. E. Bradbury, who reconstructed the traditional political system on the basis of field-work done from 1951 onwards, estimated that in the last days of Benin's independence the population of the city was less than half the 54,000 recorded in 1952. Nevertheless, it was no mean city, especially when contrasted with the little peasant villages outside its walls. From its empire Benin drew tribute in all kinds of produce, and tolls from its control of trade, particularly that in goods brought by sea from Europe. Within the capital specialist craftsmen of many different kinds, all working directly for the Oba, produced the objects which made the art of Benin famous, notably casting in brass and carving in wood and ivory; there were also weavers, leatherworkers, blacksmiths, carpenters, musicians and many others. The Oba controlled the import of guns and gun-powder, first introduced by Portuguese traders; and whereas it was originally the Portuguese demand that incited him to organise raids into the interior for slaves, he and his retainers came to capture or buy slaves for themselves and become rich through this source of manpower. There were associations of traders, each of which monopolised the trade of a particular route; these were headed by important chiefs, and the Oba was said to be a member of them all. Thus were founded all the fortunes that enable some contemporary Edo to be plantation owners.

All the free subjects of the Oba were referred to as his 'slaves', a term which was far from implying that their status resembled that of the slaves who had been captured or bought as such. It expressed one view of the Oba, as the supreme authority; and in a sense it is the converse of the view that a political career was open to any free man who could 'enter the palace' become a royal retainer, and, if he found favour, rise to an important position. Every such man inherited from his father membership of one of the three associations through whom the activities of the palace were organised. Some villager actually entered palace service, and a few rose to great heights but naturally those who had the best chances were the sons of palace officials, or at least of dwellers in the city, who were in touch with affairs and knew how to play the game of political intrigue, as well as being able to afford the necessary outlay.

PALACE ASSOCIATIONS

The palace was divided into three areas, each regarded as the domain of one of the three associations (*uto*), *Iwebo, Iwegua* and *Ibiwe-Eruerie*. A young man entered one of these by paying a fee which was distributed among the senior men and going through a seven-days' initiation, during which he was taught his duties and swore oaths to be loyal to the association and keep its secrets. Quite a number of villager took this first step, though not many actually became retainers. Within each association there were three grades, the lowest of men who had no titles and the other two, first *Ekhaen bhen* (junior chiefs) for whom there were many titles new ones being created by every Oba, and then the really important senior chiefs, who numbered twenty-two in the three associations together. The untitled section itself had

hree grades, through which one advanced by further in-
tiations and by the payment of fees to one's seniors. While a
nan was in the lower grades he did general menial work in the
balace, worked for the titled chiefs of his own association and
went as a servant with messengers (*uko*, the highest untitled
grade) from the Oba to different parts of his kingdom. When
he became an *uko* he was qualified to seek promotion to a title.
Theoretically titles were in the Oba's free gift, but since they
were the focus of political competition he was not always
ctually able to do as he pleased. The titles were ranked in an
order which was theoretically fixed, and was so in practice for
he senior ones; the Oba was allowed to create two new ones at
he beginning of his reign, and the ranking of these could be a
natter of political dispute. Roughly speaking the number of
villages attached to the title corresponded with its rank. Men
lid not advance step by step; every title that became vacant
was in principle open to any *uko*. It was also possible to move
rom one *uto* to another.

The associations were concerned in principle with different
aspects of palace life, though there was some overlapping in
practice. Bradbury has called them respectively Chamberlains,
Household Officers and Harem-keepers. *Iwebo* were respon-
ible for the upkeep of the royal regalia and for making the
beaded garments that were the insignia of high rank. *Iweguae*
was the part of the palace where the Oba lived, and its members were responsible for the commissariat. In *Ibiwe-Eruerie*
were the women's quarters, and the chiefs of *Ibiwe* conducted
negotiations for the betrothal of the many women who were
brought to the palace, some to be the Oba's wives and others to
be bestowed on favoured retainers. Many of these women
were offered to the Oba by subjects seeking favour. The two
senior *Iwebo* chiefs were responsible for controlling the trade
on the beaches with foreign ships, a duty which has no logical
connection with their palace functions and perhaps was simply
a recognised appanage of the office; they had assistants chosen
rom other *otu*.

THE TOWN CHIEFS

The palace was divided from the rest of the city by a broad

road. Beyond this lived servants of the Oba who had not 'entered the palace'. They were divided into forty or fifty wards, the members of each having their special duty; many were skilled craftsmen. Each ward had a head; as in the villages, he might be an *odionwere* or a hereditary *onogie*. The specialist craftsmen were organised in guilds, each of which was attached to one of the three palace associations; the Oba's doctors and diviners, however, dealt directly with him. There also lived in this part of the city members of the order of Town Chiefs, who obtained their titles by promotion from among the Palace Chiefs. They did not in fact administer the town, but they were regarded as the representatives of the people in general in opposition to the Oba, an opposition expressed in the tradition that the royal line was descended from a foreigner. They were expected to defend the common people against excessive demands from the palace. It was the duty of the senior Town Chief, the Iyase, formally and publicly to proclaim the entrance of any man into a titled office. This was a way of expressing the approval of both palace and town for the appointment, and by refusing or delaying to perform the ceremony the Iyase could oppose the Oba's choice. A junior order of Town Chiefs (*Ibiwe Nekhua*) was open to the sons of the Oba's daughters. Since he customarily established relations of alliance with Town Chiefs by giving them his daughters in marriage, these might almost be said to have become a hereditary class, though of course the individual titles were not hereditary, nor had the sons of *Ibiwe Nekhua* any claim to them.

THE UZAMA

In addition there was a body of hereditary chiefs, the seven Uzama. They claimed descent from the elders who brought Oranmiyan from Ife, and they were responsible for the installation of a new Oba. Although they were the highest ranking chiefs of all, they had little influence in everyday affairs. On the other hand they were independent of control by the Oba. Their villages were theirs by right; the Oba's servants could not collect tribute there, and should not give orders. The inhabitants were not called 'slaves of the Oba' but 'slaves of Uzama'. The Uzama had their own priests, and their own palaces and courts, which were patterned on the Oba's, though on a much smaller scale. They lived just outside the walls of the capital, within a further wall. The only one who was really important in secular matters was the Ezomo. He was a war captain, but not a supreme commander. The Iyase too was responsible for leading campaigns. Neither had an army at his own disposal; the Oba decided where troops were to be recruited. An Oba was expected to appoint his own eldest son to the seventh Uzama title, Edaiken; this supposedly proclaimed him as heir apparent and forestalled fighting for the throne. But no such appointment was made during the nineteenth century; the Obas seem to have been afraid that a designated heir would build up too much power, as has often happened in history.

The Palace Chiefs were the Oba's intimate advisers; in each of the three sections of the palace was a court with a dais on which he sat to hold audience and discuss with the chiefs of that section. But public decisions required the concurrence of both Palace and Town Chiefs, and they together with the Oba determined major affairs of state, and also judged disputes which lower authorities could not settle. Only the Oba, as lord of life and death, could pronounce on a capital charge, but the Palace and Town Chiefs joined with him in hearing such cases. From a reconstructed picture, such as this inevitably is, one cannot trace out the processes whereby decisions were reached or the alignment of forces in debate. Topics of discussion, as listed by Bradbury, might be 'the promulgation of new laws, the decision to conduct wars, the fixing of the dates of important festivals, the creation of new titles, the raising of special levies, and the taking of ritual measures to prevent epidemics etc.' (1967a). The Oba formally took the initiative in proposing action. The different orders of chiefs discussed the proposals separately, and when the state council met each gave an agreed opinion through a spokesman. Thus, if either Town or Palace Chiefs supported him, the Oba could do what he wanted, whereas if both opposed him he had to give way. In most of the matters to be decided there was no logical reason why the interests of the different orders as such should conflict, and one suspects that the more serious power struggles went on within rather than between them. Traditions of 'new laws' made by earlier Obas suggest that they were mainly concerned with 'constitutional' matters such as the ranking of titles or their grouping in orders. Here indeed was matter for power struggles; and if the Oba's power was supported by the territorial scattering of the chiefs' authority and by the allocation of joint activities to members of different *otu*, it was tempered by the procedure for the conferring of titles.

Numbers of competitors would apply for a vacant title, and it was awarded, in theory, simply by the Oba sending a messenger to the favoured applicant. But this man had then to pay fees to both Town and Palace Chiefs as corporate bodies, as well as to the Oba himself, and to all the individual title-holders, and to seek the blessing of each of these, in a procedure strictly analogous to that required of a villager seeking to become an elder. Hence, in practice, the approval of all the chiefly orders was necessary. After that he had to be formally inducted by the Iyase, whose action was taken to indicate the agreement of the general populace. Sometimes this process took a long time; sometimes it was never completed, and the Oba might revoke the title if opposition to the appointment was too strong. But once it had been given it could not be revoked unless the holder was charged with treason; in that case he would be ordered to commit suicide.

Thus the game of politics consisted from the Oba's side in favouring his friends where he could, associating members of different orders in the same functions, re-allotting responsibilities so that no individual could build up too much power, holding a balance between factions; and he must have had to remember that gratitude for a favour which cannot be withdrawn is not necessarily shown forever. From the side of the orders of chiefs it consisted in part of asserting any prerogatives which the Oba might wish to limit and in part of blocking the process of the final conferment of titles.

These principles applied equally in the succession to the kingship itself. There was an interregnum between the death of an Oba and the installation of his successor. Even if an Edaiken had been named he was not allowed to enter the palace until he had paid fees to all the chiefs and obtained their blessing. In the meantime it was under the control of the senior

Palace Chief, Unwague. At a gathering of all Town and Palace Chiefs, Iyase asked Unwague, who supposedly knew the late king's choice, to name the successor, and he was installed as Edaiken by Iyase when he had made the appropriate payments. After that he paid fees to the Uzama, who alone could make him Oba. Thus the formal consent of all the chiefs, and, through Iyase, of the populace in general, was publicly given to his rule. He was installed at the site of the palace of Eweka I. After this there was a mock battle between his followers and the descendants of one Ugianbhen, a chief who, it is said, rebelled against the fourth Oba and was defeated by him.

It is believed that the rule of succession to the kingship by primogeniture was introduced in the early eighteenth century. It is very unusual in Africa, where there are two common modes of succession: either any one of a dead king's sons may succeed him, and the choice is not made until after his death, or the succession rotates between two or three royal lineages, each taking it in turn to nominate the new ruler. Legend has it that the Oba who made this rule for Benin intended to put an end to succession disputes. But even this rule is not infallible. Should the heir be the oldest of *all* the sons, or the oldest born after his father succeeded? And in a large polygynous family, and a society in which births are not registered, how can one be certain who *is* the oldest? No doubt it was to avoid such difficulties that the rule quoted earlier was made, that the Oba should appoint his successor as Edaiken. But, as was mentioned, this rule was disregarded, and there was a contest, decided by civil war, on each of the last three occasions before 1897 when a Oba died.

It should be noted that *only* the kingship itself, the offices of the Uzama, one or two individual titles and the office of *nogie*, were hereditary. Those chiefs who, as holders of senior Town and Palace titles, had the greatest power, were not able to pass it on to their sons, so that there was no opportunity to build up rival lineages which might constitute a permanent threat to the Oba.

An Oba was, then, a political ruler, the head of a complex state organisation; in the great days of Benin he was the head of a wide empire, and he certainly took a full share in its management. But some would say he was also something more – a 'divine king'. Recent studies of African history suggest that a special institution described as 'divine kingship' has spread through the centuries across much of Africa from a centre in Egypt. To anthropologists, with their eyes fixed on the details of interaction by which institutions are maintained or modified, the idea of transplanting them as ready-made complexes seems rather suspect, as does the idea that kingship must have been diffused from the home of its first inventors and could not have been created from within societies by men seeking power. The existence of 'big men' among those peoples who do not recognise a common ruler would seem to most of us to support the latter view. In some cases an egalitarian ethos pulls down ambitious 'big men', in others they succeed in achieving domination.

ROYAL RITUALS

That rulers should claim a special ritual status is not at all surprising where it is believed that the social order is under the authority of divine beings. In one form or other this has always been an aspect of monarchy, and in its oldest form the idea of the legitimacy of a dynasty is often less a matter of the right to inherit a possession (the kingdom) than a special mystical quality peculiar to a particular lineage. The Oba as the head of a great empire was surrounded with elaborate rituals, but he was no more, no less, 'divine' than the Nuer priest of the earth.

Every society which recognises a unique office must have some way of expressing its conception of the uniqueness. For the Oba of Benin this took the form of the fiction that he was immune from ordinary physical needs. It was believed that he neither ate nor slept nor even washed, and that he could never die. If such actions of his had to be referred to elaborate circumlocutions were used; anyone who used the literal words might be put to death. To maintain this fiction he passed much of his life in seclusion, but of course his intimate servants, if no one else, knew it was a fiction. This was the reason why the members of *Iweguae* were not promoted into other Palace associations; they had penetrated the mysteries. It was not, however, supposed, as Frazer's view of divine kingship would have it, that he maintained the well-being of the kingdom simply by maintaining his own bodily vigour. As Bradbury puts it, it was his duty 'to foster his own magical powers and to deploy them for the good of his people', but this was done through a continuing series of rituals for which he was responsible, and in which he established communion with his own ancestors and with the collective ancestors of all the Edo.

He was indeed accorded a status on a level with the highest gods of the Edo pantheon. As 'king of the dry land' he was linked with Olokun, the 'king of the waters', the god of the sea that Edo (rightly as it happens) believe to be the source of all life. He himself was thought of as the giver of life and death, and it was, says Bradbury, to symbolise his ultimate power over the lives of all his people that so many of the rituals of Benin included human sacrifice. He might be addressed as 'Child of the Sky whom we pray not to fall and cover us, Child of the Earth whom we implore not to swallow us up'.

He was in a sense the head of a state church. Not only did he give as much time to participation in the elaborate rituals of kingship as to secular business, but he was formally responsible for many local rites. Every village had a cult association of the type that has been described among the Yakö, and made sacrifices to its deity at regular intervals. The Oba was notified of all these occasions, and sometimes sent offerings; it was one of the duties of palace officials to represent him there. Ancestor rituals throughout the country were also geared to the Oba's commemoration of his own father and of earlier Obas. Twice a year he performed a long series of rites, making sacrifices to a different past Oba every fifth day. Each of these series concluded with a public ceremony in honour of his own father, at which twelve human beings were sacrificed; they were taken from the prison where criminals guilty of the most serious offences were confined. The Iyase then held the corresponding ceremony for his forebears, and all other domestic ceremonies had to be held within the next seven days. The essence of the ritual for ordinary people was that all lineal descendants of the ancestor commemorated knelt in turn before his shrine and asked his blessing, just as anyone seeking advancement to a higher grade would kneel and ask the blessing of his seniors. A feature of the royal ritual was its dramatisation of the relation between the Oba and the Uzama. The latter symbolically claimed superiority by displaying their antique crowns. Then there was a mock battle which of course the Oba won; he offered them palm wine and kola nuts, and their acceptance betokened their submission. After this they cooperated in further rites; the Oba sacrificed a goat to the earth in which the dead elders of all the Edo were buried, and the Uzama in turn contributed to the offerings made to past Obas.

The principal ritual that was still kept up when Bradbury was in Benin was the new year ceremony, when sacrifices were made to the Oba's 'head'. The head was believed to be the source of good or bad fortune, and the Oba and the leading chiefs had altars dedicated to their heads. At the new year humans formerly, and animals more recently, were sacrificed on these altars, and the Oba was rubbed with strengthening medicines by his priests, the Ihogbe, who lived in their own village just outside the inner wall of the city. Another important rite, which was forbidden after the British conquest, was the sacrifice of a human being to give mystical power to the Oba's regalia and those of his leading chiefs. On both these occasions the chiefs contributed essential elements to the performance, and themselves shared in the mystical strength they were believed to convey. This was characteristic of all the many ceremonies, and each publicly affirmed the validity of the established order.

Bradbury has discussed with reference to Benin the contrast which Max Weber draws between two 'ideal types' of political system, patrimonialism and gerontocracy. Weber thought of the two as opposed. In gerontocracy, he said, the polity is the common possession of all its (male) members, the elders among whom administer it on behalf of the whole, whereas in a patrimonial system the ruler 'owns' his land and its inhabitants. Benin, as Bradbury shows, combined these principles. The Oba did indeed claim that all the people were 'his slaves' and all the land was his; he had servants who marked out people's boundaries. But it was the village elders who actually allotted the land. The Uzama, who claimed on their part to 'own' the kingdom, though only in the sense that they were needed to install the king, were themselves elders. Age-grade systems are by definition gerontocratic; but the grading of the titled chiefs, though superficially it resembled that of all men in the villages, and although the procedures for entering a new grade were analogous, was not actually based on age but on preferment. When a new Oba, or perhaps in the past a heir apparent, became Edaiken, he was received into membership of the Uzama and thus became a gerontocratic as well as a patrimonial ruler.

14   Stratified Polities: Rwanda and Burundi *

In the region between Lake Victoria and the smaller lakes in
the western arm of the Great Rift Valley live a number of
peoples who were ruled by kings for at least three or four centuries until, with the coming of independence to that part of
the world, kingship was rejected, in some places by internal rebellion, in others by external attack.

The most important of these were Bunyoro, Toro, and
Ankole in south-western Uganda, and Rwanda and Burundi
to the south of Ankole. Buganda, which at the time of the
European penetration was the most powerful, and is still the
largest and most populous, lies on the northern and western
shores of the great lake; it was differently organised in many
respects from the kingdoms to the west and south. To the east
of Buganda and on the south-western shores of Lake Victoria,
in the Karagwe region, there were mini-kingdoms, too small to
have been of political importance in modern times, but retain-
ing the tradition, common to all the larger units except Buganda, of the conquest and domination of an autochthonous
agricultural people by pastoral invaders.

This part of Africa is unusually rich in oral tradition. Particularly in Rwanda, long recitations extolling the achievements of past kings were preserved by professional narrators
or singers, who learned them from older men and found favour
at court by their skill in performance. Officially approved
royal genealogies were also preserved, and individual lineages
handed down similar records of their famous ancestors and
their claims to descent from royal ladies. The official records
are believed to date from the sixteenth century. Of course they
present history in a light that is favourable to the rulers. But
when they are checked against the popular history which was
also preserved in narrations, and against the traditions of
neighbouring peoples, reasonable inferences can be drawn

---

* *The Premise of Inequality.* J. J. Maquet, 1954.
  Power and Society in Africa. J. J. Maquet, 1971.
  Rwanda and Burundi. R. Lemarchand, 1970.

about the political history of the region. Dates can be fixed by eclipses, and sometimes by archaeological remains. From the earliest days of European occupation, missionaries began to collect these traditional histories, and since the second world war the work has been continued by literate Rwandese and by Belgian anthropologists and historians. Jan Vansina (1962) has reconstructed the history of Rwanda, and Luc de Heusch (1966) that of its relations with its neighbours.

Most interesting in their accounts for a student of ethnography is the tracing of the process of infiltration of pastoral peoples into the homes of cultivators and their eventual domination, that of internal consolidation, and that of the rise and fall of neighbouring peoples in a power struggle that was still going on when it was frozen by European conquest.

All these peoples call the cattle-owners and the tillers of the soil by different, supposedly tribal or ethnic, names; in Rwanda and Burundi they are respectively Tutsi and Hutu, in Bunyoro they are Huma and Iru, in Ankole Hima and Iru, and this although Rwanda and Ankole are often said to have most in common in political structure. Perhaps these names represent dominant lineages in the different immigrant and indigenous populations. It is assumed that membership of one or other category is determined by descent, that the two do not intermarry, and that they are of distinct physical type, the ruling pastoralists being unusually tall and slender. Certainly one does not expect to see this 'ethiopid' type among Hutu or Iru, but it does not follow that all the cattle-owners are recognisable by their stature. In fact the distinction depends, in modern times, and perhaps has always depended, on the possibility and the advantages of owning cattle. Where there are few cattle it has lost its importance. Where cattle are still the main source of wealth and superior status, all cattle owners may be called by the higher ranking name; this is the situation described today in Ankole. To establish a rigid boundary two conditions are necessary: that intermarriage be effectively prohibited and that only men of pastoral descent be permitted to own cattle. This was the rule in Rwanda, not only before the colonial period, but all through it; and it is Rwanda that Belgian writers have described as a caste society.

As the history of this part of Africa has been pieced together, immigrants of 'ethiopid' type infiltrated the regions where high ground gives good grazing; according to one theory, they did not arrive by the most direct route but came along the southern shores of the great lake after journeying far to the south. At first they lived in peaceful co-existence with the existing inhabitants and learned their Bantu languages. They were followed by Nilotic invaders, the Lwoo, who came as conquerors and established political domination in the lands they entered. But the Lwoo never conquered Rwanda, although they sometimes defeated it in battle. Their leading lineage, the Bito, provided the royal houses of Bunyoro, Toro (once part of Bunyoro), Buganda and Busoga. In the little kingdoms to the south of the lake the chiefs belonged to the Hinda lineage.

Bunyoro and Ankole preserve a tradition of a miraculous dynasty, the Cwezi, who ruled them for a generation or two and then suddenly disappeared. The historian Roland Oliver believes that they were indeed kings of a great empire centred to the south of the lake, which they extended into these two countries for a short time before they were defeated some time in the fifteenth century by the Lwoo invaders; then the Bito established themselves in Bunyoro, the Hima in Ankole and elsewhere. Oliver considers that the Tutsi, who alone were never conquered by the Bito, and who have no myth of the disappearance of the Cwezi, may themselves represent the last remnant of an original Cwezi immigration from somewhere in the south of Ethiopia. But the Belgian historians do not accept this view. For them the history of Rwanda begins with the entry into the country from the east of nomad herdsmen who at first lived as peaceful neighbours with the cultivators they found there, exchanging cattle products for grain as the nomad Fulani in west Africa still do. In the fifteenth century they began to build up a state, and to extend their control over more and more of the Hutu peoples, some of whom were organised as groups of autonomous feuding lineages, and were easily brought under Tutsi rule, while others recognised chiefs and were harder to subdue; some Hutu chiefs right up to the colonial period were no more than unreliable vassals. It was only in the eighteenth century that the major expansion of the Tutsi took place, and this was still continuing when Europeans encountered them in the nineteenth.

What interests an anthropologist is not so much the chronicle of victories and defeats as the question how the political institutions found in the region may have been shaped by the general insecurity that it reflects. Some traditions ascribe specific changes in organisation to particular rulers and, in the case of Rwanda, Vansina has constructed from these a picture of the stages by which the kingdom might have reached the form it had when European authority was imposed in 1910. The details of its structure were recorded by J. J. Maquet in 1950, when they were still well remembered, and further analyses of the legends have been made by Luc de Heusch.

Rwanda (with Burundi; they were treated as a single unit by their colonial overlords) was preserved by a difficult terrain and a remote situation from the Arab slave-traders whose routes the earliest explorers followed, and the first European only entered the country in 1891. It was allotted to Germany in the 'scramble for Africa', but German authority was not made effective there before 1910, and only after it passed to Belgian control in 1917 could it be said to have been closely administered. Both Germans and Belgians made it their policy to support the authority of the king (the Mwami) and his chiefs. All the country of Rwanda is more than 4,000 feet above sea level; it rises steadily from rolling hills in the north-east, on the Uganda border, to the high volcanic Mufumbiro mountains (14,000 feet) in the west. Between the steep ridges are deep valleys, some filled by lakes and river-beds, others swampy. The forests to the west are the home of the Twa pygmies, related to those of the Ituri. Lower down the land is fertile and gives the good grazing that attracted the pastoral immigrants. Food crops are maize, beans, peas, sorghum, cassava, and sweet bananas from which beer is brewed. Coffee is the most important cash crop. The population is extremely dense, and in Rwanda the conflict between the land needs of the herdsmen and the cultivators has grown steadily more acute; there has been a steady migration from Rwanda to places of employment in Buganda for thirty years or more. In 1955 the total population of Rwanda and Burundi together was 5 million.

As Vansina reconstructs the story of Rwanda, it begins with attempts by different Tutsi lineages to establish domination over one another and over the Hutu populations in the areas where they grazed their cattle, one strategy being to lend cattle to Hutu in exchange for services and political support. Thus were created mini-kingdoms on a scale similar to those of north-western Tanzania and Busoga, which were never consolidated by any extensive conquest. Ten such petty states existed in the fifteenth century in the centre and east of present-day Rwanda. Early in the sixteenth century one Mukobanya, king of a little state in the south-east, threw off his allegiance to his overlord and set off on a career of cattle raiding and expansion. One of his first successes was against Rukoma, a small country whose chief was surrounded by ritual practices unknown to Mukobanya's predecessors. The secrets of ritual and taboo were kept by a body of hereditary experts called *abiru* (singular *mwiru*). Mukobanya took over this institution, winning over to his side the leading *mwiru* lineage. The secret code of which they were the guardians is expressed in esoteric language, which would not be understood by a speaker of Rwanda without interpretation. Its secrets were preserved right up to the time when, in 1961, a republic was proclaimed in the country.

THE RITUAL SPECIALISTS

The 'college' of *abiru* became one of the most important institutions of Rwanda. No doubt the idea of his sacredness increased the power of the king over his subjects. But since each *mwiru* knew only a part of the sacred formulae, the co-operation of the whole body was necessary for any important ceremony, and this gave every one of them a hold on the king. Like the secular chiefs who administered the country on the king's behalf, the *abiru* had lands allotted to them as a source of revenue, but in their case, since their office was hereditary, they were secure in possession of their estates. New *abiru* were created from time to time. They advised the king in political as well as ritual affairs, and were responsible for naming and installing his successor. Parallels with the Uzama inevitably come to mind, although the first Uzama were conceived as having established a dynasty, not as having been appointed by a king; yet it may be that in Rukoma the *abiru* had been thought of as the Uzama were in Benin, as going back to the beginning of things. Rwanda traditions ascribe the creation of the *abiru* to a mythical first king, but as Vansina interprets the records, the institution was definitely created at the time of the conquest of Rukoma, the home of the clan which provided the senior *abiru*. The question how royal office came to be linked with ritual power is still an open one, unless one accepts the view that a complex institution came into existence in one place and was either carried over Africa by migrants or imitated from neighbour to neighbour. Where did Rukoma get *its* institutions? Beidelman sees in the Nuer the germ of a process whereby persons already credited with ritual powers could make themselves political leaders. Recent research on the history of Malawi shows how the shrines of prophets, wonder-working rain-makers, were taken over by secular rulers whose power rested largely on their control of the shrines. Elsewhere one can see lineages attaining domination because they are able to offer protection to the victims of raids, but without making ritual claims. On Vansina's hypothesis the kings of Rwanda too would have begun acquiring secular power, and seized the opportunity to reinforce it that was presented by the conquest of Rukoma.

AGENTS OF AUTHORITY

As the kings extended their domination they appointed chiefs to govern the newly conquered territories and collect tribute from the inhabitants; or they sent armies to live there; or individual Tutsi moved in where there was good grazing. Sometimes they simply made Hutu chiefs their vassals, and some of these were more submissive than others. Only in the centre of the kingdom was the royal authority unquestioned, and only there was the system operative that has been described by Maquet. In the northern areas, which had been annexed only a short time before the establishment of German rule, sporadic revolts went on even under the Germans, and Tutsi control was never wholly effective until it had the backing of the Belgian mandatory authorities.

It became the practice of the Rwanda kings to appoint as their territorial subordinates not their own kinsmen but subjects who could not claim the charisma of royalty (though they might transfer their allegiance to neighbouring kings). After they were defeated by the Nyoro there was created a standing army in which all Tutsi bore arms, while Hutu (like pioneers in the Second World War) herded the cattle on which the warriors depended for milk, but were not armed themselves. The country was divided into provinces each under a high-ranking chief, and an army was stationed on the frontier of each province. In each new reign a new army division was created, and the provinces redivided to allot an area to the new warriors. Young recruits to the army lived at court, and were instructed in tales of the heroic deeds of their forebears and in the rules of upper-class manners.

For internal administration the army chiefs appointed subordinates over districts into which their provinces were divided. They were responsible for the collection of tribute, and from some time in the nineteenth century there were two in each district, the land-chief, who was in charge of the payments in grain, and the cattle-chief. Below the land-chief was a hill-chief, usually a Hutu lineage head who was held responsible for the tribute due from the area where his descent-group lived; in much of the hilly regions of East Africa it is assumed that the members of a lineage live together on a ridge or the side of a hill, separated from their neighbours by deep valleys. In each district there was a sub-capital in which the king established one of his wives with her retinue, and appointed a special chief to look after them; often the man chosen was a Twa, one of the forest pygmies who form a third division in the population of Rwanda, and many of whom attached themselves to the court and were employed as court jesters and as spies. According to Vansina, leading Tutsi lineages competed to obtain chiefships for their members, and this fact, along with the presence of several chiefs in every district, made it hard for any rival to build up power in opposition to the king.

There seems to have been no formal council of chiefs meeting regularly to advise the king, let alone councils like those of Benin which could independently agree on a line of policy and present it to him. But a number of chiefs of recognised preeminence were summoned from time to time to discuss matters of state. First among these was the 'favourite councillor' who seems to have been more closely associated with the king. Maquet calls him a 'sort of prime minister', and the holder of such a position has also been called a 'sort of lightning-conductor'; he was expected to take the blame for unpopular decisions and thereby preserve the image of the king who could do no wrong. The institutionalised role of leading counsellor can be found in other African kingdoms; in this region the Ganda Katikkiro is the best-known example. According to Oberg, his title in Ankole was 'Nganzi', which means 'favourite', and he was responsible for the installation of a new king, the duty of the *abiru* in Rwanda. The latest writer on Ankole, S. R. Karugire (1971), asserts that no such office existed in his country until British authorities remodelled the constitutions of the smaller kingdoms in imitation of Buganda.

Where were the Hutu in this picture? Heads of Hutu lineages might occasionally be appointed as land-chiefs, and it was the duty of lineage heads to supply herdsmen to go with the armies. Hutu could herd cattle for their owners, and in Maquet's view the Tutsi got most of this work done for them by Hutu; but they could not themselves own cows and so acquire wealth. A Hutu could enter into a client relationship known as *ubuhake* with an individual Tutsi who gave him cattle to herd and general protection, in return for menial services such as building, keeping watch at night, carrying messages, cooking food on a journey. The client was entitled to all the milk and the male offspring of the cows entrusted to him, and to the meat and skin of animals which died. In this relationship the lord was called *shebuja*, the client *guragu*. It was supposed to be hereditary, though on a client's death the lord could take back his cattle. A client could also, in theory, end the relationship, but this was not easy; however, two brothers could serve different lords. The relationship was initiated by the Hutu in phrases which might imply that he expected benevolence from the lord – 'Give me milk; be my father' – but could also be taken as an undertaking to be as obedient as a son. Maquet will not allow the name of contract to these agreements, arguing that, since no Hutu could exist without the protection of a lord, there was no freedom of choice; yet a man seeking a lord for the first time could choose where he would go. Although we have no account of dispute settlement or law enforcement, it seems that there *were* courts, and that a man could appeal either to his *shebuja* or to one of the various chiefs in his area to take an interest in his case.

One can easily see how this institution could have grown up, either in the times of general disorder which must have accompanied the first conquests or later, in a situation in which all Hutu were at the mercy of any Tutsi. In the first case Tutsi themselves would be seeking to amass a following for the sake of political as much as material advantages (as they were clearly doing in Burundi right up to European times). In the second it would be the Hutu who were forced to find individual protectors against indiscriminate oppression. Maquet sees the *ubuhake* relationship in this second light, and even writes as if the Tutsi as a body, solidary against their subject people, had deliberately created it so as to prolong their ascendancy by making it not entirely intolerable.

The records of Hutu revolts in the past, and the massacres of Tutsi which accompanied the independence of Rwanda, have been taken as evidence of a resentment of Tutsi rule going far back into the centuries; but much of this violence happened in those northern areas where the Hutu had never been completely subdued, and could be interpreted equally as resistance to conquerors whose domination had not come to be taken for granted. It should also be remembered that under Belgian rule the chiefs had the support of the administration, and were encouraged to be rigorous in enforcing new forms of compulsory labour introduced as a means of economic development.

Nowhere else in the region has such a rigid division between pastoralists and cultivators been observed as was found in Rwanda. Yet even there, other writers than Maquet have recorded that it was possible to cross the line. A study of Remera (Gravel, 1968), a region in the east which was annexed only in the nineteenth century, states that certain Hutu descent groups were able to assert a prescriptive right to the position of hill-chief on their lineage land. Members of these lineages were treated with respect, and had a say in political decision. Those who became powerful were not crushed by any kind of sanction but – held to be Tutsi.

THE RYANGOMBE CULT

In contrast to Benin and indeed to most African states, Rwanda did not celebrate the sacredness of kingship by the public performance of ritual. The installation of a new king was done in secret and then proclaimed; the renewal of the sacred fire which symbolised the life of the country, the ritual hunting expeditions of the king, the blessing of the first fruits, were all secret acts announced after they had been performed to the people, who accepted the news with dancing and rejoicing. The people had and still have their own ritual, which has been interpreted in a number of different ways. This is the cult of the hero Ryangombe, and it is unlike any other pre-Christian religion in Africa in that it promises its adherents a heaven beyond the grave. Ryangombe is supposed to have founded the cult when he was dying, and to have expressly commanded all sections of the Rwanda people to honour him. It is the only institution common to all divisions of the people, though they do not combine in its rites and it is mainly practised by Hutu. Maquet, despite his general evaluation of the Rwanda political system as one resting on compulsion and not consensus, sees it in a functionalist light, as a cohesive force in an otherwise divided society. This accords with the view that the function of religion is to integrate society, as it can be seen to do in societies of very small scale, and as it often purports to do through the medium of royal ritual. But the cult of Ryangombe is neither a royal cult nor one whose rites symbolise national unity in any way. Formally accepted as it was by the kings, it could yet be called anti-royal; its 'king of the spirits' was distinct from the political king. There is a saying that the king and Ryangombe rule Rwanda together under God, but de Heusch, who has made the fullest study of this question, does not interpret that as meaning that they are partners. He regards the cult as a subversive movement which the rulers found themselves obliged to tolerate. It is a foreign introduction, as he demonstrates; he holds that it entered Rwanda two or three centuries ago. It belongs to those peoples who cherish the memory of the Cwezi, and it is not even linked to the creator god of Rwanda. Its initiates become possessed by the spirits of Ryangombe and his followers, spirits who are called *imandwa*, the name for them also in the Nyoro divination cult, and speak in their voices to people who consult them about sickness or other misfortune. The formulae of initiation assert that they are independent of the accepted norms of authority and property, though this is no more than a symbolic rejection; the followers of Ryangombe are not bandits. De Heusch regards the cult as an expression of popular alienation, 'a radical rejection of the established order'. An interpretation which comes rather closer to Maquet's was recently given by Claudine Vidal (1967), who remarks that there are close parallels between the ritual of royal enthronement and that of initiation into the cult. Although it may be true that the majority of the adepts of Ryangombe have been Hutu, Tutsi also practised the cult, even the royal family according to the testimony of one of the first missionary writers, R. P. Arnoux; and although the king could not be initiated, he attended the rituals. The head of the cult had an important position at court. Claudine Vidal sees it as a sort of mirror-image of the royal ritual, the former asserting the power of the king, the latter the recognition of it by his subjects.

BURUNDI

The military organisation of Rwanda was unique, as was the system of dual chiefship. Both these institutions, where they were operative, increased the power of the king and reduced the chance of effective opposition. In most of the other kingdoms the raising of troops was the responsibility of the territorial chiefs, each recruiting in his own area, and in none was there a standing army attached to the court. In Burundi the king could raise warriors directly only in those parts of the country that he kept as his own domains. The territorial chiefships were all held by princes (*abarganwa*). Every king filled such offices from among his own sons, and they expected to nominate successors from their own sons. A nineteenth-century king supposedly made a rule that when a new king succeeded, the descendants of his predecessor four reigns back (who had the same royal name) should give up their chiefdoms to the new king's sons. But this was never really accepted, and there was often fighting between the holders of office and newcomers. A king relied on his own sons for support against his brothers or cousins, and would place them in frontier areas to defend the country against foreign encroachments (and because they would be less likely to transfer their allegiance to a powerful neighbour). An early German writer saw the Rundi king as nothing more than a puppet of rival *ganwa*, and in fact it was only in his ritual aspect that he was unique.

In such a system, which must have been characteristic of this region as a whole in the days of constant rivalry between neighbouring kingdoms, clients were a source of political support. In Burundi excessive demands were not made on them, and the relationship could be the way to power for the ambitious, as attendance on important persons has always been. In the royal domains many Hutu were appointed as subordinate authorities, and some were said to have acted like independent chiefs.

Another institution in which Hutu could rise to positions of high status was the college, as it may be called, of *bashintagahe*, or advisers to the political authorities. One entered this body by the payment of a fee to the existing members and moved up through a series of grades. Admission to the final one was called *ukwatirwa*, the word used in Rwanda for initiation into the Ryangombe cult. At the level of a small neighbourhood it was they who settled disputes by discussion and compromise in the manner of the Arusha elders. If they failed the case went to a chief's court. Chiefs at every level had *bashintagahe* attached to their courts – 'chosen for their superior capacity or by favouritism', says Trouwborst (in d'Hertefeld *et al.*, 1962) Although the senior *bashintagahe* were usually Tutsi, some Hutu even became advisers to the king. The Rundi idea that this institution provided the elements of popular representation was expressed when they gave its name to the elected assembly that existed for a year or two after independence.

Burundi had its *abiru*, but they had less political significance as a counterpoise to the royal power. Their duty was to receive and bury dead kings in the sacred area set apart for this, and then to look after their graves. Like the *abiru* in Rwanda they had their own lands in this sacred area, and large herds of cattle which were presented to them as the representatives of former rulers, and they must have had considerable prestige. The most recently appointed are still living, though under the Belgian administration they lost much of their standing (owing to the ambitions of the princely branch which had the ear of the authorities, not to Belgian hostility to the institution). There were four *abiru*, each representing the kings called by one of the royal names which were taken in order. They were all drawn from different branches of a single Hutu clan, the Bajiji, many members of which were also high officials at court, royal herdsmen and official diviners. Whereas the *abiru* in Rwanda are thought to have been taken over from a Hutu kingdom by a Tutsi conquest, J. P. Chrétien (1970) suggests that in Burundi the Bajiji may have been a clan who offered their support to a Rundi king in order to have his protection against threats from Rwanda.

The Rundi also had their Ryangombe cult, which they appear to have taken over from Rwanda, but here there is no question of a subversive movement. Ryangombe (here also called Kiranga, the name in Rwanda of the royal drum) was thought of as the mediator between men and god, and was wholly assimilated to the official religion. One of the *abiru*, interviewed by Chrétien in 1967, said that the sacred spear of Kiranga belonged to a *mwiru*, and that a *mwiru* might speak as the mouthpiece of Ryangombe to give the order for the funeral procession of a dead king to set out. Chrétien describes the cult as one that 'mystically guarantees the permanence of Burundi' (as an entity).

A CASTE SYSTEM?

Should Tutsi and Hutu be called castes, as they have been by nearly everyone who has written about them? Certainly Rwanda and Burundi are stratified societies, one more rigidly so than the other. The question turns on the use of the word caste. If the hierarchical arrangement of named groups of people which is characteristic of India is the most important feature of the caste system there, the word can be used, as it often has been, to signify any kind of *apartheid*. If, on the other hand, one prefers to regard it as describing the complex Indian system as a whole, to which it was first applied, one must recognise that even Rwanda does not parallel this at all closely. Maquet refers to the definition of a caste as a system of endogamous groups ranked in terms of their occupation; membership is hereditary, as it logically must be if the groups are endogamous.

But is this enough? The definition was offered in 1948, and it is sufficient to cover the ideological picture of caste as dividing the whole vast population of India into four ranked sections. But the detailed studies of caste-based communities that have been made since that time show how a single community is divided into a far greater number of castes which are intricately linked in economic co-operation; and how social mobility consists in the upgrading of a caste as such and not in the movement of individuals into a higher caste. Though a man may simply work in the fields and not practise the speciality of his caste, the caste has the monopoly of its speciality. Caste superiority is defined in terms of refusal to accept food from members of less pure castes.

Descriptions of Rwanda give it the superficial appearance of a caste system by saying that there are *three* divisions, Tutsi, Hutu and Twa. I have barely mentioned the Twa, and I have done this deliberately. As a population they are not part of an ongoing system of economic co-operation. They make pots, it is said, and doubtless barter them as the Mbuti do their meat and honey. But it is never really demonstrated that Hutu do not make pots. Some Twa became court jesters or other types of royal servant, and a few of the latter must have had fairly high status. All the ethnography we have is in fact concerned with relations between Tutsi and Hutu.

Tutsi reputedly live entirely on meat and milk and honey beer, and if some of them in fact like millet porridge, they are like the high-caste Hindus who are suspected of secretly eating meat. They claim that their occupation, the only one befitting a gentleman, is herding cattle. But who does herd the cattle? Very largely the Hutu. The Tutsi have a monopoly of *ownership*, but certainly not of occupation.

This argument will not appeal to people who like to describe all forms of stratification by the name of caste.

Anthropologists are divided on this subject; I give the point of view of those who think caste is one very peculiar form which is not closely paralleled in Rwanda. Lemarchand, the author of the most recent book on Rwanda and Burundi, sometimes uses the wider and much more satisfactory term 'ethnic stratum'.

INDEPENDENCE

When the independence of Rwanda was envisaged, both Tutsi and Hutu began to form political parties, the former to defend their dominance, the latter to challenge it. Each had its militant wing. In 1959 a band of young Tutsi killed one of the few Hutu sub-chiefs, and this was the signal for rioting all over the country in which Tutsi houses were pillaged and burned down. Thousands of Tutsi fled, among them 21 chiefs and 332 sub-chiefs, some accompanied by numbers of Hutu and Twa dependents. Other chiefs organised savage reprisals. When order had been restored the Belgian authorities adopted a policy markedly more favourable to the Hutu. They appointed Hutu to the vacant chiefships, and many of these used their position to get their own back on the Tutsi, and did nothing to stop further acts of arson. Then, as part of the preparation for independence, elected communal councils headed by 'burgomasters' were set up. In these, Hutu had an overwhelming majority, and reprisals against Tutsi went on. Further elections were to have been held for the central government of independent Rwanda, but before this, in January 1961, a meeting of 3,000 burgomasters endorsed a proclamation of the abolition of the monarchy and the birth of the Rwandese republic. In the following months armed bands of Tutsi repeatedly launched attacks on Rwanda from bases across the border; each was followed by reprisals against Tutsi still living in the country. Eventually, in December 1963, after a concerted attack from several different directions had been easily driven back, the authorities of independent Rwanda executed all those Tutsi who still had any responsible position in the country, and slaughtered somewhere between ten and fifteen thousand. There are still 35–40,000 Tutsi in Rwanda, and some 200,000 in exile.

Certainly these events express extreme hatred of Hutu for Tutsi. Does it follow that life under Tutsi rule had in fact been always unendurable? A more convincing explanation is the theory of the 'revolution of rising expectations'. *Ubuhake* was not felt to be intolerable until it had been made illegal; then the fact that the Hutu gained little from the abolition made them impatient. Tutsi resistance increased in parallel with Hutu demands, and after the violence began, hatred on both sides became more and more implacable.

Burundi came to independence with a king, and a majority party which was concerned more with limiting the power of the Crown than with asserting the superiority of the Tutsi, and drew its leaders almost equally from Tutsi and Hutu. But events in Rwanda could not fail to influence its neighbour, the more so as so many Tutsi took refuge there. After the proclamation of the Rwanda republic a Hutu party was formed, and this was countered by a militant Tutsi youth league, 'little more than a gang of angry young men', who beat up and sometimes murdered Hutu politicians. In 1965 some Hutu army officers attacked the palace and the prime minister's house, apparently with the intention of proclaiming a republic, and at the same time there were attacks on Tutsi in many parts of the country, of the same type, though not on the same scale, as the earlier ones in Rwanda. There the Belgian authorities had either sympathised with the Hutu or thought they must be appeased. In independent Burundi the repression was ruthless. Up to 5,000 Hutu are believed to have been killed. In the capital 86 persons known or believed to have been behind the coup were executed; the entire Hutu leadership was liquidated. Tutsi control was complete. The final step was an army coup followed by the proclamation of a republic and the establishment of military rule. Since then there have been further massacres of Hutu in response to risings organised by refugees in Tanzania. In April 1972 part of the capital was occupied by Hutu and some 10,000 Tutsi were killed. But when the Tutsi had recovered power they embarked on a programme of mass executions in which between 100,000 and 300,000 Hutu, many of them members of the educated minority, are reported to have been put to death.

15   Old Wine in New Bottles: Bunyoro and Buganda *

Bunyoro and Buganda are neighbours, in the west of Uganda. Bunyoro is the legendary centre of the Cwezi empire, and the actual centre of a state which at its greatest extent is said to have covered the whole of the present Buganda, Ankole and Toro and territory to the north and west of Lake Albert. Nyoro legends represent the first king (Kabaka) of Buganda as a younger brother of a Nyoro king who asserted his independence; Ganda legends deny any connection with Bunyoro. Nyoro traditions record no less than eight wars against Buganda. When Speke passed through Bunyoro in 1862, the first European to enter the country, the Ganda had been having the best of the contest, and Toro and Ankole were independent. But the last independent king (Mukama) of Bunyoro, Kabarega, was campaigning to reconquer lost country, and he might have succeeded if he had not been defeated by British and Ganda troops. After this the Ganda view of the boundary between the two kingdoms was accepted, and the most heavily populated part of Bunyoro was included in Buganda; it was returned to Bunyoro after a plebiscite which was provided for before Uganda became independent and held shortly after. Even without this addition to its area and its people, Buganda is a much larger and more populous kingdom than Bunyoro. It is one of the four provinces of Uganda; Bunyoro is a district of the Western Province. Speke estimated the population of Buganda at 850,000; this is just about the number of Ganda recorded in the census of 1959 (so Speke must have considerably overestimated), but the population of the province with its many immigrants is 1,300,000. That of Bunyoro was under 200,000 even after the return of the 'lost counties'.

KINGS AND CHIEFS

The dynasty which ruled Bunyoro up to the ending of kingship

* *Bunyoro, an African Kingdom.* J. H. M. Beattie, 1960.
  The Nyoro State. J. H. M. Beattie, 1971.
  The King's Men. Edited by L. A. Fallers, 1964.

in 1966 belonged to the Bito clan. Ganda kings had no clan; each one observed the clan avoidances of his mother, an arrangement not recorded anywhere else. The kingship, nevertheless, was inherited from father to son, and the sons of kings (and their descendants) were recognised as princes (*balangira*). As was just mentioned, Ganda kings did not recognise kinship with Bunyoro.

Status distinctions in Bunyoro were something like those of Burundi. Highest ranked were the members of the Bito clan. The categories Huma and Hutu were recognised, and there is a tradition of a time when cattle were numerous, and there could have been a pastoral class. But that must have been a long time ago. Already in Speke's day there were noticeably few cattle in the country, where tsetse fly are rife. But Nyoro cherish the picture of a glorious past when there were many cattle, and believe that their herds were deliberately destroyed under British rule.

The Ganda have never distinguished a pastoral and an agricultural class. Once this was interpreted as an enlightened attitude which had been rewarded by prosperity, political preeminence and rapid 'development'. Today we are more likely to find the reason in the fact that there are fewer areas in Buganda suitable for grazing, while the excellent soils and rainfall of the part of the country near Lake Victoria make agriculture particularly rewarding. The staple food is the plantain, which fruits all the year round and does not call for arduous cultivation. One interpreter of the history of Buganda argues that this easy subsistence enabled the Ganda men to devote most of their time to warfare from which they brought back booty, including cattle. The one class distinction recognised by the Ganda is that between chiefs (*bami*) who control access to land and peasants (*bakopi*) who must serve a chief in order to have land.

Each of the two countries was ruled by a king, who delegated authority over areas of his domains to chiefs whom he appointed. Nyoro kings distributed land among their many brothers and made them responsible for the political administration of these estates. In Buganda princes were not placed in positions of authority. Records compiled by African writers give the clan membership of men holding the ten leading chiefs, and Martin Southwold (1961) has deduced from these that the oldest chiefdoms were considered to be hereditary, but that as the Kabaka's power increased he was able to disregard hereditary claims and appoint persons of his own choosing.

In both kingdoms the chiefs were entitled to call on the labour of persons living in their territory and to receive tribute from them. In Bunyoro tribute consisted in foodstuffs and beer, and as Beattie describes the system that is remembered today, the chiefs passed on a portion of this to the Mukama. In Buganda messengers were sent from the capital periodically to organise collection. Here the royal tribute consisted largely of the cowrie shells which were used as currency, and the cloths made from the beaten out bark of a species of fig-tree which the Ganda used for clothing, bedding and hangings. The chiefs received their own minor tribute of a portion of game caught and beer brewed, as well as a share of that collected by the Kabaka's messengers, who would be accompanied on their progress by a representative of the chief. They were responsible to the ruler for supplying labour when this was required for work in the capital, for recruiting troops and for keeping the peace by settling disputes among their subjects.

In both countries the major chiefs had their subordinates chosen from their own followers, with responsibility over subdivisions of their area, and it was to these men that newcomers had to apply for permission to settle. It was taken for granted that an established member of a community could pass on his land to his heirs. Chiefs were not landlords; authority to say who could live in a place carried with it authority to turn someone out, but if anyone was turned out it was for refusing to recognise authority, not for failing to pay a rent. In twentieth-century Buganda there has been a great deal of movement from one chief's area to another, and as people picture the past they say it had 'always' been so; people would leave a chief whose demands on them were excessive or his judgements unjust and attach themselves to one with a better reputation, and the Kabaka judged the worth of a chief by the numbers living under his authority. Buganda and Bunyoro had the same words for greater and lesser chiefs – *bakungu* and *batongole*. But in Buganda there was a special category of *batongole*, men who were rewarded for special services, particularly in

wars, by receiving estates and the authority that went with
them. New *batongole* were created in every reign, supposedly
receiving land that had not yet been allotted to anyone.
Mutesa the first, who reigned from about 1856, organised the
population of a number of *bitongole*, known as Kijasi, as a
standing army, responsible to a senior official in charge of an
arsenal of the fire-arms which by that time were being acquired
from trade with the Arabs. There was one Kijasi chief in each
of the ten 'counties' of traditional Buganda; he had a title corresponding to that of the administrative chief and was not subject to the latter's authority. Kijasi chiefs, like other *batongole*,
were supposed to have a special loyalty to the Kabaka and to
report to him any disaffection among the administrative
chiefs; this arrangement has points in common with the dupli-
cation of chiefs in Rwanda.

In both countries the *bakungu* were required to spend most
of their time at the capital, where each had a house; in Buganda
these were aranged in order of precedence, the senior being
nearest to the Kabaka's palace. Here they were available as
counsellors to the king and to take command of war expeditions; and their presence was a guarantee that they were not
plotting rebellion. Meantime their administrative duties were
performed by substitutes whom they selected from their own
royal followers. British governors saw a royal court of this kind
as a sort of Versailles where frivolous courtiers amused themselves at the expense of the common people, and one of the first
changes that they introduced was to insist that the chiefs
should live in their districts.

Beattie does not describe from Bunyoro a named office of
special counsellor to the king, such as existed in Rwanda and
Ankole as well as in more distant African kingdoms. Buganda,
however, had such an office, that of Katikkiro. The Katikkiro,
like the *abiru* collectively in Rwanda, was a king-maker; he was
supposed to know which of his sons his master wished to succeed him, and to proclaim this after his death. He was supposed to guide a new king in the first years of his reign; when
the new ruler had gained confidence he would appoint his own
Katikkiro. He held a court at the capital, to which cases were
brought that chiefs had failed to settle; and he controlled
access to the king by petitioners of all kinds. In the British

period the position was one of great political importance because both the Kabakas who reigned under British over-rule succeeded as minors, and in each case a Katikkiro was appointed as the senior of three regents. The British extended the title (and in some cases created the office) to other peoples of the Protectorate when they generalised a system of adminis tration which they believed to follow the Ganda model.

FEUDALISM?

Should either of these kingdoms be described as feudal? The word has been applied by anthropologists both to Rwanda and to Bunyoro. Beattie has drawn analogies between the Bunyoro of tradition and feudalism in Norman England, referring in particular to the Mukama and his chiefs. Each one on appoint ment promised loyalty to the Mukama in a ceremony that was believed to convey to him a part of the mystical power *(mahano)* that the Mukama preserved in his own person by a strict adherence to many ritual prescriptions and avoidances. This ritual aspect of chiefship, however, has no counterpart in any feudal system, nor indeed in what we read of the other interlacustrine kingdoms. Beattie finds the Mukama's position to be comparable in many respects with that of William the Conqueror. The latter was an invader who parcelled out the land of England among his followers. It was one of the duties of the fief-holders to present themselves at court when they were summoned. He would travel around his domains, as the Mukama did, moving his court from one city to another. He held feasts attended by the nobles and as many commoners as could manage it; Christian William had three a year, the Mukama one. He rewarded palace officials with grants of land; and he took commoners into his service and ennobled them (1960).

Parallels can certainly be drawn, as Beattie shows, between many aspects of eleventh-century England and nine teenth-century Bunyoro; contrasts could also be found, for example between religious institutions wholly identified with the royal power and those that depend on an external auth ority and may oppose that of the ruler. If African polities are to be called feudal, we must make up our minds what was the specifically feudal aspect of the epoch that we roughly call by that name. Beattie attaches importance to the bond of loyalty between superior and inferior (a reciprocal bond), which is created by a grant of land. For Maquet the grant of land is irrelevant. He offers 'feudality' as an ideal type (1954, p. 133), the essence of which is the offer of services by an inferior to a superior who grants him protection in return. Maquet thinks in terms of exploitation, not loyalty. What he describes is a clientage system, and this could be found in many societies that one would hesitate to call feudal.

Edward Steinhart (1967), following most mediaeval historians, takes as the essence of feudalism the contract of vassalage and the grant of the fief. The contract of vassalage, like the *ubuhake*, is made between two legally free men and creates a personal bond between them. The fief is the land granted for the maintenance of the vassal so that he can render the services due to the lord. The Ganda chiefs, however, had not offered themselves as vassals; they were nominated officials whose prime function was to exercise delegated authority; and so were those of Bunyoro. In Rwanda, he argues, the *ubuhake* was not the basis of the political system, as Maquet himself admits; and indeed his interpretation of it as a form of exploitation, which Steinhart accepts, deprives it of the character of a relationship of mutual loyalty which is essential to vassalage.

Goody for his part remarks (1971, Ch. 1) that some writers have been able to describe African kingdoms without referring to feudalism at all, and argues that we should develop concepts which are derived directly from the facts observed and not beg questions about parallels.

MODERN TIMES

In nearly all the territories governed by the British in Africa, the policy adopted for local administration was to confer limited authority on men whose status was derived from the traditions of their own people and make them agents of the superior government; at the same time their relations with their subjects were altered in various ways in the interests of efficiency and what was thought of as enlightened rule. Much of the work done by anthropologists in Africa between the wars was concerned with the effects of these changes, and when the East African Institute of Social Research was created in 1945, detailed studies were made of the process, particularly in Uganda and Tanzania. Uganda was of especial interest, because the British authorities sought there to take over what seemed to them the essentials of a particularly effective African system – that of Buganda – and extend it throughout the Protectorate. This chapter is not concerned with the results of this policy in acephalous societies, but with what happened in Buganda and Bunyoro.

The status of the Kabaka of Buganda was recognised in an agreement made in 1900. This prescribed that territorial chiefs were to be chosen by 'the Kabaka's government' subject to the approval of Her Majesty's representative (in practice the Provincial Commissioner, on whose advice the Governor acted). For purposes of twentieth-century administration the boundaries of chiefdoms were fixed, and the creation of *bitongole* came to an end. The Protectorate authorities recognised three grades of chief: *saza* or county, of whom there were now twenty in Buganda, *gombolola* or sub-county, and *miruka* or 'parish'. These ranks, with their Ganda names, and sometimes also the Ganda titles, were extended over most of the Protectorate, and in the early years of the century Ganda were appointed to the offices in parts of the country that had no such system as part of their own tradition.

The Uganda agreement also recognised a council (*the Lukiko*) to consist of three Ministers, a Katikkiro, Muwanika (Treasurer) and Mulamuzi (Chief Justice), the twenty saza chiefs, and other 'notables' nominated by the Kabaka; and a council on similar lines was set up in the other kingdoms.

For the office of chief, at least in the senior ranks, new qualities were now seen to be necessary, ideally those of the impersonal bureaucrat. The *miruka* chiefs could be local worthies, but at higher levels what was expected was some degree of education and some experience of employment in business or government service. Chiefs may have still been chosen from men who found favour with the Kabaka or the Ministers, but they earned it in a different way. Office once attained was supported by the external British authority, and the performance of chiefs was judged by its standards.

Bunyoro was treated up to 1933 as conquered territory, and was administered for some years by Ganda chiefs appointed by the Protectorate government. After the Ganda were withdrawn, local men were nominated by District Commissioners with no more than a token consultation with the Mukama. But the Agreement of 1933 gave him power to appoint and dismiss chiefs without any such checks as reference to the opinion of the body of leading chiefs, such as he could hardly have evaded in the past; and he used this power to appoint sycophants and control critics and men of independent mind. Good administration, whether by British or Nyoro standards, was no longer a road to favour.

Dissatisfaction with 'native authorities' who seek to enforce rules and regulations, and advocate policies, introduced by alien rulers has not been peculiar to these countries; it has been universal in Africa. British authorities built great expectations on the prestige of a chief's traditional position, but this did not lead the mass of the population to take his word for it that innovations were 'for their good', and a common language and local knowledge were not enough to qualify him for the subtle task of winning acceptance by persuasion.

CHIEFS AND THE LAND

But what is unique in Buganda and Bunyoro is the relation between political authority and rights over land. The Uganda Agreement allotted large areas of land in freehold to the Kabaka, four princes and others of his relatives, the Ministers and the saza chiefs, and 'the estates of which they are already in possession' to 'a thousand chiefs and private landowners'. The saza chiefs got eight square miles each, and many other men received large areas. Hence this freehold land came to be called *mailo*. Eventually some four thousand persons became freehold owners, entitled to sell the land allotted to them and to charge rent to peasants living on it. Thus great numbers of men who had no recognised administrative responsibilities were now entitled to derive revenues from land; most of them claimed the tribute of game and beer due to chiefs, and after cotton cultivation was introduced they took a share of the price received by anyone living on their land. In

1926, however, the *Lukiko* was induced to pass a law limiting their exactions.

From the point of view of the average Muganda these land-owners *are* chiefs. Large *mailo* owners have sold portions of their land to raise money for various purposes, and there are now estimated to be about 52,000 freeholders, the majority owning small areas. But all belong to the upper class in con-trast to the peasants who own no land; indeed this is said to be a reason for trying to buy land, rather than that security of tenure for development which economists see as the advantage of freehold, or even the revenue from rent which is the more obvious advantage in the eyes of the Ganda. A 'chief' in this sense cannot call on police to support his authority (though he can usually count on the moral support of the official chiefs), but he is expected to collect the taxes due from his tenants, and they expect him to settle disputes which may arise among them. Moreover, most *miruka* chiefs are *mailo* owners in some part of the area for which they are officially responsible.

The *mailo* estates have been a source of envy to men in other parts of Uganda whose social and political status would have entitled them to *mailo* in Buganda, but the Protectorate auth-orities soon came to think that security for the peasant was more important than secure tenure for the chief, and they resisted demands for the extension of the system. In Bunyoro however, the method they chose to protect the cultivator had unexpected consequences. Up to 1933 Nyoro chiefs were not paid fixed salaries, but received as official perquisites an area of land in which they collected from every man living there a money payment (*busulu*), in commutation of the traditional tribute and labour. When a chief retired he lost this source of income; so to provide the equivalent of a pension, areas of land were excised from those attached to the office and given to retired chiefs, who had a secure right to them since there was now no office to dismiss them from. Indeed they soon began to assert a right to pass them to their heirs. These areas were called *bibanja* (singular, *kibanja*). This word in Luganda simply means an ordinary family homestead. The Mukama made it a practice to grant *bibanja* to many kinds of people whom he wished to favour. Nobody interfered with the claims of *kibanja*-holders to pass on their land to their sons. By 1931 our-fifths of the population of Bunyoro were paying *busulu*; and chiefs in office tried to persuade people to live on their *bibanja* so as to have the maximum number of such tenants when they retired. *Busulu* was abolished in 1933, and at the same time the authorities rejected claims to transform the *bibanja* into *mailo*, and argued that it was the tenants who needed protection. They offered a certificate of occupancy, which would be registered for a fee of five shillings, to everyone who was actually cultivating an area of land. This protected him from eviction and allowed him to pass the land to an heir, provided that the latter also lived on and cultivated it. The issue of certificates was the responsibility of the chiefs, as the local agents of government; they issued most of them to *kibanja*-holders. Everyone believed that the registration fee was the price of the land (after all the Ganda got theirs for nothing, though – Nyoro probably did not know this – they had to pay for survey, and some had to sell part of their land to raise the money). So now the *kibanja*-holders believe they are, and behave as if they were, freehold landowners, even to the extent of selling areas of land.

Nevertheless, as in Buganda, the landlord–tenant relationship is not a purely commercial one. The landlord is called, significantly, the *mukama w'ekibanja*, and he expects and is commonly given obedience outside the field in which a landlord as such has rights. His tenants are expected to bring disputes to him before they go to an official chief, and this is not only a recognition of his authority, it is an assertion that they constitute a community which prefers to manage its own affairs without interference from outside. The *mukama w'ekibanja* is also expected to defend his tenants against official (and perfectly legal) demands for taxes or labour for communal purposes; and some of them reject any exercise of authority by official chiefs over their tenants.

Most African chiefs became increasingly unpopular during the colonial period. Conservative peasants missed the days when a man had direct access to his chief, and when some return for tribute and labour was made in largesse and feasting. Educated young men complained that chiefs did not advance progress – but peasants hated it when they tried to. Nationalists saw them as traitors who collaborated with alien oppressors.

But in Uganda it was chiefs and not kings who were thus unpopular. In the preparations for independence the Kabaka of Buganda first attempted to secede and thereby ensure that his kingdom should never come under the authority of a government elected by the whole population of Uganda. When he failed he claimed for his kingdom the autonomy of a state in a federation, and the three other kings (Bunyoro, Ankole, Toro), hanging on his coat-tails, also obtained a special status, though one inferior to his. The Kabaka became the first president of independent Uganda; its first (and only) elected prime minister was Dr Milton Obote, who came from an 'acephalous' people, the Lango. The two were at loggerheads from the start, and in 1966 Obote, who thought, perhaps rightly, that the kings were plotting to get rid of him, mounted a military attack against them. The Kabaka escaped to England, and died in poverty there some years later. Obote introduced a new constitution abolishing the kings and the special status of their kingdoms.

But the chiefs are still there. Whether or not they were ever feudal vassals, now they are a bureaucracy and as such indispensable. Under Obote they were nominated by politicians of his party; no doubt under General Amin they are nominated by army officers.

16 Religion and Society: The Dinka *

The 900,000 Dinka, like the Nuer, are transhumant pastoralists, but with a different pattern of transhumance. Their country extends more widely than that of any other Nilotic people. It stretches up the White Nile from Renk to Tombo only 160 miles from the Uganda border, and to the west it covers most of the Bahr-el-Ghazal Province and part of the Mongalla Province of the Sudan. It surrounds the Nuer country on three sides. Godfrey Lienhardt's study of the Dinka, made in 1947–50, is mainly based on the western area near Wau. The majority of the Dinka are still living now as they were then.

DINKA AND THEIR CATTLE

Much of Dinka country resembles that of the Nuer, but on its western fringes the ground is higher and the vegetation is forest savannah. In the wet season the cattle are not kept at the settlements, as with the Nuer, but moved to camps on higher ground in the forest area. Hence the young men are away from the settlements even at the time when there is enough water for people to live in them. For the Dinka it is the cattle camp and not the village that is the paradigm of political organisation. They use the word *wut* to describe both a camp site and the people who commonly camp there, a herd with or without its herdsmen, and a group of men who herd their cattle together, and they use it equally to describe a whole tribe and its territory.

The smallest herding group consists of the men of an extended family, but in any cattle camp several of these will come together, and the one whose ancestors are believed to have founded the camp will be dominant, the others being attached in some way to it. Its members are called 'the people of the centre of the camp', because they have the right to tether their cattle in the best-drained area. Similarly each named division

* *Divinity and Experience*. R. G. Lienhardt, 1971

of a tribe recognises a lineage, and each whole tribe a clan, which is said to 'have' the land that is the common territory. Their status is something like that of the Nuer aristocrats, with the important difference that they provide the ritual leaders – the 'masters of the fishing spear'. All these descent-groups are called 'people of the fishing spear', while the others are 'people of the war spear'. In Dinka theory each tribe and sub-tribe should recognise a single common ritual leader and war leader. In practice spearmasters attract their own following by their personality and the supposed efficacy of their prayers. There are many spearmaster clans, even though they are fewer than the warrior clans, and by no means all their members actually become spearmasters. Spearmaster clans are thought to be linked to warrior clans as mother's brother to sister's son.

The Dinka picture their whole history, one of expansion into empty lands, not of the conquest of neighbours, on the analogy of the division of a cattle camp. This is a political secession, not the fission of a lineage. When a lineage that has no claim to the well-drained area grows large and wealthy in cattle it secedes and founds a new camp, which as the generations go on may populate a new sub-tribal section. Such a secession is often led by an ambitious man of a spearmaster clan.

It is characteristic of cattle people that cattle play an important part in their ritual. As the most prized form of wealth they are the fittest offering to any being who is to be propitiated. But it has been shown, particularly in relation to the Nuer and Dinka, that the significance of cattle sacrifice goes far beyond this. An ox is a substitute for a man because in many ways an ox is identified with a man. Indeed the whole social system, as the Dinka themselves see it, rests on the relationship between men and herds. The metaphor of the cattle camps has been mentioned. It is in virtue of his rights in a herd that a man is a member of this or any wider political community. It is by the payment of cattle that he obtains a wife and so can continue his lineage. A man with no rights in cattle is hardly a man. The group's herd is thought to have a continuing existence parallel to that of the lineage. Men and cattle are interdependent and prosper, if they prosper, as a group; men lead the cattle to the good pastures, cattle give men milk. Prayers are offered for men and cattle together; the spearmaster of a camp should offer these prayers every night. Cattle are the means of creating new relationships (in marriage) between separate herd-owning groups, and of healing (by compensation payments) breaches between such groups; and if the matter is a serious one they are the *only* admissible means, the only creatures that may be equated with men.

They are known individually, and their passage from one herd to another in social transactions is remembered. Beyond this, every adult man has his own favourite ox, as is also the custom of Nuer and Karimojong. He takes as his own name a word that describes the colour-markings of this ox, adorns it with decorated tassels, displays it when he goes courting with his fellows, dances with his arms in the shape of its horns, and composes songs in its honour. Men are also given ox-names, that is names that describe their qualities in terms of those of oxen; to call a man by such names is to praise him.

Finally, detailed rules regulate the distribution of the meat of a sacrificed animal in accordance with the relation to the sacrificer of all those present at the ritual; and thus the body of the ox mirrors the social body. Although the ox is not the being approached in sacrifice but the means of communication with this being, this reflecting of the relationships within the congregation in the distribution of the meat of the sacrifice closely accords with Durkheim's view of the close connection between ritual and social structure.

Godfrey Lienhardt's account of Dinka religion shows how it arises from their experience both of the natural and the human environment. It interprets some aspects of this experience, enables some to be brought under control, and mirrors others. Dinka, as he remarks, do not distinguish between the natural and the supernatural; such distinctions are made by people who have enquired into physical causes and who relegate to the domain of the supernatural the phenomena that they do not know how to explain. But the Dinka do make a distinction between 'that which is of men' and 'that which is of Powers', and this is in effect a distinction between what men believe they can and cannot control. Their religion peoples the world with beings to whom they ascribe unsought and uncontrollable experiences.

DIVINITY AND DIVINITIES

The widest religious concept of the Dinka is that of 'Powers' (*jok*, plural *jaak*). The most important of these they call *yath* (plural *yeeth*). But they also use the word *nhialic*, which means the sky and that which is in the sky, and is the name of an entity that is sometimes addressed in prayers as 'father' and 'creator'. Yet this being is not in every way analogous to the Christian God, and the word does not always mean a personalised being, but sometimes a quality of being which is possessed by the many *yeeth*. Lienhardt therefore uses the word Divinity to translate *nhialic*, and divinities, in lower case, for the *yeeth*, who all alike are ultra-human.

Every clan has a divinity which belongs to its members collectively. It is believed to protect them, and is thought of as the source of its continuing existence as a body, just as Divinity is the source of all life. Men make sacrifices to Divinity and their clan-divinity together, and pray to the latter as 'you of my fathers', not to their ancestors as individuals. Each divinity is represented by some animal species or class of objects, what older anthropologists would have called a totem and Lienhardt calls an emblem. If the emblem is an animal they show 'respect' for it, and if it is a dangerous animal, such as snake or crocodile, they believe it will not attack them. The gifts made in the form of sacrifice are an expression of respect.

Many clans have more than one divinity. The most important of all is *Ring* – Flesh – which is common to all spearmaster clans. Unlike other divinities it is believed to inhabit the bodies of spearmasters and to give them the power that makes their prayers on behalf of their people effective. Such prayers are offered before the sacrifice of an animal which is the central rite of Dinka religion. An annual sacrifice is made after the harvest for the blessing of herds and people who will be moving to the dry-season camps. Other occasions for sacrifice are sickness or the failure of women to conceive. Before the beast is killed the spearmaster makes an invocation over it, calling on Divinity and on his clan-divinity to give him what he asks in return for the life of an animal. During his address the muscles of his thighs may begin to twitch, as the visible sign of the presence of the divinity Flesh in his body; and if this is unusually powerful, the Dinka believe, the tethered animal may sink to the ground under the mere force of it.

But *Ring* is thought of as something much more than flesh in the physical sense. It is said to be like light, and so like truth – truth not in the banal sense of correspondence with observed fact but as assurance of a desired state of affairs. Prayers are not always made in the form of petitions; sometimes they state that the blessing desired is already granted. Spearmasters of high reputation are those whose statements of this kind prove to be justified by the event. This is another manifestation of the power that divinity confers on the spearmaster. Essentially he is supposed to possess more *life* than other men, and to make this excess of life available to the people on whose behalf he communicates with Divinity.

It is because the spearmaster thus embodies a life in excess of his own personal life that the Dinka formerly held that he should be buried while still living; perhaps they still hold to the belief, but the ritual of burial alive was prohibited by the British administration, and it is likely to have become obsolete by now. It has often been reported of 'divine kings' that they were put to death or forced to commit suicide when some authorised person decided that their powers were failing. In one of the accounts of the deaths of Dinka spearmaster collected by Lienhardt, a wicked man who did not cherish his people was said to have been killed against his will. But this is not what the Dinka regarded as the right way for a spearmaster to die. It should be his own choice at a time when he knew that his death was near – therefore, long after his physical power had begun to weaken. By choosing the time for his death he may be said to master an event in the face of which the common run of mortals have to be passive. As a Dinka text puts it, 'He will not be afraid of death; he will be put in the earth while singing his songs. Nobody among his people will wail or cry because this man has died. They will be joyful because their master of the fishing spear will give them life so that they shall live untroubled by any evil.' In death, then, the spearmaster for the last time gives his people what his prayers had promised them whenever he made a sacrifice on their behalf. As they do not mourn him, so they do not speak of his having died, preferring some euphemism such as 'the master has gone to the earth'.

But they are not pretending he has not died or that the rite has made him immortal; rather they are making the experience of his death conform with an assertion of collective immortality, with the faith that the tribe as such will continue to exist.

The burial of a leading spearmaster brought together a larger congregation than any other Dinka ritual, all the men of his 'camp' – his tribe or sub-tribe. As well, then, as being the supreme example of a rite which brings experience under control, it images the unity of the tribe and asserts that unity. All the men were summoned at the bidding of the spearmaster, and they came, bringing their cattle with them as they must, and tethered them around the burial place, usually the centre of the spearmaster's cattle camp. The young men cut branches which formed the framework of a litter of strips of ox-hide, on which the spearmaster was lowered into his grave. Cattle were sacrificed to his clan-divinity; every major lineage represented should contribute one. The old man bade farewell and spoke his last words, and when he ceased speaking the grave was covered not with earth, but with cattle-dung.

As Lienhardt interprets this ritual, the life which it purports to preserve is that which his people receive from the spearmaster as the mediator of his clan-divinity, *Ring*. All the emphasis of the ritual was on vitality, on the triumph of life over death, a theme which all mortuary ritual expresses in one way or another. Details illustrate this. The cows were not milked, and they bellowed in discomfort; they were said to be mourning the spearmaster, but at the same time the bellowing of cows heavy with milk is a sound from the good pastures on which Dinka life depends. The *akoc* tree, used to make the litter on which the spearmaster lay, is the one that best survives the dry season and the first to put out new leaves. Some accounts refer to a fence round the grave made from *awar* grass, again a species that survives drought and is the divinity of some spearmaster clans. Finally, the young men attended the ceremony armed and ready to attack outsiders, and made displays of aggression. Lienhardt comments that for the Dinka fighting strength was itself a condition of survival. Whether this is the reason for the association of warlike dances with funerals, or whether it is enough to say that aggressive behaviour is an assertion of vitality, other African peoples too have performed

war-dances on these occasions (see Wilson, 1957, pp. 25ff).
Certainly such dances express the unity of a group in opposition to outsiders.

Malinowski saw the essence of religion in the need of individual men for comfort in the face of their own real helplessness,
and above all in the face of death, reminding them of their own
inevitable dissolution. This could be one way of saying that religion enables the believer, and the believers as a group, to interpret their experience in such a way that they feel themselves
to be in control of it. Lienhardt puts it that the invocations at
sacrifices 'assert by a combination of assertions of control and
admissions of weakness a relationship between freedom and
contingency in human life, in which freedom appears eventually as the stronger'.

DIVINITY AND EXPERIENCE

As he points out, Dinka regard experiences which we should
see as internal conditions, emotional or physical disturbances,
as coming to them from outside and so detachable from them.
Sickness for them is not 'cured' but 'removed'. All human suffering is ascribed to some agent, and this has to be identified by
a qualified person, and then removed by the appropriate act of
sacrifice. The experience of sickness is conceived as the visitation of a divinity which has seized upon the sufferer in order to
make known some demand. It may require him to make
redress for some wrong that he has done; in that case it is likely
that when he, as we should say, searches his conscience, he will
ascribe his sickness to the clan-divinity of the wronged man.
But the visitation may be from one of the Powers whom Lienhardt calls 'free-divinities' because they are not attached to
separate descent-groups. In either case the remedy will be to
make a sacrifice to the divinity that has been angered, in the
ritual of which the divinity is held to be separated from the sick
man, and the sickness, along with the guilt which has caused it,
'laid on the back' of the sacrificial victim.

Free-divinities make their presence known by causing sickness or mental disturbance, and must be identified by some
person who has been endowed with the power to do so after an

earlier visitation. The most important of them is Deng, who is also the divinity of rain, thunder and lightning, and is thus a bringer of both life and death. Some clans have Deng as one of their divinities, and their members are believed to be successful in praying for rain. New free-divinities appear from time to time, imported from neighbouring tribes or peoples. Garang is one such. His name is the name of the first man, but he is also associated with the sun. People possessed by him are able to draw out fevers from the bodies of sick men by massage. He is associated with the ashes from the fires in the cattle byres, which a man puts on his tongue when he swears a solemn oath; if such a man perjures himself he expects to be punished by death or grave misfortune. Abuk, the mother of Garang, is associated, as women are, with rivers; drowning men call on her.

Then there is an evil divinity, Macardit, the great black one; he is the explanation of misfortunes which the sufferer does not see as deserved punishments. Whereas other divinities are sources of life, its creation and continuance, Macardit is the source of death and sterility. He is propitiated not to seek blessings, but to keep him away, and the ritual of sacrifice to him reverses what is done at all other sacrifices. Whereas white oxen are sacrificed to other divinities, those for Macardit are black. Eldest and youngest sons sacrifice to clan-divinities. The right man to sacrifice to Macardit is a middle son, a man whose share in inheritance will be less than that of either his eldest or his youngest brother. In every homestead there are shrines to the clan-divinities, near the dwelling-house of the senior wife. A shrine to Macardit is set up outside the homestead, near the dwelling of the junior wife, whose last child will be the last child of the homestead. Junior wives propitiate Macardit so that their child-bearing days should not be cut short.

The association of evil with a reversal of the normal is characteristic, in another way, of the Dinka idea of witches. Witches are thought of as belonging to the bush, the wild uncultivated land that is contrasted with the settlement and homestead. They are associated with wild animals, and particularly with the cobra, the most dangerous snake; they are said to have a tail like that of the baboon who was demoted from manhood because he was so greedy. They defile the homestead by excreting within it instead of 'going to the bush'. But, unlike some peoples to be discussed later, Dinka do not often identify individuals as witches.

Various categories of person are believed to have some kind of special relationship with Powers. At the lowest level, a man may own material objects – 'medicines', dried roots and twigs – in which some Power is believed to inhere; these can be bought and sold, and their owner need not himself be associated with any divinity. Some of these substances are used in the treatment of sickness; the most famous, *mathiang gok*, can be directed by its owner against a person who he thinks has injured him. If this person is guilty he will fall sick and not recover until he confesses and makes restitution. The Dinka say the Power 'speaks to' the guilty man; it attacks his conscience as well as his body. Lienhardt shows that this idea is quite unlike the mistaken theory of physical cause and effect which Frazer supposed was the basis of magical beliefs.

Then there are men who can divine – answer questions of which they have no direct knowledge – by various means such as scattering grain on the ground and interpreting the pattern it makes. But most important of the individual vehicles of Divinity are those who have suffered some illness attributed to possession by one of the major free-divinities, and have then become its servants and able to divine the causes of sickness when inspired by it. These men are called 'men of *nhialic*', and are held to have power beyond the average both to help or injure others by word or gesture, and to reveal unknown matters or predict the future. They have the same right to the name of prophet as those described among the Nuer, and one of them, Arianhdit, was a leader in defiance of the government in its early days, but they have not played the conspicuous political part recorded of Nuer prophets. Moreover the Dinka ideal of a prophet is that of a man of peace, and indeed some of them maintain that Arianhdit was seeking peace with the government authorities when his followers disobeyed him.

The divinities with which the Dinka people their world at the same time mirror their experience of life in society and explain in terms of personal motives the experiences which come to them from outside society. As will be clear already, the association of every clan with its own divinities, and of the spearmaster clans with an especially powerful divinity through which they obtain the well-being of the whole community, expresses and reinforces the sense of common membership in both kinship (clan) and political (tribal) groups. The conception of the permanently existing clan-divinity reflects the experience of the clan as a social unit with a remembered past and a hoped-for future, and the moral obligation to participate in ritual and to supply animals for sacrifice expresses and reinforces the sense of common interest in herds and pastures, and the duty of mutual support, that is recognised by descent groups in some contexts and territorial units in others. Durkheim's argument that the god of any religion is really society itself was put in more abstract terms; as he saw it, the heightened atmosphere of a ritual gathering stimulated a sense of mutual dependence and so a willingness to accept the constraints of social life. Lienhardt shows in a more specific way how a Dinka sacrifice expresses both the unity of the whole congregation and the recognised divisions within it. The Dinka – by no means alone in this – regard it as essential that those concerned in the successful outcome of any situation, whether as kin of an individual sufferer or as themselves at risk in the dangers of the dry season, should be united in their approach to divinity. They must join in the ritual as a unit, and their hearts must be at one; no one must harbour a smouldering grievance. While the sacrificial beast is still living and itself whole, all the attention of the congregation is focused on it. As soon as it has been killed there begins the distribution of the meat, in which every participating section has its share, and about which there is room for argument. 'People begin again to see themselves in relation to others and not only to the victim'; or, one might say, the sufferer whom the victim represents.

The references to Divinity as 'father' and 'creator' can be said to express the two types of experience which are referred to this all-encompassing Power, the affective experience of personal good or ill fortune and the cognitive experience of existence in a world of human beings and other entities of many kinds. As 'father' Divinity is the ultimate source of one's individual fate; specific events that need explanation are ascribed to divinities of limited range. Divinity is conceived, as is a Tallensi ancestor-spirit, as both cherishing and punishing, and as entitled to complete submission; and this is the relationship of a Dinka son to his father, on whom he depends in religious matters as does the Tallensi son. A song which refers to the propitiation of Divinity by sacrifice addresses him as the head and protector of the homestead; it is sung during a thunderstorm. People who suffer misfortune do sometimes complain to Divinity as one might remonstrate with a neglectful father. But Divinity is essentially just, as a father should ideally be, and so is able to see through and punish human deceit.

The conception of Divinity as creator could be said to interpret the Dinka experience of a world which does not at all times impinge directly on any given individual; it may be thought of as a philosophical or cosmological notion, and some modern anthropologists would see it as an embryonic form of scientific generalisation. In this context Divinity, according to Lienhardt, stands for what is common to all humanity (in which vulnerability to non-human forces is certainly an element). 'All people are your children', says a Dinka hymn; and another 'No man hates (*sc.* ought to hate) another in the whole world.' Hence Arianhdit was recognised as a 'man of Divinity' primarily because he was able to make peace between normally hostile groups; without this ability claims to have received revelations from Divinity would have been of little account. Lienhardt does not separate what might be called the practical and theoretical ideas of Divinity as one must be driven to do if one is seeking to interpret religious belief as nascent science. Divinity as the ground of all that exists, he writes, 'images the lived experience of community and concord', and also 'truth, justice, honesty, uprightness and such-like conditions of order and peace in human relations'. Social disorder is immediately experienced and needs to be explained (where Malinowski would have said that individual suffering is immediately experienced and relief from it sought). The absence of Divinity is the answer, and once this answer has been given the remedy – to make peace with Divinity – is clear.

For the Dinka, as for everyone who postulates the existence of an ultra-human power that is essentially benevolent and just, the question why the righteous suffer and the wicked flourish has to be considered. Their answer is that everything that happens comes from Divinity, but that Divinity has a dual aspect; that aspect from which come drought, sterility and disaster (but drought and sterility are the major disasters) is Macardit. Macardit is not, like Satan, an independent being at war with Divinity; he is an aspect of Divinity, since Divinity is the ground of everything experienced. In Lienhardt's interpretation Nhialic and Macardit are not different kinds of being but images of different kinds of experience.

MYTHS

Malinowski taught us to recognise that a myth is not just a story, but a statement of events in the remote past that are seen as the justification of existing institutions; a myth asserts that things are as they should be. Dinka myths tell of the source of the clan-divinity *Ring* and the power that it conveys, and form the 'charter' for the spearmasters' monopoly of this power. Their ancestors defeated a semi-divine being, Aiwel Longar, who was engendered by a river, and he then bestowed on them the power to speak to Divinity (invoke) and to bless and curse. The myth is told in such a way as to give a prominent role in the story to the ancestor of the person telling it. Each version fits the context of the local knowledge of a small section of the Dinka; there is no way that an agreed 'official' story could be established for all this huge dispersed population. The clan that provides the spearmasters of any locality is the one whose ancestor is the hero of the myth told there.

But the features common to all or many versions relate to the experiences which are common, and particularly significant, to all Dinka. First there is dependence on rivers as the permanent source of water and pasture, and at the same time capricious forces which can be a source of death as much as of life. To get to dry-season pastures Dinka often have to drive their herds across a river which is still high; cattle and men may be drowned or seized by crocodiles. 'Crossing the river' is a metaphor for survival; 'he will not cross the river' means 'he will die'. Aiwel of the myths comes from the river, and in several versions of the story he finds water by plucking tufts of *awar* grass – the same that is sometimes planted around the grave of a spearmaster. The events of the myth are those of the dry season; cattle are dying, Aiwel offers to lead them to inexhaustible pastures and the people refuse to go. Aiwel punishes them by spearing them like fish as they try to cross a river, and the man who outwits him is given a fishing spear and the power that Aiwel confers upon it. As the river is the source of both death and life, so Aiwel first destroys people and then gives them the life that is in the spearmasters' possession.

There is also significance in the status of Aiwel as the 'eldest son' of Divinity. His relations with Divinity and with his followers mirror the Dinka experience of relations within the family. In the first place, the eldest son is regarded as the 'opener of the way' for the rest of his mother's children. If he is not successfully born his mother must die, and with her all the other children she might have borne for the lineage. In another sense here, he is both the giver and the withholder of life. The eldest son in a Dinka family, who will succeed his father, is thought of as being particularly closely associated with his father; on the other hand, he is the first to marry and set up an independent household and thus pass out of his father's control except in ritual matters. Aiwel as the eldest son of Divinity is thought to share some of his father's nature, to have authority of his own, and to be a mediator with Divinity as an eldest son is the mediator between his father and his younger brothers.

The place of women in the myths is a reflection of their place in Dinka experience, first and foremost, of course, as a source of life. In most versions of the myth it is a woman who suggests the trick that thwarts Aiwel's attempt to kill the people as they cross the river; he spears them as Dinka do fish, thrusting his spear where he sees a movement of the reeds, and he is deceived when one man carries some object which deflects the spear. Sometimes this is the sacrum of an ox, sometimes a grass pad for carrying things on the head. Both are women's implements; the ox-bone is used for stirring porridge. The ambiguous position of women, whose loyalty must always be divided between their own lineages and their husbands', is also reflected in the myths. In them a woman betrays the spearmaster to the people whose lives are saved by the betrayal. But it is she who has enabled them to take possession of Aiwel's life-giving power. In Dinka life people try to marry their daughters into spearmaster clans and thereby gain especial benefits (what might be thought unfair advantages) from their powers of invocation.

Women feature in the myths, which have their counterpart in every society, that tell how man was separated from God and death came into the world. As in all comparable myths the division came when a command of God was disobeyed, and usually it is a woman who was disobedient. In this case the command was to eat no more than a grain of millet a day. A 'greedy' woman pounded a larger quantity; Divinity was struck by her pestle, and in anger withdrew from men (but not primarily because his order had been disobeyed). To be able to pound surplus millet is evidence of well-being, and this connects women with prosperity and survival as well as with death and misfortune. Lienhardt also sees in this myth a reference to the contrast between the universal community over which Divinity presides and the lineage divisions of Dinka society, created by the separation of the sons of co-wives; again the ambiguity of the women's position is that they are the source of the strength of the lineage as well as of its divisions.

Aiwel, the river, and women, then, are equally sources of life and well-being and means whereby these blessings can be cut off. Aiwel's motive in trying to destroy his people is not discussed nor any attempt made to justify him. What matters is how he was mastered and his power controlled for the good of the Dinka, just as the river has to be mastered.

17   Religion and Science: The Kalabari *

Lienhardt's analysis of Dinka religion shows how a people can come to terms with their experience of social life, and of their natural environment, by peopling the world with ultra-human beings as the sources of this experience. Robin Horton's study of the Kalabari sees their religion not only as concerned with lived experience, but also as a detached attempt at a theory of natural phenomena.

KALABARI SOCIAL STRUCTURE

The Kalabari are one of the Ijo peoples of the Niger Delta. Today they are fishermen, as they were before the Portuguese explored the Bight of Biafra in the fifteenth century. They build their villages in the mangrove swamps, where there is land permanently above the level of high tides and river floods. Having only fish as a local source of subsistence, they have always traded with their inland neighbours, exchanging fish and salt for vegetable food. A village may contain from 200 to 1,500 people; the houses are built close together round a central area where the villagers gather for the discussion of public matters, including the trial of offences against the law – in the past murder, theft and sorcery – and for ritual. Every village is independent in the management of its internal affairs.

A village of any size is divided into wards, or 'houses' as the Ijo themselves call them, inhabited by people claiming descent from a common ancestor. The rule of descent is not unilineal. Marriage can be contracted with a high or a low payment; in the former case the children belong to the father's house, in the latter to the mother's. Hence it is misleading to call these groups lineages. The head of a ward is chosen by the heads of individual households from among the elders, and so is the head of a village; no ward claims a monopoly of the village

* R. Horton (1962), 'The Kalabari World View', *Africa* (1967); 'African Traditional Thought and Western Science', *Africa*.
    G. I. Jones, *The Trading States of the Oil Rivers*, 1963.

headship. An association called *Ekine*, which is still in existence, is described by Kalabari as 'one of our highest things'. Its members perform masquerades in honour of spirits of the water. They also have a share in village government, in that anyone who considers himself wronged by a neighbour in some matter that need not go before the village assembly can complain to them, and they will hear the case and impose a heavy fine on the party judged to be at fault. Some wards have a monopoly of particular performances, or of roles in given performances. But as far as membership itself is concerned, *Ekine* takes no account of kinship; a member who dies is not succeeded, as he would be in a Yakö society, by another of his house. Hence it is, or is supposed to be, free from the contests for predominance between houses that arise in the village assembly.

Three larger communities, Buguma, Abonnema and Bakana, are described by Horton as 'city-states'. They were once united in the trading state of New Calabar, which competed with Bonny (Ubani), the other leading Ijo centre, for the control of access to the interior and the heavy dues exacted from European traders. Both Bonny and Kalabari took an active part as middlemen in the slave trade, and their rivalry eventually led, in the early nineteenth century, to the appearance of a peculiar type of organisation known as the canoe house. In essence this was the consolidation of the older residential kin-group into a business organisation concerned with the manning and equipment of large canoes carrying a crew of fifty or more and armed with cannon. Houses now increased their manpower by buying slaves, whose children were eventually incorporated fully into the house. The house head commanded and steered the canoe, managed its trading enterprises and controlled its funds; new qualities were now required of him, and a man who had been bought as a slave, or such a man's son, might become head of a canoe house if he showed the right capabilities. No doubt only a minority of slaves had such good fortune, but the majority of the men who founded great canoe houses were slaves or the sons of slaves. As numbers increased, new houses were formed and grouped under the leadership of the founding house.

Hereditary rulers appeared in response to the demand of

European traders for an individual with whom they could make agreements and whom they could trust to enforce what had been agreed. Naturally these were heads of powerful canoe house groups, and a group which had provided a 'King', as the traders called him, sought to claim a monopoly of the office. But in fact they only held it as long as they were the most powerful.

This system came to an end when the British established the Oil Rivers Protectorate in 1884 and the Delta leaders lost their control over foreign trade; and the Kalabari, as Horton saw them after the Second World War, were once again a people of fishermen, now complaining that the Nigerian Government neglected them.

THE KALABARI WORLD VIEW

Kalabari divide their world into *tomi kiru*, 'the place of people', and another ambiance which they call *teme*. The distinction recalls the Dinka division into 'that which is of men' and 'that which is of Powers'. *Teme*, which Horton translates as 'spirit', has a range of meanings something like that of the Dinka *nhialic*; it is a vaguely conceived place 'in' which spirits are, and it is also the word for an individualised spirit.

It is worth observing that the way in which anthropologists systematise the statements made to them about objects of religious belief depends much more on different theories of interpretation than does their description of institutions. In this case, where Lienhardt begins his exposition with the all-embracing concept of Divinity and goes on to the manifestations of Divinity in different Powers, Horton begins with those spirits which are thought to be of different kinds and to be concerned with events of different types, and ends with the Great Creator who subsumes all the rest.

Kalabari believe that every individual, and indeed every material object, has a spirit, and for humans this means much more than simply 'life'. Every individual has his or her own creator, *tamuno*, who joined his spirit to his body so that he could be born. The spirit, then, existed before the person's birth and continues to exist after his death. The spirit tells the creator what kind of life it is to lead on earth, pronouncing a

destiny, *so*, for the person to be born. Like the Tallensi Bad
Destiny, it may resign itself to failure in advance, and so condemn the person in whom it is incarnated to the unsuccess of
all his ventures. Kalabari believe that spirits have a series of
reincarnations, though Horton does not elaborate this theme,
and it seems that this 'won't play' attitude is ascribed to misfortunes experienced in a previous existence. Note that this is
the attitude of the spirit (the *teme*); its possessor may be a normally or even an abnormally aspiring character; it is only when
he has suffered a series of disasters that he goes to a diviner,
who explains them by telling him what the spirit said before his
birth. Horton finds here a striking parallel with Freudian
psychology; the Kalabari explanation, that the *teme* has been
frightened off from trying to succeed in life by an earlier experience, makes one think of the unconscious fears that are
brought to light by the psycho-analyst. Like (or something
like) the analyst, the diviner performs a rite in which the
patient formally repudiates the destiny chosen for him by his
teme; then he is expected to recover. Kin-groups and villages
are thought to have a collective *so*. The *tamuno* is imagined as
female and is sometimes addressed as 'mother'.

The spirits of dead ancestors, particularly house heads, concern themselves with their living descendants, and are believed
also to control their fortunes, and not merely, like so many
other ancestors, to visit with affliction those who neglect to
give them offerings or violate the norms of kinship. As the
individual *teme* 'steers' its owner through life, so the ancestor
spirits 'steer' their descendants as a body, and the rise and fall
of a house's fortunes are ascribed to them.

Another class of spirits are those of heroes – *am'oru*. These
are not ancestors, but characters who figure in myths as having
come from some distant unknown place to live in one or other
of the villages, where they laid down a body of custom for the
people to follow. The entry of New Calabar into the overseas
trade, for example, is attributed to the hero Owamekaso. After
they had set their seal on the communities they visited, the
heroes disappeared; and nobody has suggested that these stories, like that of the Cwezi, mask defeats of an enemy. No
Kalabari hero was supposed to have founded a dynasty. The
heroes look after their villages as the ancestors look after their

own descendants, and punish people who transgress the rules they laid down; in particular the village head depends on their good will, and they will increase his authority if he deserves it. This was most significant for the wielders of real power in New Calabar; Owamekaso could give them victory in battle. Then there are the water people, *owuamapo*. They have their homes in tracts of creek or swamp, where shrines are made for them on raised heaps of mud. They are believed to have created the waters over which they preside, and still sometimes to make new ones. They are responsible for the weather and the fish population, and conspicuous persons are often thought to be incarnations of a water spirit or to be under its special protection. This applies equally to the approved and the disapproved, the admired and the despised: innovators who introduce new dances or hair-styles, men who have succeeded by fair means or foul, failures in kinship roles, idiots and morons.

Transcending all these and at the same time separate from them is the creator and controller of the whole world, *Tamuno*, who formed all things out of mud. Nothing can happen which she has not willed. The *so* with which she is identified is the destiny of the whole world, and the *tamuno* and *so* of individuals or groups are said all to be parts of a single great *Tamuno* and *so*, as the Dinka divinities are all somehow parts of Divinity. *Tamuno* is not approached in ritual; man's offerings cannot bend her will.

Using a term from western science, Horton says the three types of spirit can be seen as a 'triangle of forces' in which any two may be complementary at one time and opposed at another. Thus the ancestors are on the side of the heroes when they increase the strength of the village by blessing their descendants with children, but opposed to them when they support their descendants in the rivalries which weaken the village. When water people help the fishermen, they are siding with the heroes; when they stir up storms, they are against them. When they produce deviants and delinquents they are opposed to the protectors of the village unity; when they produce inventors they improve the quality of village life.

All three categories of spirit are the object of rituals which in the past were very elaborate. House heads are responsible for the cults of their predecessors, and village heroes have priests who are chosen for their role by diviners when a holder of the office dies. Ancestors, heroes and water people used to be celebrated in a series of festivals which followed one another in a fixed order. Today in many places these ceremonies have been abandoned or greatly curtailed, but they are kept up in the remoter villages, and Horton was able to see some of them. The essence of the celebration of village heroes is the 'spirit dancing' in which the *oru* is believed to take possession of his priests, and so to be actually present to hear the people's prayers for 'peace, strength, children, life'. His presence demonstrates his concern for their well-being.

The *Ekine* masquerades are similarly thought to bring the water people to the village, and in them too the performers, if they are skilled and successful, are believed to be possessed by the spirits they represent. But these beings, as has been made clear, are not necessarily sources of protection or good fortune, and certainly not to a community as a whole. Those which are represented in the masquerades, moreover, are not those believed to live in the waters around the home of the performers; they come from 'somewhere' far away. Some are considered to be actually obnoxious and dangerous, to have been driven away from a number of other villages before they were adopted by the people who now perform their plays. At the end of the masquerades – thirty to fifty plays if a whole cycle is given – the spirits do not withdraw of themselves as the *am'oru* do, but are formally dismissed when the performers go to the 'Pouring-out Place of the Water Spirits' and strip off their costumes.

Other water spirits are adopted as patrons by individuals, nearly all women, who are called 'spirit carriers' (*oru kuro*). It is usually young married women who are 'seized' by a spirit and become its servant, but young girls may also have this experience. It begins with mental or physical disturbances of one kind or another, symptoms which are diagnosed by diviners, but are not necessarily attributed to a water spirit. However, it happens fairly often that the symptoms persist until the woman agrees to the interpretation that she was married to a water spirit in the spirit world before her birth, and must now allow him to possess her and speak through her mouth. She then usually spends some time, sometimes a long time, in the house of an established *oru kuro* woman, where she learns to keep her spirit under control, so that it visits her only at appropriate moments, when people come to consult her, and gives them advice that is not impossible to follow. Up to five per cent of all adult women in some communities are 'spirit carriers'; they are consulted in cases of illness where spirit possession is suspected. Often an *oru kuro* woman ascribes such an illness to possession by a spirit which she says is the son or younger brother of her own spirit husband. The new adept must then make offerings not only to the new spirit but to its senior, and must attend festivals and other rites in the latter's honour. A successful *oru kuro* woman can gather a large following in this way, and the celebrations of her spirit may be as large in scale as those of village heroes. Such a woman is said to have 'become a chief in water spirit country', and in the name of her spirit husband she exercises over her followers an authority similar to that of a house head. The competition between *oru kuro* women, Horton says, resembles, and is as keen as, that for political dominance between men.

It is thought that the water-spirit resents his 'wife's' relationship with her human husband, and so may prevent her conceiving, and *oru kuro* women are proverbially supposed to make bad wives. In becoming possessed and speaking in the name of spirits, women do as individuals what the priests of the village heroes do as public officials. Horton suggests that in this way women who are frustrated in their subordinate position in society assume a masculine role. In so far as they withdraw from their human husbands they are rejecting the approved female role, and the same could be said of their inability to bear children, though some further explanation of this is certainly needed. As Horton puts it, this type of possession is 'a means whereby people miscast in their social roles on criteria beyond their power to change can get themselves to some extent properly cast again' (1969, p. 42). He adds that since there is no prescribed content for the utterances of these 'unofficial' mediums, the *oru kuro* women can become sources of new ideas.

SPIRITS AND SCIENTIFIC MODELS

Horton's interpretation of Kalabari beliefs lands us right in the middle of a controversy which anthropologists have been engaged in for the better part of this century. Are all men philosophers? Are they all seeking as best they can to explain the world in terms of some kind of theory? It was Frazer, basing his argument on a vast collection of *magical* beliefs, who first argued that primitive man evolved a 'bastard science' in accordance with which objects were supposed to produce effects resembling themselves (for example, yellow plants curing jaundice). For Frazer this was an early stage in intellectual evolution; men discovered eventually that magic was not infallible, and then invented personalised beings – gods – who they thought were interfering with it. This too was false, but Frazer did not call that type of belief a bastard science.

Malinowski asserted that primitive man *was* scientific; he learned the properties of natural objects by trial and error, and had recourse to magic only when he was not able directly to control the outcome of some practical activity. He did not speculate about the world when he was not trying to manipulate it.

Neither Frazer nor Malinowski saw *religion* as any kind of cosmological speculation, and Malinowski did not ask why religion should personify the forces of which Shakespeare said mankind was the sport; indeed it has been so much taken for granted that religion is directed towards personalised beings that the question has hardly seemed necessary. But Durkheim, who regarded Australian totemism as the most elementary religion and as one without gods, saw in it a way of classifying the objects of the perceived world, and said that this was what every religion must be.

Horton sees Kalabari religion as a mode of explanation as well as of classification, and though he does not call it either a bastard or a proto-science, he argues that what the Kalabari are doing in their cosmology, though different in many respects from what we call science, yet is closer to it than most anthropologists suppose; and he thinks it important to recognise what these two ways of thinking have in common before beginning to look at the differences. Both the Kalabari and the nuclear physicist are working out 'a scheme of entities or forces operating "behind" or "within" the world of common-sense observations'. Scientists explicitly seek to show the diversity of perceived phenomena as manifestations of under-lying principles, and to make predictions on the basis of their explanations. In developing their theories they make models (necessarily) from what they know already to explain their ob-servations. Rutherford took his model from the planetary system; Kalabari take theirs from the behaviour of the people they see around them. Scientists use a hierarchy of models, each accounting for a wider range of phenomena; Kalabari see the world of men and spirits as forming a hierarchy of more and more inclusive levels, 'the world of men', the various spi-rits, aspects of *tamuno* and *so* considered as unities. Moreover, the scientist as his work progresses finds that he has to keep amending his model so as to account for anomalies; so that the nuclear physicist's present model would give a very strange picture of the planetary system. In the same way the Kalabari have come to attribute bizarre and paradoxical qualities to their spirits.

Later Horton has developed this theory so as to make it ap-plicable not only to the Kalabari but to African religious thought in general, and he has engaged in controversy with John Beattie, who maintains that the scientific view of the world is totally different from that of the myth-maker (although of course the mechanised world is not populated wholly by scientists, nor were earlier worlds populated wholly by myth-makers). Where scientists seek to *predict*, priests seek to *influence*; the physical scientists know they are dealing with a 'nature' the 'laws' of which they cannot upset; not with a 'thou' but an 'it'. Science analyses experience, re-ligion dramatises it. The underlying order that religion finds is quite different from that of the scientist (it is essentially a moral order, though neither of these two disputants makes this point), and it is reached in a different way. Religious entities proliferate, whereas science is always seeking to limit the number of causal forces it assumes.

Horton replies that, numerous as the Kalabari spirits are, they are of only three kinds. But, says Beattie, they are still the product of a myth-making poetic imagination; and – this is the crux – their existence is not subject to any testing by experience. It is not, as far as anyone can see, as a result of modifications in the light of new experiences that the Kalabari spirits have acquired their peculiar qualities; they had them all along. Their bizarre attributes, as Horton himself says of the heroes, are integral to their definition as forces potentially opposed to the ancestors. Were they then brought in as a new category when the ancestors and *Tamuno* were found not to account for everything that happened? The analogy is not very close. To Beattie the bizarre features would be harder to account for as part of the development of a theory than they are if they are simply taken as *symbols* of features of the environment.

In his most recent writing on the subject Horton explains what Beattie would see as the crucial difference between African cosmologies and scientific theories by the absence of competing explanations of the phenomena to be understood; 'there is no developed awareness of alternatives to the established body of theoretical tenets'. But if we are talking about explanations in terms of personified beings, the Christian religion, as Beattie remarks, has been on offer in Africa, in a number of different versions, for a considerable time. Traditional thought in Horton's view *persists* where there is no (or among people who, although they might, have no) awareness of alternatives; but its *characteristics* prove to be very much those that have customarily been used to distinguish religious from scientific thinking. Thus it ascribes a special power to symbols, a power which is taken for granted and not tested by experiment. It is concerned with the explanation of particular events, not with the establishment of objectively valid generalisations. In practice it is never pure speculation, because it is expressed in such aesthetic forms as the dramatic representation of the spirits. It 'nourishes a rich encrustation of cultural growths whose underlying motives have little to do with explanation or prediction' (1967, p. 165).

Horton's theory of Kalabari religion is much more concerned with cosmology than with ritual, despite his descriptive accounts of the festivals. In these he is sometimes as much interested in their aesthetic aspects as in what they are supposed to *do*. In this latest statement of his views he tacitly admits that, even if the making of a cosmology can be compared with the construction of a scientific theory, ritual procedures can hardly be assimilated to applied science.

18   Witchcraft and Oracles: The Azande *

The peoples collectively called Azande live in an area divided between the south-west of the Sudan, the east of the Central African Republic and the north of Zaïre. From the eighteenth century onwards they were brought successively under the rule of the Ambomu, emigrants from a homeland at the confluence of the Mbomu and Shinko rivers, in the west of the present Zande area. Under leaders from their dominant clan, the Avongara, the Ambomu moved steadily eastwards, establishing their rule over more than fifty other peoples, but not maintaining an entirely separate mode of life nor refusing intermarriage with their subjects. A common language came to be spoken throughout this area, and the craft specialisations of the different subject peoples were sometimes adopted by the Ambomu; in particular they learned to make garments of barkcloth to replace the skins of their own tradition.

All Zande country consists of rolling hills watered by many rivers and streams, on the banks of which tall trees grow. Azande formerly built their homesteads on these shady banks, at some distance apart, since they are much concerned about the danger of witchcraft from their neighbours. But they were exposed to sleeping sickness spread by the tsetse fly, which breeds in thick bush, and both the Sudan and Belgian Congo authorities made them live in concentrated settlements near roads. An empty space without habitations used to mark the boundary between one kingdom and the next. The Azande are cultivators, growing maize and millet, gourds and pumpkins, groundnuts, beans and simsim. For meat they depend on hunting. The tsetse make cattle herding impossible, but they have no tradition of having ever practised it.

ZANDE POLITICAL STRUCTURE

In the last days of their independence there were fifteen king-

* *Witchcraft, Oracles and Magic among the Azande.* E. E. Evans-Pritchard 1937.

218

doms, ruled by six Avongara lineages. The one where Evans-Pritchard worked in 1927–30 was that of Gbudwe on the border of the Sudan and Zaïre. Gbudwe pursued a career of conquest for some forty years, resisting both Arab slavers and Egyptian armies, and was finally shot in 1905 by British troops to whom he was preparing to surrender. Memories of his independent kingdom, then, were still easy to recall when Evans-Pritchard was there, and Gbudwe's son Gangura was regarded by the Azande as the prince of a province in his father's territory. This was one of the larger kingdoms, with a population of about 100,000.

Zande kings, unlike those of the Interlacustrine Bantu, appointed their own sons by preference to manage the divisions of their territory. Gbudwe's kingdom had twenty-six provinces, most of them under his sons; a province, then, would have about 4,000 inhabitants. Subordinate authorities, if not princes, were usually nobles – Avongara – though they might occasionally be commoners. But the lowest level authorities, whom Evans-Pritchard calls the prince's deputies, were commoners put forward as leaders by the inhabitants of a number of neighbouring homesteads. The king had a province of his own, the largest in the kingdom, which he administered himself.

Young men were formed into war companies of fifty or so, each from a different area, and they could be summoned not only for a general war or a raid on the borders of a neighbouring kingdom, but also to work the king's land and that of the provincial governors. Each company had its house at the royal capital where the young men slept when they were on duty, but nobody except the company leader was expected to spend all his time there. When a youth wanted to marry he was free to leave his company. Married men were also summoned for labour through the prince's deputies. The time given to clearing Gbudwe's millet gardens, said to have been each over a mile long and several hundred yards broad, might have been up to a month. The provincial governors had smaller gardens, on which about ten days' work was called for. Both kings and provincial governors collected tribute in food and game from the people of their provinces, and the rulers of provinces would send on to the king a portion of what they received. The

Azande did not suppose that all this was for the personal consumption of the king and princes; it was assumed that labour and tribute went towards the provision of public hospitality for the labourers themselves and the many other people who gathered at a king's or prince's court. Tribute in craft objects, and spears, which were levied in fines and paid in bridewealth, came from different parts of the country and was also largely redistributed. When Gbudwe sent his warriors on a campaign he gave them spears from his armoury. Other objects were given to people who came to beg for them. War captives were brought to him, and were also sometimes given to favoured subjects.

The Zande kings were purely secular rulers; no ritual attaching to their office is recorded. Their main function, therefore, in addition to the organisation of warfare, was judicial, and for both these purposes they had to be equipped with some means of detecting the activity of witches. In Zande thought every enterprise of any individual is threatened by the activity of witches, and everyone employs devices, which have come to be known as oracles, the behaviour of which is held to give answers to questions about the existence of danger and the direction from which it comes. Chief among these is the administration to a chicken of a poison, called *benge*, made from the wood of a creeper that grows outside Zandeland. The kings needed a *benge* oracle for two main purposes: to be forewarned of danger in war and of sorcery from their rivals, and to judge accusations of homicide by witchcraft. The *benge* oracle must be distinguished from the much more common and widely known poison *ordeal* administered to suspected *persons*. The latter, where it was used, was forbidden at the outset of colonial rule, and it is now difficult to learn much about it; but the operation of the *benge* oracle flourished in Evans-Pritchard's day, and, judging from recent work among their nearest neighbours, it probably still does. Every prince had his official oracle operators, usually two or three, who worked for him in turns. They were required to observe strict taboos when collecting and preparing the poison as well as before operating it; it was believed that if they failed to do so the basis of all justice, confidence in the infallibility of the royal oracle, would be undermined. The truth of the answers given by the oracle was supposed to depend on the condition of the poison, and this could be affected by neglect of the taboos.

All accusations of homicide were brought to the king, or a prince, and in effect this meant that he passed judgement on every death, since every death was held to have been caused either by witchcraft or by magic used in revenge for an earlier murder by witchcraft. If the royal oracle established guilt, the king would either demand that compensation be paid on the spot or authorise recourse to vengeance-magic. Physical revenge was not allowed; the king might order an execution, but it seems that this was done only if a man had been held responsible for several deaths. Under European rule no one could be forced to pay compensation for an offence which was not deemed to exist, and persons adjudged guilty by the poison oracle suffered only in reputation. It is in fact possible to affect the answers by the way in which the poison is administered, as has been shown by detailed observations made among the nearest neighbours on the west of the Zande, the Nzakara, now in the Central African Republic (Retel-Laurentin, 1969). Hence a prince's oracle operator was a holder of considerable power. Sometimes such a man was promoted to be the governor of a province.

The belief in witchcraft, then, is the support of the whole judicial system in a way which is unusual in African or any other society. As a belief, however, it is so far from uncommon as to be nearly universal. Evans-Pritchard's study was the first serious examination to be made of such a belief as a social factor, and it remains one of the most detailed. It addresses itself to the question *why* a belief that western positivists consider ridiculous should be so tenacious; the existence of witches cannot of course be directly disproved, but the inefficacy of means of detecting and combating them could be proved to a sceptic again and again. The answer which Evans-Pritchard gives does not support the view that African belief systems are first attempts at system-building. On the contrary, he argues that Zande notions of witchcraft do not form a system, but a loose collection of assumptions from which people choose at different times the one that best suits the situation of the moment. It is largely because they are not considered as a whole that their weaknesses do not become obvious. There is no question of revising theories to accommodate new experiences. Professor Mary Douglas has recently taken us all to task for forgetting that this is the central theme of Evans-Pritchard's work, and it is true that later anthropologists, perhaps taking it for granted, have been more interested in the political manipulation of witchcraft beliefs, a subject to which Evans-Pritchard gave less attention.

WITCHCRAFT AND ORACLES

However, our interest here is in the question what the Azande think witches are and do, and in the action they take to protect themselves. As Evans-Pritchard begins by pointing out, they do not regard witchcraft as the cause or explanation of physical events; it is the explanation of the *particularity* of such events, the reason why some misfortune, readily explicable in physical terms, should afflict one man rather than another. The Azande ascribe more events to witchcraft than any other people on record; where anything at all goes wrong, small or great, they see the work of a witch. The word for witchcraft – *mangu* – 'is less an intellectual symbol than a response to situations of failure'.

Although Azande regard witchcraft as an everyday and not particularly sinister thing, as part of the world and not 'supernatural', they do find it mysterious; they do not claim to understand how it works. They hold that it is a substance in some people's bodies, of which the possessors are as much unaware as anyone else, that has the power of injuring others simply by wishing to – but that also enables its possessor, along with his fellow-witches, to eat the soul of his victim; and what he is eating is not an uncorporeal substance but that human flesh that witches are said to crave. It is inherited from father to son and mother to daughter. The Azande distinguish between witchcraft, which operates by intention alone, and sorcery, which uses charms and spells; that is to say, Evans-Pritchard has translated two Zande words by these two English words. Many anthropologists have found it useful to employ the two words in the same way, even though all the peoples whom we have studied do not make the distinction; this aids communication among anthropologists.

The Azande, in this respect being rather unusual, consult oracles about future dangers from witchcraft as well as their present misfortunes. They ask in advance whether a venture will prosper – a journey, a marriage, the choice of a site for a house or field. Most often of all they ask the oracle whether their health is in danger. An oracle is consulted by asking it yes-or-no questions. First, shall I or shall I not prosper? Then, who is threatening or actually harming me? This question is put in the form 'Is it X, is it Y?' A victim of witchcraft will naturally give the names of people he regards as his enemies, therefore people whom he dislikes, and who dislike him, perhaps with reason.

The Azande use a number of oracles. The poison oracle is universally regarded as the most reliable, but the poison is hard to come by, since it grows in the Mangbetu country, six days' journey away from Gbudwe's kingdom and beyond a frontier which in colonial days it was illegal to cross. People often get it from friends and kinsmen, but a man who bought it from a stranger had to give a large spear in 1930. Small chickens are needed too for the test, and one may not happen to have any of the right size, though most Azande keep chickens for the purpose. In order not to spoil the *benge* poison, questioner and operator must abstain for a few days before using it from sexual intercourse and from certain foods.

The poor man's oracle is called *dakpa*, after one of the trees used in it. He cuts branches from two trees called *dakpa* and *poyo*, and thrusts them into an ant-hill. The termites come out, and the consulter asks a question, addressing both them and the branches. He gets the answer next day, by finding which of the branches the termites have eaten. This is a cumbrous method; only one question can be asked at a time, and the answer is not given at once.

A less reliable but handier oracle is the rubbing-board (*iwa*). This is a device which a man can carry about with him and operate at any time. It consists of two small pieces of wood; one has legs to stand on, the other a handle by which it is moved to and fro across the stationary piece while questions are put to it. It answers by sticking and refusing to move. The rubbing-board is considered to be less reliable than *dakpa*, and neither is as reliable as *benge*. Their warnings may be heeded, but any kind of action against a witch needs confirmation from *benge*.

This is an elaborate and time-consuming affair, though also one that Azande find interesting and enjoyable. It calls for skill both in putting questions to the poison and in administering it to the chickens, and a man with a problem must have an operator for the latter task, and may seek the help of a friend to put his questions for him. Sometimes two or three men consult *benge* at the same sitting. *Benge* is addressed as if it was a sentient being, and its responses are interpreted in terms of its insights and intentions, particularly if the outcome is not what the answer was taken to mean. Thus apparent failures can be explained away, as they are through the ambiguities of a spoken oracle.

The initial address, which is a speech of five or ten minutes, puts before the oracle every detail of the situation on which it is being consulted, in much the same way as a case would be stated in the court of a chief. Then the question is put, 'If X is harming me, *benge* kill the fowl. If it is not X, *benge* spare the fowl'. (Questions are not always put in such specific terms but rather 'If it is someone from X's household, or Y's settlement . . .'). Every answer is tested by asking 'Did the oracle speak truth when . . .'.

Oracles concerning the future lead people to take evasive action, postpone a journey, reconsider a marriage, perhaps even move house. The one situation in which action must be taken is that of persistent sickness, when, as the sufferer believes, he cannot recover unless the witch ceases from persecuting him. A possible recourse here is to make a public declaration at dusk or dawn, when everyone is at home, calling on the witch to desist but without naming anyone. This is done only rarely. If it is not effective – or is not done at all – the supposed witch must be confronted directly. This is not at all a dramatic procedure. It requires official authorisation however. The person who has consulted the oracle cuts off a wing of the chicken which died when the witch's name was put before it, and takes it to the prince's deputy, asking him to send a messenger with it to the supposed witch. The messenger takes it and, without making any accusation, says he has come on account of X's illness. The supposed witch must then deny any

ntention of harming X (as he logically can, since the operation
of witchcraft may be involuntary) and ritually show his good
will by the gesture of blowing water from his mouth over the
chicken wing; he also orders his witchcraft to desist. If the
patient does not recover, his kinsmen seek a new witch (who
may have come on the scene later), or suppose that the first one
was not sincere in his denials; they never say the oracle made a
mistake.

If a man dies, however, his kinsmen are entitled to revenge
with the authorisation of the prince. Revenge is sought
through magical means, and the injured kinsmen are satisfied
when the person whom they suspect, or someone closely associated with him, dies. They report this to the prince, and if
his poison oracle confirms their interpretation, he permits
them to end their mourning. All that others know is that they
are no longer observing mourning taboos.

Every death, then, must be ascribed either to witchcraft or to
vengeance-magic, and most are interpreted both ways in
accordance with different opinions. Witchcraft being what it is
supposed to be, the only conclusive demonstration is an
autopsy, and these, it seems, used to be held fairly often. Since
a dead person could not be punished, the aim of the autopsy
was to establish innocence, particularly where the dead man
had earlier been accused of killing by witchcraft and made to
pay compensation. Theoretically, proof of the absence of
witchcraft substance cleared all his lineage mates, since it was
supposed to be hereditary. But another Zande inconsistency
was that actual accusations were not directed in preference
against the lineage mates of 'proven' witches, nor rebutted by
the argument that an autopsy had shown the lineage to be
innocent. Under colonial rule autopsies were forbidden.

WITCH-DOCTORS

There is an association of specialists who claim, in addition to
knowledge of medical and magical cures, the power to see
witches after eating a secret medicine called *mbiro*, and also to
extract from people's bodies noxious objects which have been
put there by witches and are making them ill; they also purport
to be able themselves to shoot such objects at people. They

practise the first specialisation in public séances, where they answer the same kinds of questions as are put to the oracles, and the second at the bedsides of their patients. Evans-Pritchard calls these people witch-doctors, and the term certainly suggests their combination of skills. But it is an unfortunate word, because it is so frequently used in popular writing to mean a kind of man who does not really exist – the 'dreaded witch-doctor' who terrified the community by threatening them with his evil powers. Zande witch-doctors are not especially dreaded or especially respected. They are considered to be about as reliable as rubbing-boards. But everyone enjoys the act they put on.

Men – and very occasionally women – become witch-doctors after a period of apprenticeship which ends with a ritual of initiation. The principal feature of the apprenticeship consists in taking part in the communal meals at which witch-doctors eat the *mbiro* and other medicines that give them the power to 'see' and control witches and to resist the attacks of witches on them. At this stage the apprentice does not know what the medicines are; he is acquiring magical power, not knowledge. The medicines are believed to work in the bodies of those who eat them so that they want to dance, and some think they may injure a man who does not dance at their bidding. So an apprentice begins to dance at the witch-doctors' performances as soon as he has eaten the medicines and before he has been allowed to know what they are. Little by little, in return for a gift for each new piece of information, he is taught all the medicines his teacher knows, most of these being for use in treating sickness and not in detecting witches. Also, and most important, he learns the tricks by which a witch-doctor purportedly extracts from a sick person's body the substances that have been shot into it by witches and are causing his sickness. The teacher transfers to his pupil a kind of *mangu* which is supposed to have been produced in his body by the *mbiro* he has eaten; the pupil must swallow this. Witch-doctors maintain that, although the word for it is the same, this *mangu* is quite different from witchcraft-substance. The formal initiation which signifies the recognition of a new witch-doctor as a qualified practitioner was a recent introduction from the neighbouring Baka people at the time when Evans-Pritchard was there. It consisted in burying him head downwards in the ground and dancing around him. But the essential ritual preparation for the profession consisted in the eating of *mbiro*.

The witch-doctor exercises and demonstrates his powers of divination in a performance which Evans-Pritchard calls a séance. This is held at the homestead of a man who wants to enquire about a trouble of some kind, and at the same time to earn prestige by putting on a public entertainment.

At such a séance witch-doctors dance in answer to questions put to them; the dancing is believed to activate the medicines that they eat before it begins. All witch-doctors near at hand are invited; there may be from two or three to a dozen. The performance is open to anyone who wants to see it, and others besides the host may ask questions about any matter that is troubling them. The witch-doctors are elaborately adorned with feathers in their hats, skins of small animals hung round them in a fringe that covers their everyday barkcloths, bunches of seeds tied to arms and legs which rattle as they move, and they carry handbells which they shake.

They dance and sing to the accompaniment of gongs and drums and of a chorus from the crowd. A question is put to a particular witch-doctor, who dances 'to it' in front of the questioner until he is in a state of complete physical exhaustion, and then gives his answer, often in the disjointed manner of one speaking in trance. The dance is supposed to activate the medicine, which, like the *benge*, is believed to 'see' the answer to the question. Witch-doctors rarely name a witch whom they claim to have detected, but speak in hints that only the questioner can understand. As Evans-Pritchard remarks, their success consists in giving the desired answer; they can do this because they are aware of the standard sources of enmity in the community of which they themselves are members. But he considers that they reach their conclusion not solely by cold reason; what they say is that, with several names in mind, they suddenly reach a conviction of certainty about one. They say that they make their minds blank and repeat to themselves the names among which they must choose; then, at the thought of one of them, the dancer's heart begins to beat very fast; this is the right name. At this point, Evans-Pritchard observes, they are in 'a condition bordering on dissociation'. He ascribes what the witch-doctors say they experience to unconscious association; students of parapsychology might say that telepathic communication is often effective when the receiver is in a condition of physical exhaustion.

Outside the context of the séance a witch-doctor is a cultivator and hunter like anyone else. When he has not recently eaten his *mbiro* he is as vulnerable to witchcraft as anyone else, and whether or not his claims to revelation are spurious, his belief in witches is as sincere as the next man's. This is one reason why a witch-doctor rarely names a witch; he would be afraid of retaliation outside the 'privileged situation'. Despite the theory that witchcraft can be involuntary, which all Azande do not subscribe to all the time, it is insulting to call somebody a witch, and witch-doctors have to live on good terms with their neighbours. Nor is a witch-doctor the final arbiter. The questioner who picks up his hints seeks the confirmation of a *benge* oracle, and must have that of the prince's oracle before he acts; hence the actual accusation is ascribed to an impersonal source. This is convenient for the witch-doctor, but it also shows that his revelations are not valued especially highly. He is rated on a level with the rubbing-board.

Yet there is a reason for listening to witch-doctors which does not apply to mechanical oracles. This is their possession of *mangu*. Some Azande are sceptical about the powers and professions of witch-doctors in general, but hold that a minority have *mangu* and so really can detect witches. But this argument depends on the belief that the witch-doctors' *mangu* is the same as that of the witch. Witches are able actually to see one another's *mangu*; if a witch-doctor proves to be infallible must not that be because he can recognise his (spiritual) kin? The witch-doctor's answer is, of course, that his *mangu* is different.

SCEPTICISM AND FAITH

The strength of the Zande beliefs concerning witches, as Evans-Pritchard argues, is precisely that they do not form a coherent system. A Zande is not required to maintain a consistent position in every situation, nor to refrain from contradicting himself. Nobody (except an anthropologist) ever says to him, 'But you said . . . ' So he can assert as a matter of common knowledge that witchcraft runs in lineages, and yet never consider whether the enemy he suspects belongs to a tainted lineage. The kinsmen of a convicted witch, for their part, can exonerate themselves from the taint by the argument that he must have been conceived in adultery, though his legitimacy has never been questioned before. What is more significant is that Azande are not seeking to classify the members of their community or draw up lists of 'wanted men'; as long as a man is not harming *him*, a Zande does not care whether he is a witch or not.

The belief that vengeance-magic will kill a witch is also vulnerable to logical questioning. The death of the supposed witch will itself be avenged by the magic of his kin, who assume that he is an innocent victim of someone else's witchcraft. But vengeance-magic should not kill the innocent. Some Azande, challenged on this point, argued that a death might be caused by the combined effects of witchcraft and vengeance-magic. But in practice what protects this aspect of the belief from sceptical enquiry is the secrecy that surrounds recourse to vengeance-magic. Only the prince knows against whom he has authorised its use. Individuals know of cases directly concerning themselves; they have avenged the death of a kinsman, and then they see that someone else claims to have avenged the death that their magic caused. They must be pretending, is the accepted explanation; the prince could not have authorised them to avenge the death of a witch, nor could his oracle have ascribed such a death to witchcraft.

There are also explanations for failures in the pronouncements of the *benge* oracle. The poison may have been affected by some breach of taboo. A witch may have interfered with it; this is the reason why people hold consultations away from habitations. A more subtle argument is that the oracle knows better than the questioner realised; it was referring to a danger further ahead than the one the questioner had in mind.

The question whether witch-doctors really have the powers they claim is one that arises with all claims to clairvoyance. Diviners, like mediums in western society, must not disappoint their clients, so they must simulate inspiration even when they do not feel it, as no doubt they all do sometimes. The blatant fraud in the extraction of witchcraft objects from a sick person's body might seem to be a stumbling-block even to entrants to the profession, and many Azande are aware of it. Yet one novice who was taught the trick in the process of his instruction, and in fact was somewhat distressed at the revelation, restored his own faith by the argument that *really good* witch-doctors could by their magical powers remove objects which *really had* been shot into people's bodies by witches.

Evans-Pritchard found many Azande who were sceptical about the claims of witch-doctors, some asserting that the great majority were charlatans. Many suppose that they simply invent their replies to questions without any magical inspiration. Yet their judgements shift with their circumstances. It is one thing to ridicule the profession, another to reject the only available recourse when one is ill. When he is accused a man may see the witch-doctor as a fraud; when he is the accuser he relies on the witch-doctor's powers. Everyone believes that there are genuine witch-doctors somewhere, and also, says Evans-Pritchard, that those are the ones whose powers come from their 'traffic with witches'. Scepticism, he adds, even maintains faith, because it enables failures to be explained as the work of frauds. If a man is considered a fraud, this is not because the whole belief system is baseless. He is held to have failed within the system; his medicines are not good enough, or he has no *mangu*. One explanation offered for a witch-doctor's cure was that it is effected not by the pretended removal of objects which deceives the patient, but by a compact made with the witch responsible.

There are contradictions too in beliefs about the action of witchcraft. A man who thinks he is being bewitched accuses an enemy, and naturally thinks this enemy is deliberately harming him. Others say that witchcraft can act without the knowledge of its possessor, and this is the theory as naturally adopted by a person who is accused.

This discussion of the alternative explanations that are available to maintain faith in a logically untenable system of beliefs, that is yet indispensable in the absence of more effective theories, is one of the most brilliant aspects of Evans-Pritchard's exposition. It might even be said that it is a once-for-all theory of general validity, and that later anthropologists have been right to pursue the study of witchcraft from other points of view.

19　Witchcraft and Morals: The Nyakyusa *

The country of the Nyakyusa is at the head of Lake Malawi, just inside the border between Tanzania and Malawi. It rises from a marshy plain by the lake shore into a valley walled in by high mountains, in which Nyakyusa live at heights up to 6,000 feet. Abundant rainfall makes it possible to cultivate all the year round, and the variety of crops is unusual for East Africa – bananas and plantains, millet and maize, cassava, sweet potatoes, groundnuts, gourds, cow-peas and coco-yams. They also keep cattle, though nowadays not in large herds; these are stall fed, and a prosperous man may own four or five. There were many more cattle before the rinderpest epidemic which reached them in 1894. Between the two world wars the Nyakyusa began to grow rice and coffee for sale. Godfrey and Monica Wilson worked among them from 1934–8, and Monica Wilson revisited their country in 1955 and 1971.

THE NYAKYUSA POLITICAL SYSTEM

The Nyakyusa are organised by age in a different manner from any other known people. Age-mates live together in villages. These are not created by any formal act, but by young boys moving away from their parents' homes and building by themselves a little distance away. An age-village recruits members for five to seven years; after that the next batch of boys ready to leave home must start a new one. So at any time there are a number of villages with a recognised order of seniority. Often villages are so close together that it is hard to see a division between them. But the principle that age-mates live together separate from their parents is at the root of Nyakyusa political organisation, since the villages under their headmen are the basic political units. At any one time there should be in existence villages of boys, of mature men and of old men, roughly

---

* *Good Company*. Monica Wilson, 1959.
 Communal Rituals of the Nyakyusa. Monica Wilson, 1959.
 'An African Morality'. Godfrey Wilson, *Africa*, 1936.
 The Princes of Nyakyusa. Simon Charsley, 1969.

232

corresponding to grandfathers, fathers and sons. Just as the older members of an Arusha set of murran are behaving like elders some time before their formal promotion, so the older members of a 'boys'' village have established their own young families before it is time for the group to be recognised as a 'men's' village, since the formal change takes place only once in a generation, at a ceremony known as the 'coming out', when, it is said, all things are made new. Before the formal promotion a boys' village is under the authority of the headman of the men's village from which its members have moved out.

A number of lineages in Nyakyusa country claim descent from the hero-ancestor, Lwembe, who is believed to have come down from the Livingstone mountains some ten generations ago bringing with him fire, which the Nyakyusa had not known till then. Members of these lineages are called *abanyafale*, a word which the Wilsons translate 'chiefs'. Simon Charsley, who has studied the records of the missionaries who entered Nyakyusa country in 1891, calls them princes because the latter word does not convey the impression of political power; he holds that before a small number of them were supported by external authority they had little such power, and depended on the favour of their headmen and their followers, who could easily move from one prince's area to another's.

New princes were recognised at the 'coming out' – *two* sons of each prince of the previous generation. Every prince's country was divided into two 'sides', and the villages in each went with one of the new princes. We should remember that, essentially, a 'village' is a body of people, not a fixed locality. It is this body of people who build their houses in different places at different stages in their life. The younger of the two princes was expected to move away from his father's place, perhaps into neighbouring pasture land, perhaps five or six miles to cut down the forest and make a new colony. The process, therefore, was one of territorial expansion effected in a rather unusual way. There was still some virgin land available in the hills in 1955. When the Wilsons were there there were over 100 princes, with followings ranging from 100 to 3,000 adult males. A prince's area might be only a mile or two across.

At the coming out ceremony all his followers gather at the prince's village. The headmen of the existing men's villages

choose heads for the ones which are now to be promoted; these
men may or may not already have attained informal leadership. They are seized from among the crowd and pushed into a
hut where they are secluded along with the two new princes.
The princes are admonished on the way they should behave
towards their people, and they and the new headmen are
treated with medicines to give them the desired qualities of
character, and in the case of the headmen to enable them to see
and combat witches.

The emergence of the two heirs from the seclusion hut,
which gives the ceremony its name, is the climax of the proceedings. Each receives (or in some accounts each senior headman receives) a 'spear of chiefship', and war cries are shouted.
Some accounts say that in the old days they then raided their
neighbours for cattle; Charsley doubts this, and thinks the
statement is a glorification of a past which may not have been
as warlike as it is now pictured. Each new prince with his senior
headman makes fire with a fire-drill, and when the new fire has
been kindled all domestic fires are put out. The senior headman gives the new fire to his juniors, and they in turn to their
people. This is the symbol of a 'making new' which is effected
in reality by the building of new villages, and once was also by
the redistribution of garden land. The boys' villages are pulled
down, and the inhabitants live in grass shelters, without their
wives, for a month or two. Then each group builds its new village, with better houses than they had before and a broad
avenue down the middle. The older men keep, or rebuild, their
homesteads on the periphery, and these will be abandoned one
by one as they die. The old headmen eventually become priests
at the burial places of dead princes.

Doubts have been raised on the question whether what we
have here is a 'handing over of power' such as we find in some
of the more typical age-systems. Monica Wilson notes that the
old chief and his headmen still have authority over their own
age-mates, and that difficult disputes are still referred to them.
Charsley suggests that the traditional coming out did no more
than recognise the maturity of the two new chiefs, leaving it for
them to compete for leadership in a fluid situation. The old
chief certainly did not formally 'retire', but Nyakyusa said he
was expected to die soon after the coming out. Some said the

whispers of his people that he was no longer able to lead them successfully in war would mystically kill him with their chilling breath. But it seems that sometimes he was actually put to death by his headmen, as was the Lwembe, the priest of the hero-founder of the *abanyafale*. A number of informants told the Wilsons that in the past a prince was not allowed to die naturally because if he did the fertility of the land would die with him, and a missionary record of 1924 describes an occasion when funeral parties began to arrive from some distance away when a prince was ill, though not, as it seemed to the missionaries, fatally; they brought him in to hospital, but he did die as soon as he got back to his village. The ritual manner of a prince's death was more painful and less dignified than that of a Dinka spearmaster. His hair and nails, representing the power of growth, were torn out and used as medicine for the fertility of the land; this was a secret, not a public, ritual. Charsley remarks that somebody must have had to decide when the old prince was in fact dying, and that the decision would probably be made when he was losing followers on account of his failure to lead them successfully; and that this was a matter of especial concern to the headmen, who would suffer directly from the disintegration of their villages.

From 1926 – that is some ten years before the Wilsons' arrival – six princes were recognised as Native Authorities, and given the power to hold courts where petty offences were tried and to impose sentences which the government would enforce. They were authorised to make rules for local application, were expected to promulgate government policies for local improvement, and were responsible for reporting serious crime and emergencies such as epidemics. Among the many princes who did not obtain these powers, some were made official village headmen. Each recognised Native Authority exercised his powers over a defined area; as the British authorities interpreted the situation, the chiefs' powers had been modified, but their status was what it had been in Nyakyusa tradition.

In pre-colonial days, however, the princes had no such final authority, and no such clearly bounded territory. This is the reason why Charsley will not call them chiefs. The Wilsons' own observations and the recollections of their informants attest to this. Homicide and adultery were dealt with by direct vengeance, unless the guilty party could escape to another village. Villages often fought about the boundaries of their land, and princes could not stop them. In the Wilsons' day people were as chary of going to official courts as they are today of going to such courts in Bunyoro and Arusha. They would take a dispute first to a respected friend; if he failed to bring the parties to agreement they would go to their own headman, then to the senior headman, only then to the prince. As Godfrey Wilson describes this final stage, the prince sat with all the headmen and gave a decision which expressed their consensus. The missionary Merensky, writing in 1894, said that the prince took no part in the discussion, and, if no agreement was reached, could only adjourn the proceedings.

There were ways of self-help which did not require the approval of the prince. A man to whom a debt was due might take the wife of one of the debtor's neighbours as a hostage, and go with her to his prince, explaining that he had a claim on the debtor's village. The latter would then report the matter to the debtor's prince. As Charsley points out, neither prince is here approached as a judge or even a mediator; the injured man's prince simply notifies the other. How far such a means would be effective must of course depend on the state of relations between the two princes and the two villages; the capture of a woman might simply lead to a fight. He suggests, just as Evans-Pritchard does in writing of the feud, that the possibility of peaceful settlement would depend on the practical need for friendly relations between villages close together and linked by ties of kinship. But the Nyakyusa insistence on urbanity and the 'enjoyment of good company' was very different from the Nuer readiness to take offence, and in Charsley's view reference to a peaceful settlement was preferred wherever it was possible. He thinks the Nyakyusa exaggerated the toughness of life in the days when fighting was allowed.

Princes do not directly control the allocation of land, although their domains are so small. This is a matter for headmen, who report what they have done to the prince. Nor, in the past, was their decision final in matters of war, for headmen could wage war on their independent initiative.

If the prince had been an ultimate political authority one

might have expected, as Charsley argues, that the appointment of headmen would be a matter for him, whereas accounts say either that he chose them in consultation with the existing headmen or that the headmen made the choice by themselves. After Native Authorities were created, chiefs did put forward names for government recognition as headmen; we do not know whether this was their independent choice. In one incident in the early missionary days, a prince had to take refuge at the mission from the anger of his headmen, and another was beaten by them; on yet another occasion the headmen arraigned and tried their prince.

Charsley remarks that the proliferation of princes made it necessary for them to compete for followers, and maintains that the coming out did not establish a prince but merely authorised him to enter the competition. This was not a competition for the control of trade such as was so important for the Kalabari. The main way to secure followers was the generous distribution of meat and beer, and by the making of cattle sacrifices on occasion when their welfare called for it. According to one statement of Monica Wilson, the distribution of meat satisfies the ever-present, every-greedy witches, and so is a way of protecting people from their attacks. Hence a prince had to have many cattle. Charsley suggests that he must have got these partly from the marriage of his daughters to commoners (for which the bridewealth was ten cows, whereas he gave only three for his commoner wives), and partly from successful raids on the herds of his fellow princes; also, and presumably with the approval of the headmen, he could seize the cattle of a man accused of witchcraft. The son of a successful prince, inheriting his cattle and his wives, a labour force in the dispensing of hospitality, would have a good start in the race. But at the time of the coming out most of them would not yet have attained that inheritance. Hence the need to prove and establish themselves by successful raiding; hence perhaps, also, the theory that the old prince should not live too long.

THE BELIEF IN WITCHCRAFT

The main theme of this chapter is the place of the belief in witchcraft in Nyakyusa religion. Monica Wilson was the first anthropologist to remark that to study African religion without witchcraft would be like studying Christianity without Satan. Witchcraft, as seen by the Nyakyusa, is an evil power which some people are able to activate to harm their fellows, not out of righteous indignation but out of pure spite. It is not simply the dark side of a god who is the cause of everything. It is not, however, the cause of all misfortunes, but of undeserved misfortune, particularly sickness; some sicknesses are punishments for wrongdoing. There is a hint of this possibility in Evans-Pritchard's account of the Azande, but he does not develop it.

Zande and Nyakyusa beliefs have a good deal in common. Both distinguish between sorcery and witchcraft, and both suspect their enemies of witchcraft rather than sorcery. Nyakyusa believe that witchcraft is a material substance which its possessors inherit; they think it is a python in the intestines. Like the Azande, they hold that the power of witchcraft and the power to combat witches are essentially alike, if not one and the same. Headmen also are believed to have pythons in their intestines; these are given them by the medicines they drink at the coming out. The most potent of all, called *inyifwila*, is believed to have in itself power similar to that of witchcraft. It is put into the giraffe and zebra tails that a prince used to wear attached to his arm when he went to war; if there is too much, it will make him fierce towards his own people. What is worse, it may give the tail independent power, and then it, like a witch's python, will fly through the air at night attacking people and sucking the milk from the cows. There is supposed to be an endless nocturnal war between the pythons of the witches and those of the headmen.

Witches are believed to be inordinately greedy for both meat and milk, but they are not thought to eat the flesh of corpses as witches are in many other societies. What they want is roast meat such as is distributed at feasts and sacrifices. If they cause someone's death this will be the occasion for a funeral feast, but they also satisfy their hunger by mystically eating the flesh of living people, whom they attack by sending out their pythons at night. They can also blight grain crops simply by passing the field; they somehow consume the goodness of the crop. With the inconsistency that one finds in most witchcraft

beliefs, it is thought that they bring home the flesh of their victims to roast at their own fire; when they do this the fire
becomes contaminated, and there was traditionally an annual
ceremony of clearing out the ashes to remove possible conta-
mination, and lighting new fires. This was done also in times of
public disaster such as an epidemic.

In other African societies witches are suspected of sexual offences as well as of excessive greed; the Nyakyusa make little of
this aspect. Monica Wilson relates this difference to differences in territorial organisation. The Nyakyusa age-system is
such that the members of a herd-owning body – the lineage –
do not live together. Rich and poor are cheek by jowl, and a
poor man cannot fail to know when his rich neighbour is roasting meat. The *smell* of roasting meat is what excites the
witches, Nyakyusa say. On the other hand, the age-village
system is a protection against illicit sexual relations; in fact
that is what it is said to be for. It removes the temptation for
young men to seduce their fathers' wives and old men their
sons'. So the Nyakyusa need not have feelings of guilt on this
score which they project on witches. In contrast, people who
live in extended family homesteads (specifically the Pondo in
South Africa, where Monica Wilson did her original work) are
surrounded by sexually prohibited persons.

This argument may account for the Nyakyusa lack of interest in the sexual proclivities of their witches, and one may agree
that since their territorial organisation is unique their ideas on
witchcraft may be so too. But it would be hard to find an African society where witches are not thought to be greedy for
human flesh. This is what explains their victims' sensations of
weakness; their inner substance is being consumed. One might
argue that greed and sexual desire are the two drives that all
social beings must learn to control, and that witches, to whom
all that is evil is attributed, are more likely to be credited with
excess in both directions.

When someone falls sick and does not quickly recover,
various explanations are discussed. The sick person himself,
like a Zande, may simply wonder which of his enemies has
attacked him, but others will consider alternative possibilities.
The clear alternative is between witchcraft and the 'breath of
men' – adverse comment from neighbours which somehow

materialises as a chilling wind. But 'the breath of men' remains mere talk *until* the witches, along with the headman and with some other individuals who claim the power to see witches in dreams, back it up with what Monica Wilson has called 'the legitimate use of python power'. If a sickness is caused by the 'breath of men' it can be cured when the sufferer repents, admits his fault and offers a feast to his neighbours at which he should be reconciled with them. At this feast the neighbours who are supposed to be responsible must on their side say publicly that their anger is over; as such a reconciliation is described they say clearly, and so put on record, what it was that caused the anger. The Wilsons' informants stated that this was what should happen, but there are no records of actual incidents.

Another possible cause of sickness or other misfortune is the anger of the ancestor spirits, whom Monica Wilson calls 'the shades'. This may be incurred by failure to perform a due ritual, in particular to sacrifice a beast of the appropriate value, or by quarrelling among kinsmen. When the gardens of one chiefdom were ravaged by wild pigs, this was ascribed to the anger of the shades at a quarrel between a priest and his brother. The shades, it is believed, directly control procreation and so are responsible for reproductive troubles. They are thought to be actually in the bodies of a husband and wife and to be the source of sexual desire; but, if they are angry, they 'bind' the man or woman, making him impotent or her barren. This is specifically the punishment for omissions in the ritual of a girl's puberty and marriage.

To find the cause of sickness Nyakyusa resort to oracles such as the rubbing board operated by specialists, to whom they put the alternative explanations that have occurred to them. But accusations of witchcraft may be made without any such consultation. Some people claim the power to see in dreams a witch at his evil work, and Nyakyusa say that such a 'defender' gets up at once and rouses the village with his shouts; here again no actual instances are recorded. Suspicions are privately canvassed when anyone is seriously ill, and sometimes when the milk yield of the cattle drops. A headman may call his villagers together and warn the witch to desist; this is supposed to make him ashamed rather than afraid. Sometimes a witch is named on the word of a 'defender'. Sometimes a suspected person is denounced without any explicit accusation. A banana stem with banana leaves wrapped round it is set up outside his house; this is a notification that he is a witch, and he is not expected to be brazen enough to stay in the village. Or he may come back from a day in his garden to find his door barricaded with thorny branches.

If a direct accusation is made it is taken before the prince. British law prohibited the accusation, let alone the trying and punishment, of witches, but when the Wilsons were there cases were taken to chiefs' courts and simply not recorded in the books kept for the District Commissioner's inspection. But the test that has been regarded as infallible in so many African societies, the ordeal of drinking poison, has been effectively suppressed. People who had undergone this ordeal and survived spoke to the Wilsons, and a number of their informants had seen the poison administered. This was done on the orders of the prince, in the presence of 'official witnesses' (no doubt persons nominated by the prince, perhaps headmen). Both accused and accuser had to drink, and the one who vomited was vindicated. But people who did not vomit did not necessarily die, as a number or recollections indicate.

The ordeal was not, then, what an early writer called it, 'judge and executioner in one', and if it convicted anyone there remained the question what his punishment should be. The possibility that the prince might seize his property has been mentioned. One informant said he might have been speared. But the impression is certainly not given that all cases were treated in this drastic manner. Nowadays, of course, none can be. The seizure of property was not allowed under British administration, and the worst that could be done was to drive him out of the village. In Monica Wilson's view what happens depends on the status and popularity of the individual in each case, a conclusion that has been confirmed since by observation of the treatment of witchcraft in other African societies. Moreover, exile is not a serious hardship; there is no question of 'perishing in the bush'. A man who has had to leave one village may be welcomed in another. Witches are supposed to injure their enemies; a newcomer has no enemies – yet. Whether or not the Nyakyusa work it out that way, they are content to say, 'Whatever he may have done, he hasn't done it here.' Furthermore the belief that witchcraft and the power of defence are essentially the same leads people to think that in accepting an admitted witch as a neighbour they may be gaining a defender. Women witches may or may not be repudiated by their husbands; if they are, they can usually find a new mate. On the other hand, to have once been publicly accused makes one an object of suspicion on later occasions.

Here we see the essential difference between the African and the medieval attitudes towards witchcraft. In Africa an act of witchcraft is a crime committed in a peculiar way by a person who supposedly has a physical quality that not all men have. This physical quality is thought to go with a disagreeable disposition – morose, ungenerous, consumed with envy. But no society has ever held that to have such qualities was a capital offence. It was only in medieval Europe that to *be* a witch was to be unfit to live; and in so far as this was so, the reason was that they were thought to be the allies of Satan, the enemy of God. Although Monica Wilson rightly emphasises the parallel between the place of witchcraft in African religion and that of Satan in Christianity, there is this large difference that the African witch is conceived as the enemy only of his fellows and not of divine authority.

WITCHCRAFT AND SOCIETY

The Nyakyusa distinguish clearly between witchcraft and sorcery. The latter is the use of medicines against an enemy as opposed to the direction of an inherent power against him. Just as witches in certain circumstances may combine with the defenders against an evil-doer, so harmful medicines may have a legitimate use. But these will be of different kinds from the illegal ones; sorcery has recipes. Nyakyusa doctors purvey medicines to be used against unknown adulterers and thieves. One had a medicine which he said would prevent a thief from leaving the scene of his crime. Most of us call such a use of substances for legitimate purposes harmful magic, with the implication that magic is the legitimate use of medicines, whether to help or harm. Nyakyusa believe that sorcery operates over a wider range than witchcraft. The latter strikes against neighbours, the former can come from outside the village. This idea is sometimes discussed as if it was a scientific theory: 'It can't be witchcraft because . . .' as who should say 'It can't be measles because . . .'; or as Monica Wilson puts it, 'witchcraft *can only be used* (my italics) against a neighbour'. It is surely more realistic to say that only neighbours are accused of witchcraft; if an outsider is to be accused, he will be accused of sorcery. Where people from different villages are in close contact, working in offices or in labour camps, they ascribe their misfortunes to sorcery, and in these situations, much more competitive than those of the village where it is a rule of good behaviour not to try to surpass your fellows, the sorcery is supposed to be prompted by envy at another's success, perhaps in promotion. Anyone who found a nugget on the Lupa gold-field, and claimed the reward offered, was expected to die the next day, and occasionally someone did. The belief in sorcery is considered more 'rational' than that in witchcraft, and it is so to the extent that the medicines used may be poisonous, and that someone who is held to have died from sorcery may actually have been poisoned. It is, therefore, a more popular explanation with people who have had some education and know that the intelligentsia don't believe in witchcraft.

A more profitable way of looking at the distinction which so many peoples make between witchcraft and sorcery is to think of it in social rather than spatial terms. Witchcraft is nearly always thought to operate within a small community; in so far as it is ascribed to hidden grudges, it must do so. Only people in regular contact develop reasons for grudges. But these are just the people among whom there should be good will. This is why witchcraft is thought to be so heinous. For the Nyakyusa, who explicitly value good neighbourliness and even have a word for it (*ukwangala*), it violates a most cherished norm of behaviour. Elsewhere it is more commonly thought that witches attack their own kin; again, they disrupt a group who in principle are bound by what Fortes calls 'the axiom of amity'. Misfortune coming from outside this closed circle is attributed to sorcery, and sorcery in turn to jealousy at others' good fortune rather than to personal grievances. A recent writer on the subject, who as it happens draws his material from a people close to the Nyakyusa, the Safwa, offers as a general proposition that when a distinction is made, witches will be persons with whom ego's relationship is incorporative and sorcerers those with whom he has a transactional relationship (Harwood, 1970). One might simplify this proposition further by saying, as Philip Mayer has said, that the witch is 'the enemy within the gates', the traitor who hides hatred under a mask of friendship. Then the sorcerer is the outsider who has no obligation even to pretend friendship.

References

Beattie, J. H. M. (1960) *Bunyoro an African Kingdom*. New York.
   (1971) *The Nyoro State*. Oxford.
Beidelman, T. O. (1971) 'Nuer Priests and Prophets' in *The Translation of Culture* ed. Beidelman. London.
Bradbury, R. E. (1967a) *The Benin Kingdom and the Edo-speaking Peoples of Western Nigeria*. London.
   (1967b) 'The Kingdom of Benin' in *West African Kingdoms in the Nineteenth Century* ed. C. D. Forde and P. M. Kaberry. London.
   (1969) 'Patrimonialism and Gerontocracy in Benin Political Culture' in *Man in Africa* ed. M. Douglas and P. M. Kaberry. London.
Charsley, S. (1969) *The Princes of Nyakyusa*. Nairobi.
Chrétien, J. P. (1970) 'Les tombeaux des Bamis de Burundi'; *Cahiers d'Etudes Africaines* pp. 40–79.
Colson, E. (1960) *Social Organization of the Gwembe Tonga*. Manchester.
   (1971) *Social Consequences of Resettlement*. Manchester.
Copans, J. et al. (1971) *L'anthropologie, science des sociétés primitives?* Paris.
Douglas, M. (1963) *The Lele of the Kasai*. London.
   (1969) 'Is Matriliny Doomed?' in *Man in Africa* ed. M. Douglas and P. M. Kaberry. London.
Douglas, M. and P. M. Kaberry (1969) *Man in Africa*. London.
Dyson-Hudson, N. (1966) *Karimojong Politics*. Oxford.
Evans-Pritchard, E. E. (1937) *Witchcraft, Oracles and Magic among the Azande*. Oxford.
   (1940) *The Nuer*. Oxford.
Fallers, L. A. (ed) (1964) *The King's Men*. London.
Forde, C. D. (1941) *Marriage and the Family among the Yakö*. London.
   (1964) *Yakö Studies*. London.
Forde, C. D. and P. M. Kaberry (1967) *West African Kingdoms in the Nineteenth Century*. London.
Fortes, M. (1945) *The Web of Kinship among the Tallensi*. London.
Gluckman, M. (1955) *Custom and Conflict in Africa*. London.
Goody, J. R. (1969) 'The Classification of Double Descent Systems' in his *Comparative Studies in Kinship*. London.
   (1971) *Technology, Tradition and the State in Africa*. London.
Gravel, P. (1968) *Remera*. The Hague.
Gulliver, P. H. (1963) *Social Control in an African Society*. London.
   (1971) *Neighbours and Networks*. Berkeley, Calif.
Harwood, A. (1970) *Witchcraft, Sorcery and Social Categories among the Safwa*. London.
Heusch, L. de (1966) *Le Rwanda et la civilisation interlacustre*. Brussels.
d'Hertefeld, M., Trouborst, A. and Scherer, J. (1962). *Les Anciens Royaumes de la zone Interlacustrine Meridionale* p. 148. London.

Horton, R. (1962) 'The Kalabari World-View', *Africa* pp. 197–219.

(1967) 'African Traditional Thought and Western Science', *Africa* pp. 155–87.

(1969) 'Types of Spirit Possession in Kalabari Religion' in *Spirit Possession and Mediumship in Africa* ed. J. Middleton and J. Beattie.

Howell, P. P. (1954) *A Manual of Nuer Law*. London.

Jones, G. I. (1963) *The Trading States of the Oil Rivers*. London.

Karugire, S. R. (1971) *A History of the Kingdom of Nkore*. Oxford.

Lemarchand, R. (1970) *Rwanda and Burundi*. London.

Lienhardt, R. G. (1971) *Divinity and Experience: The Religion of the Dinka*. Oxford.

Maquet, J. J. (1954) *The Premise of Inequality*. London.

(1971) *Power and Society in Africa*. London.

Middleton, J. and J. Beattie (1969) *Spirit Possession and Mediumship in Africa*. London.

Retel-Laurentin, A. (1969) *Oracles et Ordalies chez les Nzakara*. Paris.

Richards, A. (1935) 'A Modern Movement of Witchfinders', *Africa* pp. 448–61.

Scudder, T. (1962) *Ecology of the Gwembe Tonga*. Manchester.

Southwold, M. (1961) *Bureaucracy and Chiefship in Buganda*. Kampala.

Steinhart, E. (1967) 'Vassal and Fief in Three Lacustrine Kingdoms', *Cashiers d'Etudes Africaines* pp. 606–23.

Turnbull, Colin (1965) *Wayward Servants*. London.

Vansina, J. (1962) *L'évolution du royaume rwanda des origines à 1900*. Brussels.

Vidal, C. (1967) 'Anthropologie et Histoire: le cas du Rwanda', *Cahiers Internationaux de Sociologie* pp. 145–57.

Wilson, G. (1936) 'An African Morality', *Africa* pp. 75–98.

Wilson, M. (1951) *Good Company*. London.

(1957) *Rituals of Kingship among the Nyakyusa*. London.

(1959) *Communal Rituals of the Nyakyusa*. London.

Worsley, P. (1956) 'The Kinship System of the Tallensi: a Revaluation', *Journal of the Royal Anthropological Institute* pp. 37–75.

Index

DATE DUE